A Software Engineer Learns Java & Object Orientated Programming

DANE CAMERON

A SOFTWARE ENGINEER LEARNS JAVA & OBJECT ORIENTATED PROGRAMMING

Copyright © 2015 Dane Cameron

Original and modified cover design by Karuanka Rayker and CoverDesignStudio.com

Cisdal Publishing

1st Edition

All rights reserved.

ISBN-13: 978-1505671940

ISBN-10: 1505671949

The butterfly lands

Company for the evening rite

Silent till the dawn

CONTENTS

	Preface	9
1	Introduction to Java	11
2	About this book	15
3	Getting started with Eclipse	19
4	Hello World!!!	23
5	Classes and Objects	33
6	Data-types	51
7	Language Fundamentals	67
8	Operators	75
9	Looping and Branching	81
10	Debugging	93
11	Object References	99
12	Inheritance	111
13	Composition	141
14	Constructors	145
15	Exception Handling	155
16	Methods	165
17	Collections	175
18	Generics	195
19	Unit Testing	201
20	Enumerated Types	207
21	Inner Classes	211

22	Lambda Expressions	221
23	Streams API	233
24	Dates and Calendars	247
25	Date and Time API	255
26	Input and Output	265
27	Properties Files	279
28	Default Methods	285
29	Threading	291
30	Parallel Programming	303
31	Java Doc	309
32	Annotations and Reflection	315
33	Building and Deploying	325
34	Logging	331
35	Conclusion	337

INDEX OF DESIGN PATTERNS

Template	131
Abstract Factory	137
Factory Method	150
Singleton	151
Clone	152

Visitor	169
Iterator	193
Command Pattern	219
Builder	243
Decorator	271

PREFACE

Tell me and I forget. Teach me and I remember. Involve me and I learn.

Benjamin Franklin

I wrote my first Java code in 1998, just 2 years after its initial release. In the subsequent 17 years I have continued to use Java, including as a professional software engineer for the last 16 years.

A lot has changed in the world of technology in the last 17 years, but in many ways Java has remained a beacon of stability. The code I wrote 17 years ago does not look vastly different from the code I wrote last week, and that code I wrote 17 years ago would still run on modern versions of Java (for the most part).

Despite the fact that the Java language has remained relatively stable, the role Java plays in the work of IT has changed dramatically. Java first came to prominence as a language for writing browser based applications (called Applets). Applets created a huge sense of excitement around the language through the later part of the 1990s and the dotcom boom, but have fallen by the wayside as native browser-based technologies have continued to improve.

Instead, Java became the dominant language for server-side programming, and is now the driving forces behind many of the world's largest and most visited web sites, along with the business applications powering the world's largest corporations.

In 2014 Java underwent a number of dramatic changes with the release of Java 8. This is the most significant release of Java since the initial release of the language, and has the potential to fundamentally change the way Java is used. This book has been written from the ground-up to incorporate these features, and treats them as integral to the language.

This book is my attempt to pass on what I have learned over the last 17 years. It is not intended as a simple primer on the syntax of the Java language (although the syntax of the language is covered in detail), it is intended to introduce you to the way a software engineer thinks about Java, and the way they structure their code in a world of large-scale, and increasingly complex software.

The intention of this book is to leave you in a position where you can write useful, real-world Java programs that solve interesting problems. This book will not teach you everything you know to become an expert Java programmer; much of that knowledge can only come through experience. I have, however, tried to write the book I would want to read if I was starting from scratch with Java.

Febuary, 2015

1 INTRODUCTION TO JAVA

Java is a statically typed object-orientated programming language. That sentence may mean a lot to you, or it may mean nothing. Rest assured, this sentence will make sense to you by the end of this book.

Java was originally created by Sun Microsystems in 1995. It has subsequently undergone a number of major revisions, most recently in 2014 with the release of Java 8, and has become one of the most widely used programming languages.

Sun Microsystems was purchased by Oracle in 2009, and they have continued to support and extend Java.

It is very difficult to describe the fundamental features of Java in an introduction. Like anything complex, Java is best explained once it is understood to some degree. This chapter will, however, provide some background on what Java is and how it works - but you may want to return to this section once you have progressed some way through the book.

Compiled vs. interpreted languages

Programming languages can be classified in many ways; one form of classification is whether they are compiled or interpreted.

In order for any software to run on a computer it must be converted into machine code: the sequence of 0s and 1s representing a set of instructions that can be comprehended by a computer processor. A compiled language is one where the source code is converted into machine code by a tool called a compiler, and packaged as a program that can be distributed directly to end-users.

Because each operating system is different, compilers need to be written for each operating system. The beauty of compilers, however, is that the same source code can be used to create executable programs for different operating systems. Examples of compiled languages are C and C++.

Interpreted languages also need their source code to be converted to machine code in order to be run on a specific operating system, but with interpreted languages this happens in real-time as the program executes. This means that the same code can be executed on any operating system supporting an interpreter for that language (which is the software that converts the source code into machine code in real time).

Interpreted languages are generally slower than compiled languages, because the compilation step is effectively happening while the program executes. Examples of languages that can be run by interpreters are JavaScript and Perl. Many interpreted languages can also be compiled, however, therefore the line between interpreted and compiled languages is sometimes blurred.

Java does not easily fit into either of these categories. Java is a compiled language: all source code must be compiled before it can be executed. As you will see, the Java Development Kit (JDK) contains a utility program called `javac` that is responsible for compiling Java source code.

Unlike traditional compilers however, the Java compiler does not produce machine code for a specific operating system. Instead, it produces Java *bytecode*.

Java bytecode does contain a set of instructions, just like machine code. Unlike machine code, however, Java bytecode cannot be executed directly by a computer. Java requires an intermediary called the Java Virtual Machine – which is provided by the Java Runtime Environment (JRE).

Any computer that wishes to run a program written in Java must have a JRE installed, and this will perform the task of converting the Java bytecode into machine code for the specific operating system as the program executes.

If you use Windows or OSX you have probably noticed that you are often requested to install a new version of Java: this is the Java Runtime Environment. Once Java is installed you can run any application written in Java.

You may be wondering why Java uses this approach? Java bytecode can be thought of as a halfway house between source code and machine code. It contains a set of instructions that can be executed by an interpreter more efficiently than regular source code.

Java chose this approach as part of its "write-once, run-anywhere" philosophy. The same compiled version of the program can be executed on any computer that has a JRE installed: it is not necessary to build different versions of the program for each platform. This has been immensely valuable, because JREs are available not just for desktop computers, but for mobile phones, set-top boxes, and home appliances. In fact, Oracle claims some 3 billion devices run Java.

This approach was also intended to make the language more secure. Traditional compiled programs can do anything on the operating system that the user running them can do – including deleting files, or sending them over the Internet to a hacker. The JRE by comparison provides a sandbox that programs run inside of, and it is possible to control what the program can do inside this sandbox, or make it request the ability to perform certain operations. This approach has become standard with Android and iOS in recent years, but was built into Java from the very beginning.

Because Java bytecode is converted to machine code as the program executes, Java shares characteristics with interpreted languages. When Java was first released this was a reasonable way to look at it, and Java was marketed as an interpreted language.

As mentioned earlier, however, interpreted languages tend to be slower than compiled languages. Even though Java bytecode is more efficient to convert to machine code than raw source code, there is still some overhead. As a result, early versions of Java were slow compared to compiled languages, and this perception has stuck to some extent. Any discussion of Java on Slashdot still immediately descends into a flame war on the performance of Java.

Java has not been an interpreted language for a long time however. Almost all Java runtimes now use an approach called Just-in-Time (JIT) compilation. The Java bytecode is compiled into machine code as the program runs, just before it is needed. Although there is still some overhead in this process, Java tends to perform as well as compiled languages; with the added benefit that the same Java bytecode can be run on many different operating systems.

One interesting aspect of Java bytecode is that languages other than Java can generate it. There are now many languages that generate Java bytecode, including several mainstream languages such as Scala. In fact, the latest version of Java comes complete with a JavaScript engine called Nashorn that integrates with the Java language, and allows you to write JavaScript code that executes on the Java platform.

Although the version of Java most commonly used is owned by Oracle, anyone can technically write a JDK and JVM. The most common alternative to the Oracle version is OpenJDK, which is an open source implementation of Java.

Statically vs. dynamically typed languages

Another way to categorize languages is as statically typed or dynamically typed languages: Java is a statically typed language.

When using a statically typed language, the programmer is responsible for beginning by defining a type-system representing all the different types of data that the program will work with and manipulate. As an example, imagine you were writing software for a rental car company: you might start by defining types such as Car, Rental Agreement and Customer. As you will see shortly, these are called classes in Java, and they describe the types of data the program will use as it executes.

Once you have defined your type-system, you can start using these types (by generating objects from them). In a statically typed language the compiler can always determine which type you are referring to. If you attempt to invoke behavior that is incompatible with the type you are using the compiler will know. For instance, if you try to rent a Customer to a Car, the program will know this is invalid and generate an error. This means you never ship the faulty version of the software to your customers.

With a dynamically typed language the compiler does not know what types you are using, and therefore you can invoke any operation on any type. It will not be until the program actually runs that the language will determine whether the code is valid, and as a result dynamically typed software can be more error prone.

Statically typed languages tend to produce fewer errors at runtime because the compiler acts as a safety net and warns us that our code is attempting to do something it shouldn't. Statically typed languages can be more cumbersome to use however, and many programmers prefer the flexibility of dynamically typed languages.

There are strong arguments in favor of both statically and dynamically typed languages. This is not the time to discuss those arguments, but you should be aware that Java is statically typed. As it happens many other dynamically typed languages do produce Java bytecode, but these are outside the scope of this book.

Programming paradigm

A final important way to categorize languages is by their "family" or "paradigm", for instance:

⇒ Imperative programming language (think C)
⇒ Object-orientated programming language (think C++ and Smalltalk)
⇒ Functional programming language (think LISP and Haskell)

As you will see, Java started life an object-orientated language (don't worry if you do not know what this means at this stage, I will cover the important aspects of object-orientated languages shortly).

Java has, however, become a multi-paradigm language; it shares many traits with imperative programming languages, and, since Java 8, has incorporated many aspects of functional programming languages.

This is not uncommon – many modern languages are multi-paradigm languages. When done right this can add tremendous benefits to a language, because it allows the language to incorporate the best parts of each paradigm, and allows the programmer to use the paradigm that is best suited to their task at hand.

Throughout this book we will look in-depth at the multi-paradigm nature of Java, and look at how these different paradigms can be used effectively together.

That is all that you need to know about Java to begin – its time to write some code.

2 ABOUT THIS BOOK

Who is this book for?

The books in the "Software engineer learns" series are typically intended for existing programmers and software engineers transitioning from other languages or technologies. This particular book is also appropriate for anyone aspiring to become a software engineer, and who wishes to use Java as his or her starting point.

If you do not have any programming experience some of the material in the early chapters may feel daunting. My advice is to stick with it: it will start to make sense the more you progress through the book. Even the simplest Java program contains a number of advanced concepts, and it simply is not possible to convey all these concepts in a couple of pages, or even a couple of chapters.

The key purpose of this book is to provide you the skills required to become a competent software engineer. This means gaining a firm understanding not only of the language fundamentals, but also an understanding of how the language should be used to create a maintainable and adaptable code base

Java is a complex programming language. It cannot be learned in a day, or even a week. In fact, I have seen many other programmers make assumptions about how particular language features work, and maintain these assumptions for years without even realizing the problems these assumptions were causing them. It is not difficult to learn these features, and there is no better time to learn them than when you are starting out with the language.

This book will include many code examples, and it is recommended that you work through these examples yourself. One of the keys to learning a language is to experiment with it, and try things out. The simple act of typing code, even if it is copied word for word, is an important way to learn the language.

I encourage you to use the code examples as a starting point. Try changing features in these programs, or think of alternative ways to write the same functionality. The thought processes this will lead to are an important component in consolidating your knowledge of the language.

What is covered?

This book will not provide an introduction to the entire Java language – although the vast majority of the language will be covered. There are some features in Java that I have never used, and am unlikely to ever use; therefore there is very little point providing information on these features for the sake of completeness. Once you know the fundamentals of the language, you will find these features if you need them.

Java is now largely a server-side language rather than a client-side language. Java EE (Enterprise Edition) is a set of APIs that are commonly used to implement server-side Java components (running on web servers or application servers): these APIs are also outside the scope of this book, although I will be publishing a *Software Engineer Learns* edition for Java EE in the near future.

Java is now seldom used to implement rich GUI applications that run natively on desktop computers (although it is widely used to write native mobile applications via the Android SDK). For this reason this book will not examine the two main Java APIs for creating desktop applications: Java FX and Swing. This is a shame; because it is always nicer to write programs that can be interacted with via a GUI, but the reality is that you are unlikely to use these APIs in professional environments.

This book will also not focus on exhaustive lists of APIs. Web based resources have improved significantly over the years, and they are now by far the best source of information on specific APIs when you need them. What these web based resources are not so good at, however, is providing you the bigger picture of when the API should be used, and what its trade-offs are. This is where a book such as this can become valuable.

Before you start it is best that I warn you that Java is a large and complex language. A similar book for many other programming languages would be at most half the size of this book. I have tried to write the shortest book that I could, but I simply couldn't make it any shorter than I have without omitting important material.

I also would like to apologize up front for the fact that many of the programs in this book, particularly in the early chapters, are not solving interesting real-world problems. It is difficult to write interesting programs until you have a grasp of large portions of the language, and therefore the early chapters use simple examples.

Versions of Java

This book will focus on Java 8, because this is the latest release of the language, and contains many significant additions. Throughout the book I will specifically point out features that relate to Java 8 (and even Java 7 to some degree), because it is important for you to know that these are recent additions to the language. There are massive amounts of Java code already written in earlier versions of the language, and it may be your job to work with these at some stage, therefore you need to know the limitations of earlier versions of the language.

Although versions of Java are technically backwards compatible, it can take significant effort to upgrade a large Java program to a newer version of Java, therefore a lot of programs continue using older versions of the language.

Resources

All resources for this book can be found at the following website:

www.cisdal.com/java.html

Source code has been provided in HTML pages rather than Java code files. The idea is that you can copy and paste this code in cases where you do not want to type an entire example

Conventions

Code in this book will utilize the following font:

```
This is code
```

Instead of endnotes, this book will use the following convention for asides that are related to the main content, but are not directly associated with the main content.

> This is an aside

Feedback

I would love to hear your feedback (positive and negative) on this book. Please email me at dane@cisdal.com. Additionally, reviews are always appreciated because they are the most important way an independent publishing house such as ours can gain traction for its books.

3 GETTING STARTED WITH ECLIPSE

Technically all you need in order to write Java programs is a text editor and the Java Development Kit (which includes a Java compiler and a Java Runtime Environment for executing Java code). In reality, almost all software engineers who use Java to write non-trivial programs use an Integrated Development Environment (IDE).

An IDE provides an environment where code can be edited, built, run and debugged. In the Java world, the open source Eclipse IDE has become the most widely used, and therefore it will be used throughout this book. If you have a preference for another IDE you are welcome to use this instead of Eclipse.

The Eclipse IDE contains everything you will need to write and execute Java code, including a Java compiler and code editor. This section will guide you through the process of installing Eclipse.

Installing Eclipse on OSX

Before installing Eclipse, it is important to ensure you have the latest version of Java installed. Specifically, you need to ensure you have a Java 8 JDK installed (a Java JRE is not sufficient), this can be downloaded from the following web site (or search "Java 8 JDK" on Google):

http://www.oracle.com/technetwork/java/javase/downloads/jdk8-downloads-2133151.html

Once downloaded, install the dmg file just like any other OSX application.

You should now download Eclipse: open your favorite browser and navigate to http://www.eclipse.org/. Click the "Download" button on the homepage, and select to download the latest version of Eclipse for your platform. I will use the "Luna" release of Eclipse (version 4.4), but if a more recent version is available you can choose to use it.

The downloaded version of Eclipse is in the form of a zipped tar file. Once the file has been downloaded, copy it to the directory where you would like Eclipse to be installed, and double click on the file. This it will unzip the Eclipse application inside a folder called "eclipse".

In order to run Eclipse, simply double click on the Eclipse application (the one with the purple icon) inside this folder. You will likely receive a warning that Eclipse has been downloaded from the Internet, which you need to accept before continuing.

When Eclipse first starts it will ask you to select a workspace. An Eclipse workspace is the directory where your code will be saved, so choose an appropriate location on your computer, as seen in figure 3-1:

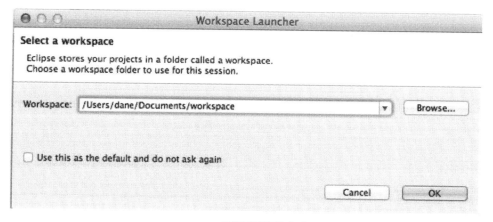

FIGURE 3-1

It is also worth checking the "Use this as a default" option so that you do not receive this prompt every time you start Eclipse.

Install on Windows

Before installing Eclipse, it is important to ensure you have the latest version of Java installed. Specifically, you need to ensure you have a Java 8 JDK installed (a Java JRE is not sufficient), this can be downloaded from the following web site (or search "Java 8 JDK" on Google):

http://www.oracle.com/technetwork/java/javase/downloads/jdk8-downloads-2133151.html

Once downloaded, install the downloaded file just like any other Windows application.

You should now download Eclipse: open your favorite browser and navigate to http://www.eclipse.org/. Click the "Download" button on the homepage, and select to download the latest version of Eclipse for your platform. I will use the "Luna" release of Eclipse (version 4.4), but if a more recent version is available you can choose to use it.

On Windows the download file is in zip format. Once the download completes, copy the zip file to the location you wish to install Eclipse. Once there, right click on the file and choose to extract its contents.

Eclipse does not need to be installed, the act of extracting it places all files in the appropriate location, and it can be run immediately.

Inside the Eclipse folder that has been created you will find a file called Eclipse.exe. Simply double click on this file to launch Eclipse.

When Eclipse first starts it will ask you to select a workspace, as seen in figure 3-2. An Eclipse workspace is the directory that you wish your code to be saved to:

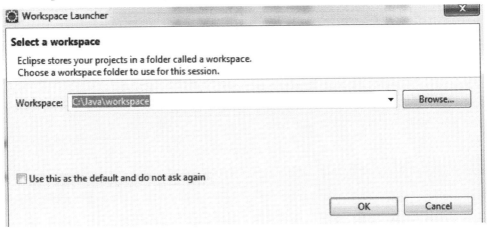

FIGURE 3-2

It is also worth ticking the "Use this as a default" option so that you do not receive this prompt every time you start Eclipse.

Getting started with Eclipse

Eclipse is a platform for software development. Although it is most closely related to Java (and is written in Java itself), Eclipse is a platform for writing software in many programming languages.

As such, Eclipse has a certain level of complexity built into it. Throughout this book I will introduce you to the most important aspects of the IDE, but be sure to take the time to explore for yourself – you will find lots of useful and time saving features.

When Eclipse opens for the first time you will be presented with the screen seen in figure 3-3:

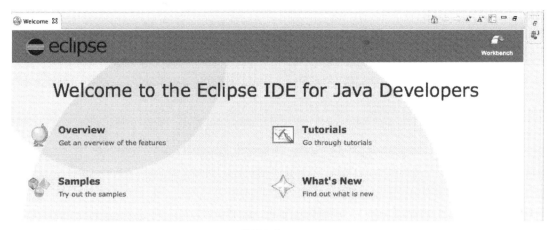

FIGURE 3-3

Click the "Workspace" icon in the top right hand corner of the screen: this will take you to the Eclipse workbench, which will appear as per figure 3-4:

FIGURE 3-4

Once you have Eclipse up and running you are ready to start working with the examples in this book.

4 HELLO WORLD!!!

There is a common convention when learning a new programming language that the first program you write is one that prints "Hello World!!!" to the console.

There is actually a very good reason for this. The act of producing the most trivial program possible introduces you to many important concepts, and involves the steps of writing source code, compiling that code, and executing it.

Before writing any code, first create a project in Eclipse. Projects are an Eclipse concept rather than a Java concept, and provide a container for all the code and libraries that constitute a program.

From the main menu choose `File -> New -> Java Project`. This option is shown in figure 4-1:

FIGURE 4-1

Inside the popup, use `helloworld` as the name of the project. It is also important to ensure at this point that the execution environment JRE is JavaSE1-8, as seen in figure 4-2.

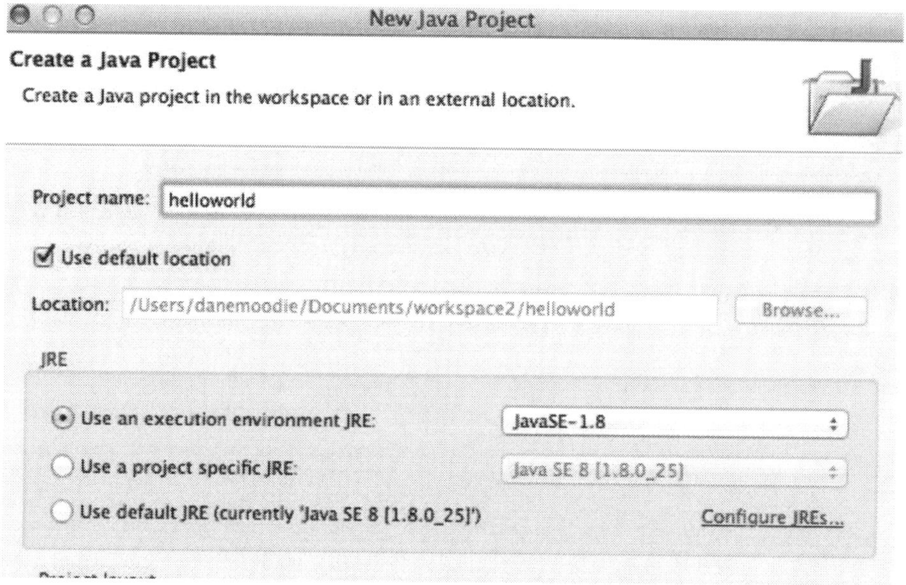

FIGURE 4-2

Once the project name has been entered, simply press the "Finish" button at the bottom.

You can now write the code to print "Hello World!!!" to the console.

All code in a Java program must be inside a *class*. I will explain what a class is in detail in the next chapter, but for now just think of it as a file containing Java source code. Each class has a name, and must be created inside a file with this exact same name, along with the file extension of `.java`.

Eclipse will always ensure that the name of the class and its filename are the same, but if you were using a text editor instead of an IDE it would be important to ensure this yourself.

When a class is compiled it will create a file with the same name, but a `.class` extension: this contains the Java bytecode that will be executed by the JRE.

There is a strict convention that classes should begin with capital letters, and utilize camel case (where each word is capitalized). For instance a class may be called `HelloWorld`, but should never be called `hello_world`: even though this is technically a valid name for a class.

Along with these conventions, Java does enforce a set of rules for class names. A class must begin with a character, but can then contain digits and the special characters "$" and "_". It is also worth mentioning at this point that everything in Java is case-sensitive – so `HelloWorld` and `Helloworld` could coexist as two separate classes.

Anything but the simplest Java program will contain many classes, therefore it is customary to group classes inside "packages". A package is essentially a folder or directory, and is represented by a directory on the file-system. Just like directories, packages can be nested inside one another.

In this example the class will be placed in a package called `hello`. By convention package names are entirely lower-case.

To create a class, use the `File-> New-> Class` option from the main menu. Alternatively, you could right click on the project name on the left of the screen and choose `New-> Class`.

After selecting this option you will be presented with a dialog box, as seen in figure 4-3, where you can specify the basic details of the class. Enter `hello` as the package name, `HelloWorld` as the class name, and ensure that you check the option `public static void main(String args[])`: I will explain this option shortly.

FIGURE 4-3

Once these values have been provided, press "Finish".

Eclipse will create the HelloWorld.java source file, and populate it with relevant code. This will be displayed to you in the editor, as seen in figure 4-4:

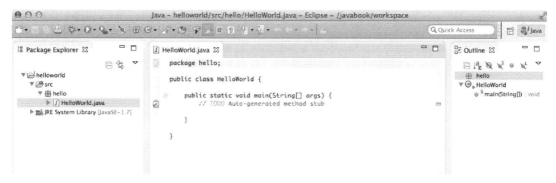

FIGURE 4-4

Additionally, if you look at the directory structure that has been created on the file system it will look like figure 4-5:

FIGURE 4-5

- The top-level folder is the Eclipse workspace.
- Inside this is a folder for the project called `helloworld`. This in turn contains two subfolders: a `src` folder for all source code, and a `bin` folder for the compiled version of the program. These are simply Eclipse conventions; the class files could just as easily be written to the `src` directory.
- Inside the `src` directory is a directory for the package created called `hello`, and finally, inside this is a file called `HelloWorld.java`. Notice that Eclipse has automatically added the `.java` extension for you, because this is a requirement of the language.

One convenient aspect of Eclipse is that it compiles a class every time it is saved (or attempts to at least). This means that if you look inside the `bin` directory, you will find an identical structure to the `src` directory hierarchy, except their will be a file called `HelloWorld.class`, because it is the compiled version of the class.

You are now ready to look at the code that has been generated by Eclipse. Because all Java classes contain the same basic structure, Eclipse is able to generate some code for you: if you had been writing this code with a text editor you would need to write this yourself.

Eclipse should have generated the following code:

```
package hello;
```

```
public class HelloWorld {

    public static void main(String[] args) {
        // TODO Auto-generated method stub
    }
}
```

The first line of each class is the package declaration:

```
package hello;
```

Technically this line is optional, because the code could be placed directly in the `src` directory, and would not be in a package. It is advised to always place code inside packages however, because even simple programs tend to grow over time, and packages are an important way of maintaining the structure of a program.

You will also notice that the package declaration ends with a semi-colon. All Java statements must end with semi-colons. Unlike some languages (I'm looking at you JavaScript), semi-colons are not optional in Java.

The empty line after the package declaration is not required, but since white space is ignored in Java, adding an empty line such as this can improve readability.

The next line provides the declaration of the class:

```
public class HelloWorld {
```

You can ignore the keyword `public` for now, I will explore this in detail in subsequent chapters. The next keyword `class` indicates that you are declaring a class, while `HelloWorld` is the name of the class. All Java class files will begin with a similar declaration, although, as you will see, there are many variants of this declaration.

This line of code ends with a curly bracket rather than a semi-colon. Curly brackets are used in Java to wrap *blocks* of code: a "{" indicates that a code block is beginning, while a "}" indicates that a code block is ending. A code block is a grouping mechanism for a set of statements.

Although blocks can be nested inside one another, curly brackets must always go in pairs because every code block must eventually end. The entire class is considered a block of code; therefore the closing curly bracket on the last line of the file signifies the end of this block, and therefore the end of the class.

The next line of code is slightly more complex:

```
public static void main(String[] args) {
```

This is a method declaration. A method provides a container for code, and therefore encapsulates the behavior of the program when it executes. Classes can contain many different methods.

A method can be thought of as a function or a procedure if you are familiar with these concepts in other languages, although as you will see, there are important differences.

It is worth noting that these lines of code only exists because you clicked the `public static void main(String args[])` option when you created the class. You clicked that because you wanted to add a special kind of method to this particular class.

When a computer program executes it needs to start somewhere. In some languages execution simply begins at the start of a specified source file, and continues until the end of that source file. Java always begins execution inside a method called `main`, and that method must have the *signature* seen in this example. When you run the Java program you will tell the JRE which class contains the `main` method, and this will be implicitly executed when the program begins executing.

> A method signature is the combination of its name, and the types (and order) of parameters it accepts (`main` accepts a single parameter of type `String[]`). Each method in a class must have a unique method signature.

Technically multiple classes can contain `main` methods, but when the program runs only the `main` method in the specified class will be executed.

I will ignore the `public` and `static` keywords until later chapters. The next keyword in the signature is `void`: this indicates the type of data returned by the method when it finishes execution. Because the `main` method does not return any data, it is always declared as returning `void`.

The next identifier in the signature, `main`, is the name of the method. Method names are usually arbitrary, with the exception that they conventionally start with a lower case character. As mentioned, the `main` name is not arbitrary in this case, because the Java Runtime Environment will look for a method named `main` when the program starts executing.

The `main` method accepts a parameter, as indicated by the following syntax (`String[] args`). Parameters provide a mechanism for passing data to methods. Each parameter has a type, in this case `String[]` which means it is an array of character strings (i.e. zero or more character strings), and a name: `args` in this case. The name of the parameter is not important, this line could have just as easily been declared:

```
public static void main(String[] arguments) {
```

The parameter accepted by `main` provides an important feature. When any Java program begins execution it can be passed a set of arguments: these will then be made available in this array. Passing arguments to a program at runtime allows the same compiled program to behave differently depending on the values passed to it. For instance, in this case you could pass an argument specifying that the program should print its output in capital letters.

You will not pass any arguments to this program, but it is still necessary to declare that the `main` method accepts this parameter.

The `main` method also contains a block of code, therefore it uses open and closing curly brackets to denote its start and finish: anything inside these curly brackets is the method body.

Notice that these curly brackets are nested inside the curly brackets for the class itself. Because Java code can consist of many nested blocks of curly brackets, it is important to indent each block, as seen in this example.

This is not a requirement of the language, but it makes it much easier to find the closing bracket for an opening bracket because, as you will see in future chapters, the nesting can sometimes be many levels deep.

The final line of code that Eclipse has generated for us is a comment:

```
// TODO Auto-generated method stub
```

Comments can either be denoted with a double forward slash (as in this case) or using the following construct if they span multiple lines:

```
/* This comment
spans multiple
lines */
```

Naturally comments have no bearing on the program at run time, but they are an important way of conveying the meaning of code to other programmers.

In order to print `Hello World!!!` to the console you need to add a line of code to the `main` method as follows:

```
public static void main(String[] args) {
    System.out.println("Hello World!!!");
}
```

I will not explain the full complexity of this line for now, but `System` is a class that comes built into Java. The code `.out` accesses a utility object held by the `System` class called a `PrintStream`, which acts as the standard output for the program. The code `System.out` therefore can be thought of as a mechanism for accessing the standard output of the program.

The next portion of this line `.println` is invoking a method on the `PrintStream` object called `println`. This method is just like the `main` method you have written, except it is provided by the Java platform.

The `println` method can be passed an argument of type `String`. In this case you will create a *literal* `String` by simply enclosing a set of characters inside double quotes. Notice that the argument is enclosed within `()` brackets.

> The terms parameter and argument are subtly different.
>
> When methods are defined, the list of *parameters* is specified. When the method is invoked, a set of *arguments* is passed to these parameters.

The `println` method will print the string it is passed to the standard output of the program, which in your case will be the Eclipse console. If you were running this program from an operation system console or shell, the standard output would be that console or shell.

You can now run the program by selecting `Run -> Run` from the main menu. When you choose this option, Eclipse will look for a class in the project with a `main` method and run it.

Alternatively you could have right clicked on the `HelloWorld` class and chosen `Run As -> Java Application`.

When the program runs it will produce the output seen in figure 4-6 to the Console tab of Eclipse:

```
Problems  @ Javadoc  Declaration  Console
<terminated> HelloWorld [Java Application] /Library/Java/JavaVirtualMachines/
Hello World!!!
```

FIGURE 4-6

Congratulations, you have just written and executed your first Java program!

Trouble shooting

Even with simple programs such as this, it is important to know how to trouble shoot problems that may arise. In order to demonstrate this, go back to the editor and remove the semi-colon from the end of the following line:

```
System.out.println("Hello World!!!")
```

This has introduced a syntax error into the code; meaning Eclipse is unable to compile it.

Eclipse will warn you that a problem exists in the code by adding a red dot to the margin of the editor at the appropriate line, as seen in figure 4-7:

```
public static void main(String[] args) {
    System.out.println("Hello World!!!")
}
```

FIGURE 4-7

If you click on the red dot, Eclipse will tell you what the problem is:

```
Syntax error, insert ";" to complete
```

In this case the error tells you exactly what the problem is. Eclipse is not always so helpful, but usually knowing where the problem is provides enough information to know how to fix it.

You will also notice that you cannot run a Java program if it contains any compilation errors. Attempting to run the program now produces the following message:

```
Exception in thread "main" java.lang.Error: Unresolved compilation problem:
    Syntax error, insert ";" to complete BlockStatements

    at hello.HelloWorld.main(HelloWorld.java:6)
```

Conclusion

The Hello World program demonstrated in this chapter is not as simple as Hello World programs in many other languages. Not only is it several lines longer than many languages, it is difficult to concisely explain many features of this program without understanding more of the language. In fact, I have not explained many of the keywords used in this program.

This in itself does not make Java a good or bad language, but it does stem from an important principle in Java: everything is a class. Many languages, including object orientated languages such as C++ allow arbitrary code to be included in a source file and executed: Java insists that all code is placed within a class structure. In many languages this program could be written as a single line of code, for instance:

```
print("Hello World!!! ")
```

In the next chapter you are going to take a closer look at classes, and the related concept of objects, this will include a look at some of the keywords I skipped over in this chapter.

5 CLASSES & OBJECTS

As mentioned in the introduction, Java is an object-orientated programming language. Object-orientated programming is a paradigm that uses the concept of an object to encapsulate the data and behavior of a program. Objects are reusable modules, and can interact with one another as the program executes.

This differs from many other programming languages that use functions or procedures to encapsulate the behavior of the program: these languages are called functional-orientated and imperative languages respectively.

Object-orientated programming was already well established when Java was created, and can be traced all the way back to the 1960s. Java was notable for being a more pure object-orientated language than many of its direct competitors, however, most notably C++..

The most important concept to grasp in this chapter is the difference between a *class* and an *object*. A class acts as a template for objects: it declares the data that will be held by an object, and the methods that operate on this data. Put another way, once a class is defined, many instances of the class can be constructed, and these are called objects.

You can think of classes as molds. Once you have constructed your mold you can use it to create as many objects as you like from the mold.

Some object-orientated languages let you create objects without classes (yes, I am looking at you again JavaScript). With Java, however, you always need to start with a class.

Each object created from a class is independent from the other objects constructed from the same class, but the methods available remain the same. Before explaining the concepts of classes and objects in more detail it is worth doing so with examples.

Classes are usually thought of as the "nouns" of a program. You may remember from grammar class that nouns are used to name "things" such as people, places, ideas or animals. These are opposed to verbs, which describe actions.

When you first sit down to write a Java program you need to think about what the nouns will be. For instance, in a rental car program the nouns may be Customer, Car and Rental agreement. In a banking program the nouns may be Customer, Account and Branch.

Once you have defined the nouns, you next start thinking about the data each of these nouns needs to hold. You describe the data that will be captured by defining *fields* on the class. For instance, a Rental agreement class might contain fields that capture the daily rate, the date the agreement was signed, and any special charges that will be applied to the rate. The class defines the fields, while each object will be assigned specific values for these fields.

Finally you need to think about what behavior is required from the class; the behavior will be captured in the class's *methods*. For instance, the Rental agreement class might have a method that calculates the total cost to the customer. In order to achieve this, methods can read and modify the data held by an object.

You will remember from the Hello World example that you declared a class called `HelloWorld`. Before beginning the examples in this chapter it is worth pointing out a quirk of the Hello World program. In that program you did not create an object from the `HelloWorld` class, yet its `main` method could still be invoked. This is because the method was declared as `static`:

```
public static void main(String[] arguments) {
```

Static methods are different from most of the methods that you will look at in this book because they can be invoked directly on the class, rather than instances of the class (its objects). This is a subject I will return to in later chapters.

Declaring a class

You will begin by creating a new project in Eclipse called `ObjectsAndClasses`.

Inside this project, create a new class called `Car`, and place this class inside a package called `vehicles`.

Because you now have multiple projects in Eclipse, Eclipse needs to know which project the class should be added to. The easiest way to ensure that the class is created in the correct project is to select that project in the "Package Explorer" on the left hand side of Eclipse: this automatically selects that project as the "current" project.

Unlike the `HelloWorld` class from the previous chapter, you will not check the `public static void main(String[] args)` option when creating this class.

When you click "Finish", Eclipse will generate the following code:

```
package vehicles;
public class Car {

}
```

Everything about this code should look familiar from the `HelloWorld` example in the previous chapter: the class resides in a package, and consists of an empty code block.

The first step for defining a class is adding its fields. The fields that the class needs will depend on the program in which the class will be used. For instance, a Car in a vehicle registration program might hold very different data to a Car in a taxi booking system.

The process of determining the fields that are relevant for the program being written is called data-abstraction. This is because you are creating an *abstraction* of a Car that models just the information and behavior that is relevant for the context you are using it in.

Although computer programs often represent concepts in the real world, they do not have to represent every aspect of the real world. One of the most important skills you will need to acquire as a programmer or software engineer (regardless of the language you are using) is the ability to abstract the relevant features and characteristics of real-world entities that are important for your task at hand.

In this particular case you will focus on the fields that may be relevant for a car in a vehicle registration system, therefore add the following fields:

```
package vehicles;

public class Car {
    private String registrationNumber;
    private String make;
    private String model;
    private int engineSize;
    private short yearFirstRegistered;
}
```

You have added five fields to this class. Each definition contains three component parts:

- ❖ **An access modifier**: `private` in this case
- ❖ **A data-type**: this indicates the type of data that each field holds
- ❖ **A name**: this can be used to reference the field

These component parts will be described in more detail shortly.

Due to the fact that this is a class (or a template for objects), you do not need to assign values to the fields; the values will be assigned to each instance (or object) you create from this class.

In some cases it may make sense for a field to have a *default* value. A default value is an initial value that you want all objects to have. This can be achieved by adding an equal sign and then a value after the field definition, for instance:

```
private short yearFirstRegistered = 2015;
```

Each field that you define has a data-type. A data-type defines the type of data that can be stored in that field. Java is a statically typed language, therefore you must declare the type of every field, and this can never be changed once the program begins executing. For instance, you cannot decide you want some `Car` objects to use an `int` for `registrationNumber`.

The type of each field can either be a class (as seen in the first three fields that are defined to be of type `String`), or a primitive type, as seen on the last two fields that use `int` and `short` respectively.

Primitive types are the basic building block of the Java language: they consist of a simple, atomic value such as a number, a character or a boolean (`true` or `false`). It is not possible to define your own primitive types; you are limited to those defined in the language. Classes on the other hand aggregate a set of primitive values or other classes together, and assign meaning to the set of values (as you are doing with the `Car` class).

You will look at primitive data-types in more detail in later chapters, but the following list briefly describes each primitive data-type:

- `boolean`: stores the value `true` or `false`
- `byte`: holds an 8 bit signed integer (i.e. -127 through to 128)
- `short`: can be assigned a 16 bit signed integer (i.e. 32,768 through to 32,767)
- `char`: can be assigned a 16 bit Unicode character
- `int`: can be assigned a 32 bit signed integer (i.e. -2^{31} through to $2^{31}-1$). This is the default choice for integer numbers in Java
- `long`: can be assigned a 64 bit signed integer (i.e. -2^{64} through to $2^{64}-1$)
- `float`: this can be assigned a 32 bit signed floating point number, defined in accordance with the IEEE 754 specification. There is no definitive range for this type, since it depends how much precision the number needs to be recorded to
- `double`: this can be assigned a 64 bit signed floating point number. This is the default choice for floating point numbers in Java

> Strings are not primitive types, because they are constructed as an array (list) of `char` values.

In the `Car` example you will see that the `engineSize` field is defined as an `int`, while `yearFirstRegistered` is a `short`, because it will contain a year (for instance 2010 - you will see later in the book, however, that there are better ways of representing years in Java). All other fields are defined as `Strings`.

You may also notice that each field has been declared as `private`. I will explain the meaning of this later in the chapter, but essentially it is a way of controlling access to the data held in the field.

Finally, each field has been assigned an appropriate name, always beginning with a lower-case character, and utilizing the camel case convention (each word starts with a capital letter). As mentioned earlier, this is not a requirement of the language, but is a near-universally accepted standard.

The naming requirements for fields are the same as classes: they must start with a character, and then can contain characters, numbers the underscore character and the dollar sign character. It is not possible for two fields in the same class to have the same name (even if they have different types), but there is no problem if two different classes have fields with the same name.

Now that you have added fields to the class, you need to think about the methods needed by the class. The methods define the behavior of the class, or the things it can do. Methods will often represent the "verbs" of the program. In this class you will define two methods:

⇒ A method to change the registration of the Car
⇒ A method to return the details of the Car as a formatted String so that it can be printed out

The method for changing the registration number should be defined as follows:

```
public void changeRegistrationNumber(String newRegistrationNumber) {
    registrationNumber = newRegistrationNumber;
}
```

The best way to think about a method is a block of code that:

- Optionally accepts a set of arguments
- Performs some processing with these arguments and/or any fields defined on the class
- Optionally returns data to its invoker

You should add this code to the body of the class (before the final curly bracket). It is customary to add all the fields at the top of the class, and the methods at the bottom of the class.

The first line of this code defines the signature of the method:

```
public void changeRegistrationNumber(String newRegistrationNumber)
```

This is slightly more complex than a field definition, and consists of the following:

- The access modifier of the method, public in this case. This will be explained shortly
- The type of data the method returns when it finishes executing, or void if the method does not return a value
- The name of the method, changeRegistrationNumber in this case. The name of the method should attempt to concisely describe what the method does.
- The list of parameters accepted by the method; in this case a single parameter called newRegistrationNumber that should have the data-type String.

In the method body, the argument passed to the method will replace the existing value of the registrationNumber field:

```
registrationNumber = newRegistrationNumber;
```

The = operator is referred to as the assignment operator, and is used for assigning a new value to a variable or field.

An alternative way to write this method would be as follows:

```
public void changeRegistrationNumber(String registrationNumber) {
    this.registrationNumber = registrationNumber;
}
```

Notice in this case that the parameter has the exact same name as the field defined on the class. Within the body of the method, `registrationNumber` will refer to the parameter, therefore in order to refer to the field you need to prefix the field name with `this`.

> Remember, although the field is declared on a class, this method, when called, will change the value of that field for a single object (or instance of that class).

The value `this` is a special keyword that refers to the object itself – therefore `this.registrationNumber` refers to the `registrationNumber` field on the object the method is being executed against.

It is good practice to use `this` when referring to fields because it avoids issues that can arise when parameters or variables share the same name as fields on the object. For instance, the following code does not change the `registrationNumber` field:

```
public void changeRegistrationNumber(String registrationNumber) {
    registrationNumber = registrationNumber;
}
```

It simply sets the `registrationNumber` parameter to have the value it already has.

The method returning the details of a `Car` will return a `String` encoded as follows `VDY666 (2012-Toyota)`. It therefore needs to *concatenate* together details from three different fields. There are multiple ways to concatenate `Strings` in Java, but the simplest is by using the + operator.

```
public String getDescriptionOfCar() {
    return registrationNumber +
        " (" + yearFirstRegistered + "-" + make + ")";
}
```

> Notice in this case that a single statement has been split across two lines in order to improve readability. This is possible due to the fact that white space, including carriage returns, is ignored by Java.

The use of the + operator here is an example of *operator overloading*. If the + operator is used on two or more numbers it performs addition. If any of the operands are `Strings`, however, they are concatenated (or joined) together to create a new `String`.

This line of code concatenates fields on the object, such as `registrationNumber`, with literal `Strings` such as `" ("`.

Notice that the statement begins with the `return` keyword. This means that once the `String`s are joined together, the result will be automatically returned from the method, and made available to whoever called the method.

An alternative way of writing this method would be as follows:

```java
public String getDescriptionOfCar() {
    String result = registrationNumber +
        " (" + yearFirstRegistered + "-" + make + ")";
    return result;
}
```

On the first line of this version a local variable is declared inside the method called `result`: this has the data-type `String`. The result of the concatenation is then assigned to this variable.

Local variables are private to the method itself, and can be used to store the state of intermediary operations as the method executes. Local variables are always destroyed when the method finishes executing, therefore it is not possible to store state in one invocation of a method, and use that state in another invocation of the method.

On the second line of the method the value of the `result` variable is returned from the method to its invoker. From the point of view of the invoker these two implementations are identical.

You now have a class with fields and methods. You are still missing one ingredient however: you need a way of setting the values of all the fields when you first construct objects from the class. Put another way, you need a mechanism for setting the initial *state* of each object.

In order to set the value of fields when the object is created you will use a feature called a *constructor*. A constructor is similar to a method: it accepts parameters, and encapsulates a block of code. Unlike methods, however, it is invoked only when an object is first created.

A constructor always has the same name as the class (including the capitalization of the first letter), and unlike a method it does not declare a return type, because a constructor can never return a value. The following is an example:

```java
public Car(String initialRegistrationNumber, String initialMake,
          String initialModel, int initialEngineSize,
          short initialYearFirstRegistered) {
    registrationNumber = initialRegistrationNumber;
    make = initialMake;
    model = initialModel;
    engineSize = initialEngineSize;
    yearFirstRegistered = initialYearFirstRegistered;
}
```

Again, this is more commonly written as follows:

```java
public Car(String initialRegistrationNumber, String initialMake,
          String initialModel, int initialEngineSize,
          short initialYearFirstRegistered) {
    this.registrationNumber = initialRegistrationNumber;
```

```
    this.make = initialMake;
    this.model = initialModel;
    this.engineSize = initialEngineSize;
    this.yearFirstRegistered = initialYearFirstRegistered;
}
```

Using `this` makes it clear that you are setting fields on the object.

It is not mandatory to have a constructor on every class: as you will see, there are other ways to set the initial state of an object. It is also possible to have multiple constructors on a single class. You will look at constructors in considerable detail in the coming chapters.

With the constructor in place the entire `Car` class should look like this:

```
package vehicles;

public class Car {
    private String registrationNumber;
    private String make;
    private String model;
    private int engineSize;
    private short yearFirstRegistered;

    public Car(String initialRegistrationNumber,
            String initialMake, String initialModel,
            int initialEngineSize,
            short initialYearFirstRegistered) {
        registrationNumber = initialRegistrationNumber;
        make = initialMake;
        model = initialModel;
        engineSize = initialEngineSize;
        yearFirstRegistered = initialYearFirstRegistered;
    }

    public void changeRegistrationNumber(String registrationNumber) {
        this.registrationNumber = registrationNumber;
    }

    public String getDescriptionOfCar() {
        return registrationNumber + " (" +
            yearFirstRegistered + "-" + make + ")";
    }
}
```

Constructing objects from a class

Now that the `Car` class has been defined, you can start creating objects from it. Remember, the class acts as a template for the objects that are constructed from it.

In order to start using this class you will create a new class called `Main`, and give it a `main` method, because (as mentioned in the previous chapter) all programs need to start in a class with a `main` method. This will be similar to the class you created in the previous chapter: you will not create objects from this class; you will simply take advantage of its `main` method:

```
package vehicles;
```

```
public class Main {
    public static void main(String[] args) {
    }
}
```

Inside the `main` method you can create an instance of the `Car` class and assign it to a local variable called `car1`:

```
public static void main(String[] args) {
    Car car1 = new Car("HGS928", "Ford",
        "Focus", 1800, (short) 2010);
}
```

There are a number of things worth mentioning about this new line of code:

- ❖ The *variable* `car1` is declared to be of type `Car`. As mentioned earlier, variables are different from fields, because they are defined inside methods, and local to that method.
- ❖ The `new` keyword is used to indicate that an object should be instantiated from the designated class. The type of class that should be constructed follows the `new` keyword: `Car` in this case.
- ❖ The arguments inside the `()` brackets are passed to the parameters defined by the constructor of the `Car` class. Notice that you do not name the arguments, therefore the order in which they are specified must be the same order they are defined on the `Car` constructor. You are passing literal values to the constructor, but you could also pass local variables if they were of the appropriate type.
- ❖ The last parameter passed is `(short) 2010` rather than simply `2010`. When an integer is defined as a literal value, it automatically has the data-type of `int` (which is a 4 byte signed integer). You are passing this to a parameter that is defined as a `short` (which is a 2 byte signed integer), therefore, technically the number may be too big to fit the parameter. Adding the `(short)` declaration before the number is a way of telling the compiler that you are confident the number will fit into a `short` parameter. This process is called *casting*.
  In the case of a literal such as `2010` you could argue that the compiler should know that the number will fit into a `short` value, but the number could have been constructed via a complex mathematical operation, therefore the compiler errs on the side of simplicity and insists numbers are always cast from larger to smaller data-types.

> I have specified the engine size in cubic centimeters rather than cubic inches, as is more common in North America. This highlights another important issue with data-abstraction: it is important to agree how a value should be interpreted, and document this in the class itself via comments. Later chapters will examine an important concept called JavaDoc that allows you to document an API.

Once the line of code has executed you have an instance of the `Car` class assigned to the car1 variable, and this has the *state* of the values passed to the constructor. You can now start using the object my invoking its methods:

```
public static void main(String[] args) {
   Car car1 = new Car("HGS928", "Ford",
      "Focus", 1800, (short) 2010);
   System.out.println(car1.getDescriptionOfCar());
   car1.changeRegistrationNumber("ZZZ999");
   System.out.println(car1.getDescriptionOfCar());
}
```

Notice that you invoke a method on an object by specifying:

- The variable holding a reference to the object, `car1` in this case
- A dot
- The method name
- The arguments you wish to pass to the method – you always need to add `()` even if the method does not accept any arguments

You will also notice that if you type `car1.` Eclipse will automatically provide you a set of method names that it knows you can invoke, as seen in figure 5-1:

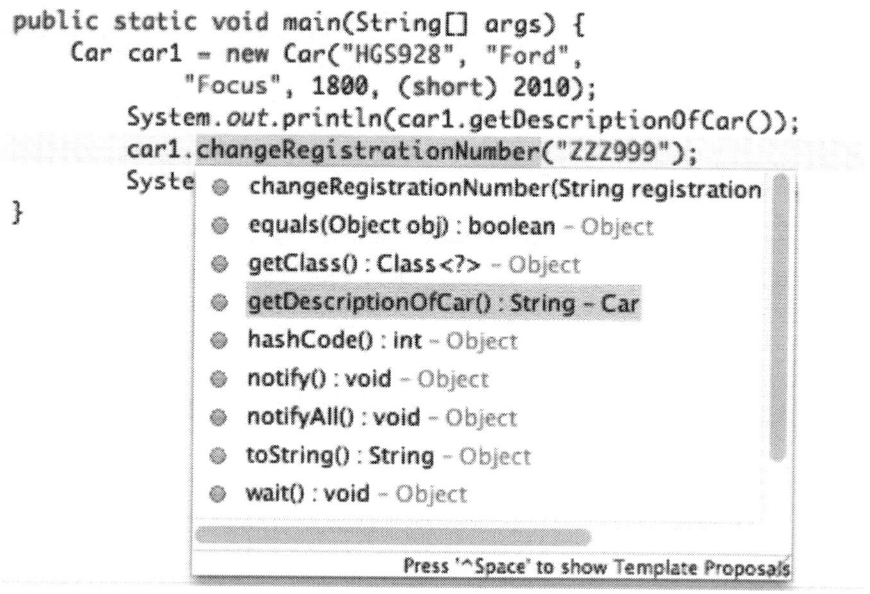

FIGURE 5-1

> This list contains a number of methods you did not create, such as `equals` and `getClass`. I will explain the presence of these methods later in the book.

If you run this program it should display the following output:

```
HGS928 (2010-Ford)
ZZZ999 (2010-Ford)
```

Because classes are templates for objects, the same class can now be used to create more `Car` objects. Each object created from the `Car` class is independent of the others, and will have its own state. They will, however, all expose the same methods:

```
public static void main(String[] args) {
    Car car1 = new Car("HGS928", "Ford",
        "Focus", 1800, (short) 2010);
    System.out.println(car1.getDescriptionOfCar());
    car1.changeRegistrationNumber("ZZZ999");
    System.out.println(car1.getDescriptionOfCar());
    Car car2 = new Car("GGG666", "Mazda",
        "CX5", 2000, (short) 2013);
    Car car3 = new Car("JKL333", "Toyota",
        "Corolla", 1800, (short) 2012);
    System.out.println(car2.getDescriptionOfCar());
    System.out.println(car3.getDescriptionOfCar());
}
```

Notice that you always specify the specific instance of the object you wish a method to be invoked on.

This will produce the following output:

```
HGS928 (2010-Ford)
ZZZ999 (2010-Ford)
GGG666 (2013-Mazda)
JKL333 (2012-Toyota)
```

This demonstrates that each instance of the `Car` class has its own completely independent state: changing the registration number on one instance will not have any impact on other instances of the class.

Encapsulation

Now that you have a working example of a class, and have begun creating objects from it, it is possible to start explaining the keywords `public` and `private` that you have seen several times. These keywords are referred to as *access modifiers*, and control the visibility of methods or fields.

Consider a case where you want to change the `engineSize` of `car1` inside the `main` method. It may seem sensible to use the following code:

```
Car car1 = new Car("HGS928", "Ford",
    "Focus", 1800, (short) 2010);
car1.engineSize = 1900;
```

The dot notation can be used to access fields just in the same way it can be used to access methods, so there is nothing inherently wrong with this code. Additionally, this is essentially following the same approach employed by the `changeRegistrationNumber` method when modifying the `registrationNumber` field; you are simply altering the value of the field.

If you try to write this code, however, Eclipse will generate the error seen in figure 5-2:

```
public static void main(String[] args) {
    Car car1 = new Car("HGS928", "Ford", "Focus", 1800, (short) 2010);
    car1.engineSize = 1900;
    Syste
    car1.  The field Car.engineSize is not visible
    Syste  2 quick fixes available:
    Car c                                                    000, (short) 2013);
    Car c    Change visibility of 'engineSize' to 'default'
    Syste    Create getter and setter for 'engineSize'...    a", 1800, (short) 2012);
    Syste
}
```

FIGURE 5-2

The reason for this is that the `engineSize` field on the `Car` class has been declared as `private`:

`private int engineSize;`

This means that the `engineSize` field is not visible outside of the `Car` class. Despite this, methods inside of the `Car` class can access and modify the `engineSize` field. For instance, the following method could be added to the `Car` class:

```
public void setEngineSize(int newEngineSize) {
    this.engineSize = newEngineSize;
}
```

It is possible to make the `engineSize` field visible outside the class by changing its access modifier to `public`:

`public int engineSize;`

There are in fact 4 access modifiers. When applied to fields and methods these access modifiers have the following meaning:

⇒ **public** means that any code with a reference to instances of the class have visibility of the method or field. For instance, because the methods on `Car` were declared as `public`, the `Main` class is able to invoke them. If the methods had been declared as `private` they could not have been invoked from outside the `Car` class.

⇒ **protected** means that any code in the class itself, or in code extending the class has visibility of the fields or methods. This will be explained further when we discuss inheritance.

⇒ The absence of an access modifier means that any code inside the same package has visibility of the field or method. This access modifier is referred to as the *default* access modifier, but is rarely used. Because the `Main` and `Car` classes are in the same package, the methods on `Car` could have used this access modifier.

⇒ **private** means that the field or method is only visible to other code inside the same instance of the class.

Rather than changing the `engineSize` field to `public`, it is first worth asking why you would want to mark a field or method with anything other than `public` in the first place. To put it another way: why do you want to restrict access to fields or methods?

The key answer to this question is *encapsulation,* or as it is sometimes called, *data-hiding.* Encapsulation allows you to expose some of an object's features, while hiding its internal details from the outside world.

A key reason for encapsulation is that each class should expose a well-defined API (application programmer interface) to the outside world, while hiding its internal logic and state. This allows the internal logic of the class to change without impacting any other code that uses the class.

Let's consider a very simple example. The following is a class that acts as a counter and could be used by any piece of code to count how many times an operation has occurred:

```java
package counting;
public class Counter {
    private int count = 0;

    public int getNextValue() {
        count = count + 1;
        return  count;
    }
}
```

This can be used as follows:

```java
package counting;
public class Main {

    public static void main(String[] args) {
        Counter c = new Counter();
        System.out.println(c.getNextValue());
        System.out.println(c.getNextValue());
    }
}
```

With this implementation of `Counter` you can be sure that if one call to `getNextValue` returns 1, then the next call will return 2. Imagine, however, what could happen if you made the `count` field `public`. All of a sudden it would be possible to manipulate the state of a `Counter` object, and therefore the behavior of `getNextValue` becomes unpredictable:

```java
package counting;

public class Main {

    public static void main(String[] args) {
        Counter c = new Counter();
        System.out.println(c.getNextValue());
        c.count = 0;
        System.out.println(c.getNextValue());
    }
}
```

Similar problems could be imagined with the `Car` class. Consider the `yearFirstRegistered` field: if this was made `public` any code could change it to any value, including negative values. If you wish to allow it to be modified you should instead provide a `public` method that first validates the new value before accepting it.

> Naturally the constructor should perform the same range checks. Data validation is a subject I will return to once you have a greater understanding of fundamental concepts.

Understanding encapsulation is one of the keys to understanding Object Orientated Programming, and will be explored in more detail in the chapters that follow. Although encapsulation does not provide any real benefits in the simple programs you are writing at the moment, it becomes increasingly important as programs grow in size and complexity.

In Java, it is conventional to always declare fields as `private`, even if you do not care how the field is accessed or modified. A pair of methods is then provided for each field called a *getter* and *setter*. These allow the field's value to be accessed and modified respectively. You can easily generate these methods by right clicking on the `Car` class, and choosing `Source -> Generate Getters and Setters...`, as seen in figure 5-3:

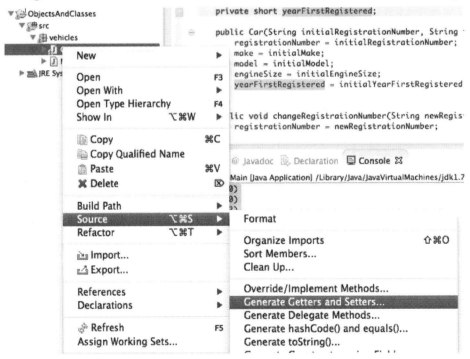

FIGURE 5-3

You can then choose the fields that you wish to expose via getters and setters, as seen in figure 5-4:

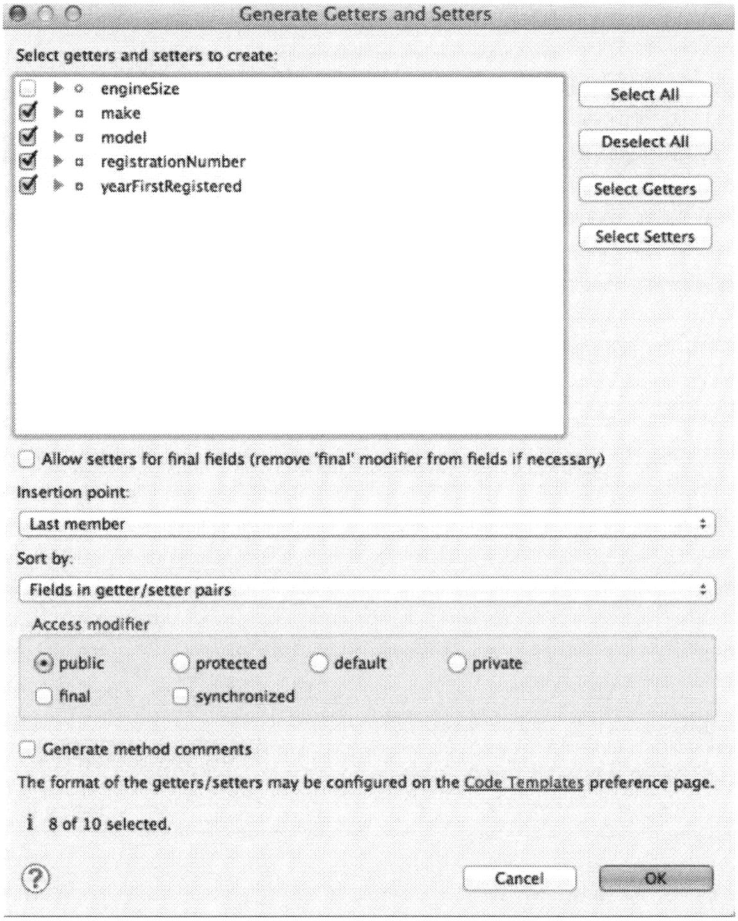

FIGURE 5-4

When "OK" is selected, the following code will be generated:

```
public String getRegistrationNumber() {
    return registrationNumber;
}

public void setRegistrationNumber(String registrationNumber) {
    this.registrationNumber = registrationNumber;
}

public String getMake() {
    return make;
}

public void setMake(String make) {
    this.make = make;
}

public String getModel() {
    return model;
}
```

```
public void setModel(String model) {
    this.model = model;
}

public short getYearFirstRegistered() {
    return yearFirstRegistered;
}

public void setYearFirstRegistered(short yearFirstRegistered) {
    this.yearFirstRegistered = yearFirstRegistered;
}
```

You will find many cases where it is convenient to have Eclipse generate code for you. This highlights a further advantage of using an IDE such as Eclipse over a text editor.

As can be seen, getters and setters follow a strict pattern. The fields are prefixed with either `get` or `set`, and the field name is capitalized. With these in place, you can now change the make of a `Car` inside the `Main` class:

`car1.setMake("Ford");`

The convention used for the getters and setters in this example is actually part of a programming standard called the JavaBean specification. Many libraries rely on classes following the JavaBean specification; therefore if assessors and modifiers are required for a field, they should follow the naming convention demonstrated here.

There is one main exception to the naming convention shown here: if the field is of type `boolean`, the getter can optionally use `is` rather than `get`, for instance `isFieldName()`.

You may be wondering what the point is of providing getters and setters in this manner if you don't really care how the field is accessed or modified: why not just make the fields `public`? The main answers are as follows:

⇒ It ensures that extra logic can be added to the getters or setters in the future (such as validation) without changing external code.
⇒ Many other libraries and tools expect classes to follow the JavaBean specification.
⇒ Once I introduce the concept of debugging a program it will become obvious that it is easier to debug changes to a field when it is modified through a setter rather than directly.
⇒ It is possible to provide different access modifiers to the getter and setter. For instance, the getter may be `public`, but the setter `protected`. It is also possible to only provide a getter, and therefore essentially make the field read-only.

In reality, 99% of the getters and setters I have written are of the generic kind seen above, but the arguments in favor of getters and setters (and the fact it is easy to generate the code) mean it makes sense to stick with this approach.

You will have also noticed that classes have access modifiers: all of the classes you have created so far are `public`. Access modifiers work slightly differently with classes, and will be discussed in later chapters.

Static code

At this point it is worth stopping to take a more detailed look at another important concept: the `static` keyword. You have seen one example so far of a `static` method: the `main` method of the program. The `static` keyword can in fact be used on any field or method.

The `static` modifier means that the method or field exists on the class itself, rather than instances of the class. If a field is `static`, therefore, it only ever has a single value, no matter how many instances of the class are created.

To see this in action, add a new field to the `Car` class as follows:

```
public static int staticField = 1;
```

Now add the following code to the `main` method of `Main`:

```
car2.staticField = 5;
System.out.println("The static field on car 1 is "+car1.staticField);
System.out.println("The static field on car 2 is "+car2.staticField);

car1.staticField = 10;
System.out.println("The static field on car 1 is "+car1.staticField);
System.out.println("The static field on car 2 is "+car2.staticField);
```

This will produce the following output:

```
The static field on car 1 is 5
The static field on car 2 is 5
The static field on car 1 is 10
The static field on car 2 is 10
```

As can be seen, modifying a `static` field on one object affects the field's value on all of the objects – this is because `staticField` is an attribute of the class itself.

A more correct way to modify this field is without even referencing an object. To see this approach, place the following code at the very beginning of the `main` method (before any objects are created):

```
Car.staticField = 20;
System.out.println("The static field is "+Car.staticField);
```

Methods can also be `static`. For instance, you could add the following method to `Car`:

```
public static void addToStaticField(int number) {
    staticField = staticField + number;
}
```

This method accepts a number as a parameter, and then adds that number to the current value of `staticField`. This can be used as follows in the `main` method:

```
Car.addToStaticField(10);
```

It is very important to understand, however, that although a `static` method can access or modify a `static` field, it cannot access a non-static field (or other non-static methods).

This is because non-static fields only exist on objects, whereas a `static` method can exist independent of objects.

`static` methods and fields do have their place, but as you will see in the chapters to come, it is generally best to avoid them where possible because they break important object orientated principles that we will discuss shortly.

If you come from an imperative programming background you may be tempted to write Java programs entirely with `static` methods, because this allows you to ignore the object-orientated nature of Java. This is a mistake, and hopefully you will be convinced of this by the end of the book.

6 DATA-TYPES

This chapter will introduce you to many of the most important data-types built into the Java language. A solid understanding of these data-types, and more importantly, when each should be used, is essential for any Java programmer.

If you are migrating from dynamically typed languages such as JavaScript or PHP you probably haven't needed to think too much about data-types: in a dynamically typed language the data-type of a variable is determined by the context in which it is used. For instance, the following line of JavaScript creates a variable called `var1` that has the data-type `number`:

```
var1 = 10;
```

This, on the other hand, creates a variable that has a data-type `string`:

```
var1 = "10";
```

In a statically typed language such as Java you are responsible for defining the data-types you wish to use, and this decision will impose certain restrictions on you.

In the previous chapter you learned how to create your own classes, and instantiate objects from these, for instance:

```
Car car1 = new Car("HGS928", "Ford",
    "Focus", 1800, (short) 2010);
```

In this case I referred to the variable `car1` as being *of type* `Car`. When you create classes, therefore, you are creating your own data-types.

You have also seen that there are a number of data-types built into the language. These ranged from primitive types such as `int` and `short`, to classes built into the language such as `String`.

Numbers

Numbers are fundamental to virtually all computer programs. You have already come across the basic numeric types, and looked at the differences between them. This section will provide a more in-depth look at numbers.

I will begin with the primitive numeric data-types built into Java. These are split into two distinct categories: integer data-types (which can only contain whole-numbers), and floating point data-types (which can hold numbers with a decimal place).

Integers

The following integer based data types are available in Java: `byte`, `short`, `char`, `integer` and `long`. For the most part, the only difference between these types is the number range they can represent, and by extension, the space they take up in memory.

As you have already seen, a literal integer (for instance 7, 89) in a Java program is of type `int`. The next thing to note is how Java behaves if two different numeric data-types are included in the same expression. Imagine the following two variables were defined inside a method:

```
long num1 = 43243;
int num2 = 22;
```

What data-type would be returned by an expression that added these two numbers together? The answer to this question can be seen by trying to assign the result to an `int`:

```
int result = num1 + num2;
```

The compiler will complain in this case `Type mismatch: cannot convert from long to int`. You can deduce from this that the result is a `long` rather than an `int`.

This is following a general rule with any expression involving integers of different data-types: the resulting data-type is the largest data-type of all the data-types included in the expression. Because a `long` is 64 bits, while an `int` is 32 bits, the result is of type `long`. Notice that it does not matter in this case that the result would easily fit into an `int`.

It is always possible to cast the result of an expression if you are confident it is compatible with a smaller data-type:

```
int result = (int)(num1 + num2);
```

> Notice that the brackets in this case ensure that the expression is evaluated before the cast is performed.

Because literal numbers have a data-type of `int`, any expression that operates solely on literal integers will produce a result of type `int`. This is true even if the result is assigned to a variable of type `long`.

For instance, 2147483647 is the maximum positive number that can be held in an int. Adding 2147483647 to itself produces a number that can easily fit into a long, but if you execute the following code, the result will be -2:

```
long l = 2147483647 + 2147483647;
System.out.println(l);
```

This is because the data-type returned from the expression is an int, and the result cannot fit into an int data-type. It is only after the expression has been evaluated, and the result constructed, that the value is assigned to the long variable: therefore the type of the variable the result is being assigned to has no impact on the expression itself.

This is an example of operator precedence. Both the + and the = are referred to as operators. The = operator is the assignment operator, and has the lowest precedence of any operator. This means they are the last part of the expression to be evaluated. If you think about this it makes sense: you want the entire expression on the right-hand side of the = sign to be evaluated before the result is assigned to a variable on the left-hand side.

It may still be somewhat surprising that the result of the previous expression is -2. If a value exceeds the range that can be captured by the data-type it is said to *overflow*. Effectively this means that the language does not notice that it has exceeded the number of bits it has available, and just continues updating the lower order bits in the result as though nothing happened. When numbers overflow they essentially contain garbage, and therefore it is important to prevent this from occurring.

There are two ways around this problem. The easiest way is to tell the compiler that one (or both) of these numbers are long values by appending an L to them:

```
long l = 2147483647 + 2147483647L;
System.out.println(l);
```

> Technically this can be a lower case L, but this looks like a 1, which sometimes causes confusion.

This now prints the expected result: 4294967294. Because you have indicated that one of these numbers is a long, the result of the expression will also be of type long.

The other way around this is to cast one of the literal integers to the type long before the addition occurs:

```
long l = (long) 2147483647 + 2147483647;
```

The reason this works is because casting is also an operator, but it has a higher precedence than addition, therefore this line of code:

⇒ Casts the first integer to be of type long.
⇒ Adds the long value and the int value together to produce a long value as a result.
⇒ Assigns the long value to the l variable.

> The number needs to be cast before the expression is evaluated. The following would not work:
>
> ```
> long l = (long)(2147483647 + 2147483647);
> ```
>
> In this case two `int` values are added together producing an `int` result (which overflows). This is then cast to a `long`, but the precision has already been lost at this point.

The other important point to note about the integer data-types is the uniqueness of the `char` type. Unlike the other integer data-types, the `char` type cannot hold negative numbers. The reason for this is that the `char` type is intended to hold a character in the Unicode 16 (UTF16) character set: char is the shorted form of "character".

The Unicode character set holds the characters for virtually all written languages – along with numerous symbols. When Java was originally created it was envisioned that all characters, in all written languages, would be representable in a 16-bit number (allowing 65,536 characters). This has since become infeasible, and Unicode has since been extended to allow 1,112,064 characters! Java does have an approach for getting round this called "supplementary characters" – but it is unlikely you will encounter a need for these unless you use very obscure languages.

`char` variables can be assigned a literal character where that character is available on the keyboard:

```
char c1 = 'c';
```

Notice that this expression uses single quotes rather than the double quotes.

Or prefixed with \u where it is not available:

```
char c2 = '\u00A5';
```

The four digits included in the number are hexadecimal (and therefore have possible values 0-F, rather than 0-9), allowing 16 bits of information to be held in each position. Because 16x16x16x16 equals 65,536, it is therefore possible to express a 16-bit number with 4 hexadecimal characters.

Given that the `char` data-type represents a character it may look like they are quite distinct from the other integer data-types. In fact chars can be treated like numbers, and used in any numeric expression:

```
char c1 = 'c';
System.out.println(c1+1);
```

The result of the expression c1+0 is 100, because the lower case c character is the 99th character in the Unicode character set (the first 128 characters in Unicode are also the first

128 characters in the ASCII character set).

When choosing which type of integer to use I almost always restrict my choice to `int` or `long`. There are very few cases in real-world programming anymore where memory use is of such critical importance that it should lead you to use `byte` or `short` values. Even if I knew that a number would only ever hold the values 1 or 0 I would still generally use an `int`. The main reason for this is that it saves the hassle of casting the number anytime it is used in an expression with literals. I prefer clean code to saving a small amount of memory.

Number systems

The numeric literals you have used up until this point have all used the decimal number system, where each number is in the range 0-9. This is also called base-ten.

Although we tend to take the decimal number system for granted, it is just one of a multitude of number systems, and Java supports three other important systems:

The *binary* number system (base-2) is the basis of all computing, and therefore there are cases where it is useful to construct numbers using the binary number system. In binary, each position of the number contains either a 0 or a 1. The following code constructs an integer with the value 9:

```
int binaryVal = 0b1001;
```

The 0b prefix indicates that the numbers to follow are in binary format. The actual value of the number can be determined by working backwards through the number as follows: (1 + (0*2) + (0*4) + (1*8) = 1 + (1* 8) = 1 + 8 = 9.

The *octal* number system allows each position in a number to have a value between 0-7 (8 possible values). The following code constructs a number using octal notation:

```
int octalVal = 010;
```

Octal numbers look somewhat confusing, because it is the 0 prefix that denotes the fact that it is an octal number. The value of the number above is actually 8: (0*0)+(1*8).

Finally, the *hexadecimal* number system allows each position to hold one of 16 distinct values, each of which is represented with the values 0-F. I have already introduced an example of hexadecimal numbers when constructing Unicode characters. The following is an example of a hexadecimal number:

```
int hexVal = 0x2b;
```

The 0x prefix denotes that this is a hexadecimal number. The value of this can be calculated as follows: (11*1) + (2*16) = 43

Regardless of which number system is used for constructing a number, Java still uses the same internal representation for storing the number once it is constructed. For instance, the number 32 constructed using the binary number system is identical to the number 32 constructed from the hexadecimal number system.

A final feature of literal numbers that is worth mentioning is the underscore character:

this can appear anywhere in the middle of a number (except adjacent to the decimal place in floating point numbers). The underscore has no specific meaning, it is just a way of splitting up a number to improve readability, and therefore functions much like a comma (which is explicitly disallowed):

```
int bigNum = 999_999_999;
```

Floating-point numbers

As mentioned earlier, Java supports two primitive floating-point number types: the 4-byte `float` type and the 8-byte `double` type. Any time a literal number contains a decimal place it is considered a floating-point number.

Unlike literal integers, which default to the 4-byte `int` type, literal floating-point numbers default to the 8-byte `double` type. This means that the following line of code is invalid and will not compile:

```
float f = 3.0;
```

This line of code is attempting to assign an 8-byte value to a 4-type data-type. The following is however valid because it assigns a 4-type integer to a 4-byte floating point number:

```
float f = 3;
```

Just as you were able to append an L to a literal integer to instruct the compiler it is a `long`, you can append an F or f to a number to indicate it is a `float`; therefore the following is valid:

```
float f = 3.3f;
```

If you have not worked with floating-point numbers before it is important to understand that the way they are stored inside a computer can lead to anomalies. For instance the following expression should equal 0.33 repeating.

```
1.0 - (2.0/3.0)
```

In fact, it equals `0.33333333333333337`. Not only that, the following expression is false:

```
1.0 - 2.0/3.0 == 1.0/3.0
```

The double equals == operator tests whether the expressions on either side are equal to one another. Although the statements are equal in a pure mathematical world, they are not equal in the less pure world of computer-based floating-point numbers.

When high levels of precision are required you should favor the `BigDecimal` data-type that will be introduced shortly.

Java expressions only produce floating-point numbers where one of the operands is a floating-point number. For instance, the expression below produces an integer result (3), because both the operands are `int`s. The result of this is then assigned to a `double` (producing 3.0):

```
double d = 10/3;
```

The following expression, on the other hand, produces a floating-point number with the value 3.3333333333333335, because one of the operands is a `double`:

```
double d = 10/3.0;
```

If a floating-point number is assigned to an `int` it is rounded down. For instance, after the following 2 lines of code are executed, the variable `i` has the value 9:

```
double d = 9.99;
int i = (int)d;
```

Notice in this case you needed to cast the `double` to an `int`. Whenever you convert from a floating-point number to an integer type you need to perform a cast, even if you are converting from a `float` to a `long`. This is because you are losing the precision on the right-hand side of the decimal place.

If you would like to round a `double` to an `int` you can use the `Math.round` helper method. This uses the conventional rounding approach whereby numbers less than 5 round down, and greater or equal to 5 rounded up:

```
long val = Math.round(d);
```

The `Math` class contains a large number of useful helpers, and should be your first port of call whenever you are looking for mathematical operations in Java. The helpers on this class are all `static`; therefore you do not need to instantiate the `Math` class.

Finally, floating-point numeric literals can use scientific notation where required, for instance:

```
double d = 1.234e5;
```

Initialization

It is possible to use a primitive variable that has never been assigned a value. For instance, in this example the variable `i` is never assigned a value, but it can still be used in an expression inside the `main` method.

```
package numbers;

public class Integers {
    private static int i;
    public static void main(String[] args) {
        System.out.println(i);
    }
}
```

In many programming languages the value of `i` would be unpredictable: it would take on whatever value existed in the memory reserved for the variable before it was declared.

This has been a well-known source of bugs in other languages, so Java decided to always initialize primitives to 0: therefore the code above will print out the value 0.

If a primitive is declared inside a method it must be assigned a value before it is used. The following is not valid code, and will not compile:

```
public static void main(String[] args) {
    int i;
    System.out.println(i);
}
```

In this case the compiler knows that i has never been assigned a value, therefore it cannot be used in an expression.

Wrapper classes

As mentioned earlier, primitive data-types are fundamentally different from class-based data-types, most notably, they do not support methods.

There is, however, a way to wrap primitive data-types inside objects using a set of classes found in the java.lang package:

⇒ Byte
⇒ Short
⇒ Character
⇒ Integer
⇒ Long
⇒ Float
⇒ Double

The following is an example showing the use of the primitive wrappers:

```
Integer num1 = new Integer(23);
Long num2 = new Long(30);
Long num3 = (num1+num2)*2;
```

Notice that all the wrapper classes have constructors that accept their corresponding primitive type. The first line therefore creates a new Integer object, and assigns it the value of 23. The second line creates a new Long object, and assigns it the value of 30.

The interesting line here is the third line: this shows two features:

⇒ The result of an expression can be assigned directly to a wrapper type, rather than a primitive type if required: although the result of the expression is a long it is assigned to a Long.

⇒ An expression can contain wrapper types and primitive types.

This feature is called *autoboxing*, and allows the automatic conversion between the primitive types and their wrapper types (and vice versa). This is a relatively new feature of Java (introduced in Java 5), and greatly eases the burden of dealing with the object wrappers.

Because the wrapper objects are genuine objects, they contain methods:

```
Float f = 43.44f;
System.out.println(f.longValue());
```

And they also support `static` helper methods such as these (as of Java 8):

```
Integer.max(20, 30);
Integer.sum(20, 10);
```

It is also important to understand that the wrapper objects are *immutable*. This means that once an object is constructed, the value it contains can never be changed. This even applies where you appear to be changing an object's value:

```
Long num2 = new Long(30);
num2 = num2 + 10;
```

Although it appears you are changing the value of the object declared on the first line, you are actually creating a new object. This may not sound like an important detail, but as you will see in the coming chapters, it can have important implications.

Unlike the primitive data-types, the wrapper objects do not automatically initialize to 0, therefore the following code prints `null`:

```
package numbers;

public class Integers {
    private static Integer i;
    public static void main(String[] args) {
        System.out.println(i);
    }
}
```

Converting to and from Strings

It is common to convert numbers to and from `Strings`. The easiest way to do this is via a set of `static` helpers on the object wrappers. For instance, the following constructs an `int` from a `String`:

```
int i1 = Integer.valueOf("999999");
```

While this produces a `String` from the same `int`:

```
Integer.toString(i1);
```

Later chapters of this book will look at how you can convert numbers to more human readable formats such as `999,999` and `$999,999.00`.

BigInteger and BigDecimal

There are two problems with the number types you have examined so far:

⇒ The range of numbers they can store is limited, for instance, the maximum value that can be held by a `long` is `9223372036854775807`. This is big enough for many purposes, but not all.

⇒ Expressions involving floating-point numbers can result in the loss of precision.

Java includes two classes designed to alleviate these issues: `BigInteger` and

BigDecimal. As their names suggest, these are used for integer and floating-point numbers respectively. Both of these classes are defined in the `java.math` package, therefore the examples below need to `import` these packages – you will look at imports in the next chapter, so do not focus too heavily on this feature for now.

In order to construct new objects of these types you can utilize static helper methods available on each class:

```
package arithmetic;
import java.math.BigDecimal;
import java.math.BigInteger;

public class LargeNumbers {
    public static void main(String[] args) {
        BigInteger num1 = BigInteger.valueOf(9223372036854L);
        BigDecimal num2 = BigDecimal.valueOf(4324.34324324324324);
    }
}
```

This approach works if the number can be represented in one of the standard primitive types, but is not particularly useful if the number cannot be represented as an 8-byte number. In these cases the following constructor can be used:

```
BigInteger num3 = new BigInteger("9223372036854775807732131232");
```

Just like the wrapper objects from the previous section, these objects are immutable: once a value is assigned to a `BigInteger` or `BigDecimal` it cannot be changed. Any operation that appears to change the value of these objects is actually constructing a whole new object.

The great thing about `BigIntegers` and `BigDecimals` is there is no limit on the size of the number they can hold. As long as the number can fit into the physical memory of the computer it can be captured in these objects, it doesn't matter if it is a billion digits long, or contains a billion digits after the decimal place.

Unlike the wrapper classes, it is not possible to use autoboxing with these types, therefore it is not possible to use the standard Java operators such as +, -, * or /. This makes `BigDecimals` and `BigIntegers` less convenient to program with.

Instead of using the standard operators, both `BigInteger` and `BigDecimal` expose a set of methods than allow them to be used in mathematical operations:

```
BigInteger num1 = BigInteger.valueOf(9223372036854L);
BigInteger num2 = new BigInteger("9223372036854775807732131232");
BigInteger num3 = num1.add(num2);
BigInteger num4 = num3.multiply(BigInteger.valueOf(32432));
System.out.println(num4);
```

Due to the constraints of these methods, it is not possible to add a `BigDecimal` to a `BigInteger` (or vice versa). Therefore, it is necessary to decide in advance if any numbers will be floating-point: if so then the `BigDecimal` type must be used.

It is also possible to convert a `BigDecimal` or `BigInteger` back to a primitive value via utility methods:

```
int i = num1.intValue();
```

The biggest danger with these methods is that they do not fail if the number is too large for the type it is being assigned to. This results in a garbage value being assigned to the variable. In order to alleviate this, Java 8 has introduced a new set of methods with `Exact` appended to their names, for instance:

```
int i = num1.intValueExact();
```

These new methods produce an error if the resulting number overflows – which is generally more helpful than just automatically overflowing and producing an incorrect value.

Boolean

The only non-numeric primitive type in Java is the `boolean` type, which simply represents `true` and `false` values. In some programming languages numbers are used to represent Booleans: typically 1 is true and 0 is false. Java does not use this convention: the only data-types that can evaluate to `true` or `false` are Booleans.

Just as Java supports numeric literals, Java supports Boolean literals using the keywords `true` and `false`. This is one mechanism that can be used for initializing `boolean` variables:

```
boolean b = true;
System.out.println(b);
```

Notice that `true` is not surrounded with quotes: it is a keyword in the language. If a `boolean` is not initialized to a value it defaults to `false`.

You will encounter many cases where `booleans` are returned from expressions. Boolean expressions are fundamental to implementing looping and branching within computer programs – as will be seen in the next few chapters.

Java also supports a wrapper type called `Boolean`, as can be seen in the example below:

```
Boolean b2 = new Boolean(true);
System.out.println(b2);
```

Just as with numbers, Java supports autoboxing between the `boolean` primitives type and the `Boolean` wrapper.

Arrays

Arrays are fundamental data-types in most programming languages. They provide a data structure that encapsulates a group of values inside a single data-type. For instance, an array can allow you to group together a group of `int`s, or a group of `String`s.

The data-type of the values inside the array must be declared when the array is defined, and can either be a primitive type or a reference (class) type. All elements in the array must then conform to this data-type.

Arrays themselves are objects, so they have methods and fields just like any other object.

The values inside an array are stored in a specific order. In addition, the size of an array is defined when the array is constructed (although this can be after the array is declared), and cannot be increased in size. For instance, you may define an array of 10 `ints`. In this case the array can never contain more than 10 elements.

Due to the limitations of arrays (particularly the fact that their size needs to be declared in advance), arrays are not widely used in Java, and instead an alternative API called the Collections API is generally used. This will be examined in-depth later in the book.

The easiest way to define an array is to declare the array and define its elements in a single statement. The following example shows the declaration of an array containing 10 `ints`. The `ints` are listed after the declaration in curly brackets:

```
package arrays;

public class ArrayDefinition {
    public static void main(String[] args) {
        int[] nums = {3,6,33,1,4,5,78,6,5,9};
        System.out.println(nums[8]);
        System.out.println(nums.length);
    }
}
```

The variable `nums` is defined as an array of the data-type `int` by the use of square brackets within its declaration. This line would fail without the inclusion of the square brackets, because the compiler would think you were declaring a single `int` value.

The second line of the method prints out the element at position 8 in the array. Because counting starts at 0, this will actually print the 9th element in the array, and therefore prints the value 5.

The final line of the method prints out the size of the array, which is 10. Notice that `length` is a field on the array rather than a method, as seen by the fact you do not need to use brackets after it.

This approach works well when all the members of an array are known when the array is defined. Often, however, the array declaration and the definition of the elements will occur as two separate steps. In this case it is necessary to specify the size of the array before adding any elements:

```
package arrays;
public class ArrayDefinition2 {
    public static void main(String[] args) {
        int[] nums = new int[10];
        nums[8] = 5;
        nums[3] = 6*6;
        System.out.println(nums.length);
        System.out.println(nums[8]);
        System.out.println(nums[9]);
    }
}
```

Notice that the first line of the method declares that the array will hold 10 `int`s. The next two lines then populate two of the available positions by specifying the index of each element within the array.

Even though only two of the ten slots in the array have been populated, the length of the array is still listed as 10, because the length never changes.

On the final line of the method the program accesses an index of the array that has never been set. Due to the fact that `int` values default to 0, this line prints out 0. If the array was declared as holding objects (such as `String`s), this line would print `null`.

If you attempt to access an index of the array that doesn't exist (e.g. 10 or -1) an exception will be raised. You will learn a lot more about exceptions shortly, but essentially they can be thought of as a runtime version of a compilation error: they indicate that the program has performed an invalid operation, and the current thread of execution must be aborted.

The arrays that we have used up until this point have been one-dimensional. It is also possible to create multi-dimensional arrays. In order to visualize a multi-dimensional array, consider what the arrays introduced previously would look like if each element were not an `int`, but an array of `int`s.

A multi-dimensional array can be declared and defined in a single step as follows:

```java
package arrays;
public class MultiArrayDefinition {
    public static void main(String[] args) {
        int[][] nums = {{1,2,3},{4,5,6},{7,8,9}};
        System.out.println(nums[1][2]);
    }
}
```

Notice that two sets of square brackets are used to define the array, and curly brackets embedded in curly brackets when the array values are specified.

The second line of the method prints out the third value of the second array (6).

It is also possible to separate the definition from the population of the array, but in this case you need to define the size of each dimension:

```java
package arrays;
public class MultiArrayDefinition2 {
    public static void main(String[] args) {
        int[][] nums = new int[3][3];
        nums[1][2] = 6;
        System.out.println(nums[1][2]);
    }
}
```

Java also provides a helper class for working with arrays called `Arrays`. This contains a set of `static` methods that can be invoked on arrays to perform common tasks such as initialization, searching, printing and sorting, for example:

```
package arrays;
```

```java
import java.util.Arrays;

public class ArraysHelper {
    public static void main(String[] args) {
        int[] nums = {3,1,5,3,7,5,8};
        System.out.println(Arrays.binarySearch(nums, 8));
        Arrays.sort(nums);
        System.out.println(Arrays.toString(nums));
    }
}
```

Because this is declared in the `java.util` package an `import` has been included at the top.

Strings

Strings are a primitive data-type in many programming languages. In Java a `String` is an object because it can be represented as an array of the `char` primitive type. For instance, the `String` "hello" could be represented as follows:

```java
char[] s1 = {'h','e','l','l','o'};
```

Obviously this is rather painful, and is why Java supports `Strings` as a built-in type:

```java
String s1 = "hello";
```

Strings in Java are immutable: once they are constructed they can never be changed. This may sound implausible, given the following valid lines of Java:

```java
String s1 = "Hello";
s1 = s1 + " World";
```

Although it is a subtle point (and will be explained in great detail in the chapters to come), no `Strings` have been modified in this example. The only thing changing in this example is the underlying `String` that the variable `s1` refers to.

The variable `s1` starts out referring to a `String` object with the value "Hello". On the second line, Java first constructs a new `String` object with the value " World". Next, when the concatenation is performed, Java creates a third String object with the value "Hello World", and points the variable `s1` at this.

Because `Strings` are objects, they support methods. It is important to realize that although these methods perform operations with the value of the `String`, due to the fact that `Strings` are immutable, they never change the value of the `String` – instead they construct new `Strings`:

```java
package strings;
public class Strings {
    public static void main(String[] args) {
        String s1 = "Hello World";
        System.out.println(s1.toUpperCase());
        System.out.println(s1.substring(6));
        System.out.println(s1.indexOf("W"));
    }
}
```

The program above prints out:

```
HELLO WORLD
World
6
```

Some of the more useful methods supported by `String` are as follows:

⇒ `length`: this returns the number of characters in the `String`
⇒ `matches`: this tests whether the `String` matches a given regular expression. Regular expressions are outside the scope of this book, but are a standard way of expressing textual patterns
⇒ `replaceAll` and `replaceFirst`: replace instances of a specified `String` with a new `String`
⇒ `split`: splits the `String` based on a delimiter (for example, a comma) and returns an array of `Strings`
⇒ `substring`: returns a portion of the `String` based on a starting and (optionally) end index. As with arrays, the first character in the `String` is at position 0
⇒ `trim`: removes leading and trailing whitespace from the `String`

`StringBuilders` are similar to `Strings`, except they are mutable: A `StringBuilder` is an object, and encapsulates a string of text, but this string can be modified after the `StringBuilder` has been created:

```java
package strings;
public class StringBuilder {
    public static void main(String[] args) {
        StringBuilder sb1 = new StringBuilder ("Hello");
        sb1.append(" World!!!");
        sb1.reverse();
        System.out.println(sb1);
    }
}
```

This produces:

```
!!!dlroW olleH
```

The main reason `StringBuilders` are used is due to their performance advantage over `Strings` when concatenating many values together. String concatenation is a relatively common task, and there are cases when hundreds or thousands of strings must be concatenated together. In these cases the `append` method on `StringBuilder` will generally offer superior performance to string concatenation using the + operator.

There is a similar class to `StringBuilder` called `StringBuffer`. These two classes are essentially the same except `StringBuilder` is not thread safe. Do not worry if you do not understand that concept yet, it will be explained in the Threading chapter. As a general rule `StringBuilder` offers superior performance to `StringBuffer`.

Unless I am concatenating a large number of strings together I generally prefer the simplicity of `Strings`. The speed of modern computers means it is seldom worth optimizing relatively simple operations when there is a trade-off in terms of code simplicity.

Conclusion

This chapter has introduced you to some of the most important Java data-types, but is by no means a complete list. There are many other important data-types that will be introduced as you progress through the book, for instance, you still have not seen how date and time values can be represented in Java.

The most important feature to take away from this chapter is the fundamental distinction between primitive and reference (or class based) types, and what the basic primitive types are.

With an understanding of the basic data-types introduced in this chapter you are well on the way to being able to write more advanced programs, but there are a few more fundamental subjects that need to be addressed first. These will be covered in the next chapter.

7 LANGUAGE FUNDAMENTALS

You have made significant advances towards understanding the Java language, but there are some important concepts that I still have not covered, or have not covered in sufficient detail to allow you to write more complex programs. This chapter is a chance to step back and gain an understanding of some of these concepts before progressing further with the language.

Naming

You have already seen many examples of naming in the programs that you have written: you have named classes, methods, fields and variables.

Java has a set of rules that must be adhered to when defining these names. I have alluded to these rules in passing, but there is slightly more to these rules than mentioned so far.

As a first rule, names cannot use any of the reserved keywords in Java. The list of keywords includes `class`, `public`, `new`, `static`, and all the other words that have special meaning in the Java language. The full list of keywords can be found here:

http://docs.oracle.com/javase/tutorial/java/nutsandbolts/_keywords.html.

In addition, programmer defined names must always begin with a character, the underscore character or the dollar sign. Subsequent characters can be any of these, plus numbers.

Packages

As you have seen in earlier examples, classes are placed in packages. Packages provide a grouping mechanism for related classes, but they also provide unique names for classes. A class is uniquely identified by both its name, and the package it is declared in.

It is not uncommon for two classes to have the same name. For instance, the Java libraries contain two classes called `List`: one is an array like construct; the other is a GUI component. These two classes are however defined in different packages:

```
java.awt
java.util
```

The fully qualified names for these classes, therefore, are as follows:

```
java.awt.List
java.util.List
```

As long as a package does not contain two classes with the same name there will never be duplication of class names.

This is still not a foolproof mechanism, however, because it is common to import libraries from multiple sources. Therefore, two different people may write a set of utility classes and use the package name `util`, and make these available as a library. Theoretically, they may name classes identically, and theoretically both libraries may be imported into the same program, resulting in duplicate class names.

There is a common convention to avoid this problem: prefix the package name with your domain name in reverse. For instance, my company's domain name is cisdal.com, so I place my utility classes in a package called `com.cisdal.utilities`.

Imports

Due to the fact that there can be more than one class with the same name, you may be wondering how Java determines which class to use. For instance, if I want to use the class `java.util.List` (it is actually an interface – but ignore that distinction for now), how can I signal to Java that I wish to use this class instead of `java.awt.List`?

There are, in fact, three ways I can achieve this.

The first approach is to refer to classes by their fully qualified name. For instance:

```
package importing;
public class ImportExample {
    java.util.List list = null;
}
```

This approach is the most foolproof way to ensure you are using the class that you expect, but it is also the most long-winded.

The next approach, and probably the most common, is to use an import statement for the explicit class:

```
package importing;
import java.util.List;

public class ImportExample {
    List list = null;
}
```

A class can have any number of `import` statements, and these always occur before the `class` definition, but after the `package` definition.

It is not necessary to import classes if they are in the same package as the class you are writing, but it is always necessary to import other classes, even if their name is unique within the program.

> The one exception to this is classes declared in the `java.lang` package such as `Integer`. These are automatically imported into every class.

There is actually a simple way to `import` relevant classes in Eclipse. In order to demonstrate this, enter the code above without the import:

```
package importing;
public class ImportExample {
    List list = null;
}
```

There will be a compilation error on the line declaring the `List`, because Java cannot locate this class. Now, type:

⇒ Ctrl-Shift-O (on Windows)

⇒ Command-Shift-O (on OSX)

This command will launch the "Organize imports" feature of Eclipse. This will automatically import any classes where a single match is identified, or offer an option to import the relevant class where multiple matches are found, as seen in figure 7-1:

FIGURE 7-1

The other nice thing about this feature is that it will group imports from related packages together, and remove any imports that are not actually being used, which helps keep code tidy.

The third way to import classes is via a wildcard:

```
package importing;

import java.util.*;

public class ImportExample {
    List list = null;
}
```

This example implicitly imports all classes in the `java.util` package – therefore `java.util.List` can be referred to as `List` in the body of the class.

The three approaches outlined here are listed from most specific to least specific. For instance, consider the following example:

```
package importing;
import java.util.*;
import java.awt.List;

public class ImportExample {
    List list = null;
}
```

The variable `list` will be an instance of `java.awt.List`, because it has the most specific `import`. Notice that this has nothing to do with the order of the `imports`; it is purely related to how specific the `import` is.

Additionally, consider the following example:

```
package importing;
import java.util.*;
import java.awt.List;

public class ImportExample {
    List list1 = null;
    java.util.List list2 = null;
}
```

The variable `list1` will have the type `java.awt.List` (as per the explicit import), while `list2` will be of type `java.util.List` (because it is explicitly named).

Classpath

When a program is running it has access to many different classes. Some of these you will have written yourself, others will have been provided by Java itself, while a third party vendor or an open source library may provide others.

The collection of all the classes available to a running program is referred to as its *classpath*. Java will load these classes on an "as-needed" basis as the program executes in a process called *class loading*.

It is possible that classes will be available at compilation time, but not available when the program actually executes. For instance, when packaging your Java program you may forget to include some required libraries. In this case the class loader will fail to load classes when the program executes, and generate an exception as a result.

Standard output and input

The programs written in this book are command-line programs rather than GUI based programs: they will simply produce textual output to files or the Eclipse console.

Java adheres to traditional UNIX standards and provides three streams to programs that they can utilize as needed:

⇒ **Standard input**: this is where the program reads input from. The default standard input is the keyboard, but the program must be explicitly listening for input in order to read it. This stream can be accessed via `System.in`.

⇒ **Standard output**: this is where the program writes output. The default standard output is the command shell the program is running in, or, in the case of Eclipse, the Console view. This stream can be accessed with `System.out`, as seen in numerous examples already.

⇒ **Standard error**: this is where the program will write any error messages. This has the same defaults as standard output, but in Eclipse the text will be output in red. This can be accessed with `System.err`.

It is possible to redirect these streams. For instance, it is possible to redirect standard error to a file rather than the console. This topic will be revisited in later chapters.

This book will largely ignore standard input. It is relatively rare to require inputs while a command line program is running: typically all information required by the program is provided as arguments. If a program does need input while it is running it is typical to use a GUI, but, as discussed, this is outside the scope of this book.

Up until this point you have written to standard output as follows:

```
System.out.println("Hello world");
```

The `println` method, which, as discussed earlier, is defined on the `PrintWriter` class, automatically inserts a line break at the end of the text. `PrintWriter` also supports a method called `print`, which is identical, except it does not include an implicit line break.

The `PrintWriter` class also contains another very useful method called `printf`. This will be familiar to any C or C++ programmers, because it is the equivalent of `sprintf`. This method provides a mechanism for including parameters inside the `String` being printed, without resorting to `String` concatenation. For instance, consider the following method:

```
public class Printing {
    public static void main(String[] args) {
        int i = 10;
        double d = 20.2;
```

```
        System.out.println("The value of i is "+
            i+" and the value of d is "+d);
    }
}
```

Although there is nothing wrong with this code from a functional point of view, the `println` statement is both messy, and prone to error (it is easy to forget the spaces before and after the variables). This code can be rewritten as follows:

```
public class Printing {
    public static void main(String[] args) {
        int i = 10;
        double d = 20.2;
        System.out.printf("The value of i is %d and the value of d is %f\n"
            , i, d);
    }
}
```

In this example I have provided a placeholder for an `int` with the special sequence `%d`, and a placeholder for a `double` with `%f`: I then provide the values for these placeholders, in the order they appear in the `String`, after the `String` is terminated.

You will also note that I have added `\n` to the end of the `String`. `printf` does not include a line break, but it is possible to force one with `\n`.

> The backslash character is a way of informing Java that the next character in a `String` has special meaning, and is referred to as the escape character. For instance, `\t` creates a tab.
>
> It is also possible to add double quotes to a `String` using `\"` – the backslash ensures that Java will not confuse the double quotes with the end of the `String`. In addition, if you need to add a backslash to a `String`, you can do so by using a double backslash - `\\`.

The following additional placeholders can be used with `printf`:

⇒ `%c` : used as a placeholder for a character
⇒ `%s` : used as a placeholder for a `String`. If `%S` is used, the `String` will be automatically converted to uppercase.
⇒ `%n` : can be used as an alternative to `\n`. This form should actually be favored, because different platforms sometimes use different sequences to force new lines. As an example, Windows typically uses `\r\n` (carriage return, new line), whereas UNIX uses `\n`. `%n` is therefore a platform neutral mechanism of forcing a new line.

Everything is an object

A commonly made statement about Java is, "In Java, everything is an object". As it happens, this is quite literally true. The Java platform contains a class called `Object`, and this is the implicit parent for all other classes declared in Java.

> The only exceptions are the primitive types, which are not descended from anything.

The `Object` class contains a number of utility methods, and because every other Java class is descended from this class, every class automatically has an implementation of these methods, as the next example demonstrates:

```
public static void main(String[] args) {
    Car car1 = new Car("HGS928", "Ford",
        "Focus", 1800, (short) 2010);
    Car car2 = car1;
    System.out.println(car1.toString());
    System.out.println(car1.equals(car2));
}
```

This example uses the `Car` class created in earlier chapters: but the methods it invokes were never defined on this class. Even though you did not write the `toString` and `equals` methods on the `Car` class, they are available because they are *inherited* from `Object`, and `Car` automatically *extends* `Object`: a process called inheritance.

You will look at inheritance a lot more in the coming chapters, but for now think of it as a way of adding functionality from one class to another class. In this case, functionality from `Object` has been added to `Car`. You will also see that it is possible to change the definition of these methods to meet your own specific needs if the implementation provided by `Object` is not sufficient.

I will introduce the methods defined on `Object` at the appropriate points in the book, and you will also learn about other implications stemming from the fact that all classes are derived from the `Object` class.

Passing arguments to a program

Passing arguments to a program is one way to make your programs more generic. Arguments passed to a program let the same compiled code behave differently based on the values provided at runtime.

As a simple example, consider a program that needs to add together two values passed to it. This program will assume that the arguments are both integers:

```
package adder;

public class Adder {
    public static void main(String[] args) {
```

```
        int i1 = Integer.valueOf(args[0]);
        int i2 = Integer.valueOf(args[1]);
        int result = i1+i2;
        System.out.printf("The result is %d", result);
    }
}
```

If you run this program like the ones you have run up until this point it will fail. This is due to the fact that the `args` array has zero elements and the program attempts to access elements at position 0 and 1.

When you run this program, you need a way to provide arguments to it. In order to demonstrate this, right click on the class in the package explorer view and choose `Run As -> Run Configurations...`

This will present you a dialog. Choose the `Arguments` tab, and enter two numbers (separated by a space) in the `Program arguments` box, as shown in figure 7-2:

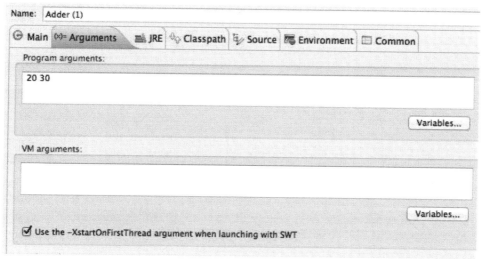

FIGURE 7-2

If you now choose `Run` at the bottom of the dialog, the program will print out the result of adding the two numbers.

Once you learn more about looping through arrays you will appreciate that it is possible for a program to accept and process an arbitrary number of parameters. For instance, you may let the user pass as many numbers as they want, and have the program add them all together.

8 OPERATORS

Java has a large set of operators for performing operations on one, two or three operands. You have already seen examples of the + and = operators, but it is important to gain an understanding of all the core operators supported by the language.

This section will examine these operators by splitting them up into their relevant categories. If you have used other programming languages this section will probably look very familiar, because the operators available tend to be consistent from language to language.

Arithmetic Operators

The most familiar operators in any programming language are the arithmetic operators. Java supports the 4 core arithmetic operators (+, -, * and /) along with the modulus operator (%), which returns the remainder of a division operation involving integers. Java uses conventional operator prescience, but this can be overridden through the use of brackets ().

The following program shows the arithmetic operators in action:

```java
package arithmetic;
public class ArithmeticExcample {
    public static void main(String[] args) {
        // prints 2
        System.out.println(1+1);
        // prints 5
        System.out.println(1+2*2);
        // prints 6
        System.out.println((1+2)*2);
        // prints 1
        System.out.println(10%3);
        // prints 3
```

```
        System.out.println(10/3);
        // prints 3.3333333333333335
        System.out.println(10.0/3);
    }
}
```

Remember, if all the numbers are integers, the result is an integer. If one of the numbers is a floating-point number, the result is floating-point. This only impacts the / and % operators, and is why the last two operations in the example produce different results, despite the inputs appearing to be the same.

As mentioned elsewhere, the + operator has been overloaded in Java: if one of the two parameters is a String, the operator performs String concatenation on the two operands. This is the only operator that has been overloaded in this manner: for instance, it is not possible to use the * operator with Strings.

Unary Operators

A unary operator performs an operation on a single operand.

The ++ and -- operators are used to increment or decrement an operand by 1. The following program shows an example of the ++ operator:

```
package unary;
public class UnaryExample {
    public static void main(String[] args) {
        int num = 10;
        int num2 = num++;
        int num3 = ++num;
        System.out.println(num2);
        System.out.println(num3);
    }
}
```

There is a subtle but important difference between the 2nd and 3rd line of the main method. The 2nd line places the ++ operator after the variable, while the 3rd line places it before the variable. This looks like a small difference, but is actually important:

- ❖ The second line states: assign the value of num to the variable num2, *and then* increase the value of num by 1.
- ❖ The third line states: increase the value of num by 1, *and then* assign the value of num to the variable num3

From the point of view of the num variable these lines are equivalent (its value is increased by 1), but to the variable assigned the result of the operation, the result is different. This is why the program prints out:

10
12

The -- operators is identical to the ++operator, except the value of the operand is decreased by 1.

The - operator can also be used as a unary operator, and will turn a positive value into a negative value. For instance, the following line of code prints -2:

```
System.out.println(-(1+1));
```

The unary + operator exists, but does not actually do anything (because numbers are positive by default). The + operator does not turn a negative number into a positive number; the Math.abs method can instead be used to achieve this.

The final unary operator is the ! (not) operator. This is used to negate a boolean value: turning true to false and vice versa. For instance, the following prints true:

```
System.out.println(!false);
```

Equality and Relational Operators

Equality and relational operators are used to compare two operands. This includes:

⇒ Two operators that compare whether the operands are equal or not-equal (== and !=)
⇒ Four relational operators (<, >, <= and >=)
⇒ A type comparison operator (instanceof)

The result of any operation using these operators is a boolean value. For this reason it is common to use these operators in conjunction with branching and looping operations, as will be demonstrated in the next chapter.

The following program demonstrates the equality operators. Every operation in this program returns true:

```
package comparison;
public class Equality {
    public static void main(String[] args) {
        System.out.println(1==1);
        System.out.println(1==1.0);
        System.out.println(1!=2.0);

        StringBuffer sb1 = new StringBuffer("Hello");
        StringBuffer sb2 = new StringBuffer("Hello");
        StringBuffer sb3 = sb1;
        System.out.println(sb1 == sb3);
        System.out.println(sb1 != sb2);

        System.out.println("hello" == "hello");
        System.out.println(new String("hello") != new String("hello"));

        System.out.println("hello" instanceof String );
        System.out.println(sb2 instanceof StringBuffer );
    }
}
```

There are a few interesting points to note here:

❖ When comparing numbers, the data-types do not need to be the same for two numbers to be equal: this is why 1 (an int) is equal to 1.0 (a double). Due to

precision issues with floating-point numbers, however, it is generally a bad idea to compare integer and floating-point values for equality.
- ❖ Two objects are equal when they refer to the same object: this is why `sb3` is equal to `sb1`: they both refer to the same object, but `sb2` is not equal to `sb1`, because it refers to a separate instance of the `StringBuffer` object (even though it holds the same value). To fully comprehend this it is useful to understand the difference between an object and a reference to an object - a topic that will be explored in depth in coming chapters.
- ❖ `Strings` are a special case: due to the fact they are immutable, Java holds all `String` literals that are created by the program in an in-memory pool. If the same literal is constructed more than once, the same instance from the pool is used. As a result of this `"hello"` is equal to `"hello"` – they are literally the same object. This subject will also be examined in detail in future chapters, so feel free to ignore this point for now.
- ❖ If `Strings` are constructed via their constructor, however, they bypass this pool, and for this reason `new String("hello")` is not equal to `new String("hello")`.
- ❖ The `instanceof` operator is a useful utility for determining whether a variable is an instance (or type) of a specific class.

The following program demonstrates the relational operators, again, all operations in this program return `true`:

```java
package comparison;
public class Relational {
    public static void main(String[] args) {
        System.out.println(1 >= 1);
        System.out.println(2 > 1.0);
        System.out.println(1.99999 < 2);
        System.out.println(1.9 <= 2.0);
    }
}
```

Conditional Operators

Java also contains two conditional operators: `&&` (and) and `||` (or) which can be used in conjunction with `boolean` values, or expressions that return `boolean` values. For instance, they can be used to return `true` if two `boolean` expressions are both `true`. Alternatively, they can be used to return `true` if at least one of two `boolean` expressions are `true`.

As with arithmetic operations, brackets can be used to define precedence. The following statements all return `true`:

```java
package conditional;

public class ConditionalExample {
    public static void main(String[] args) {
        System.out.println(true && true);
        System.out.println(1 > 0 && 1 >= 1);
```

```
        System.out.println((0 > 1 && 0 > 2) || 0 == 0);
        System.out.println("hello".length() == 5
            && "hello".charAt(0) == 'h');
        int[] nums = {};
        System.out.println(nums.length == 0 || nums[1] > 5);
    }
}
```

The last statement in `main` is interesting. The expression `nums[1] > 5` would cause an exception if it was executed, because it is accessing an element at index 1 in an array that contains 0 elements (try it out on its own if you want to be sure).

The line as a whole executes without any problems, however, and returns `true`. This is because the first expression `nums.length == 0` returns `true`, and therefore there is no need to execute the second expression, because, regardless of its result, the result of the overall "or" expression will be the same (`true`).

This is called short-circuiting, and also occurs if the first expression in an `&&` expression returns `false`, because regardless of the outcome of the second expression, the `&&` expression must return `false`.

Assignment Operators

As discussed earlier, the equal sign is the assignment operator:

```
int num = 10;
```

Java also supports a number of other assignment operators that are useful for adding brevity to some statements. For instance, the following line of code:

```
num = num + 10;
```

Could be replaced with:

```
num += 10;
```

The other operators in this family are -=, *=, /= and %= .

DANE CAMERON

9 LOOPING AND BRANCHING

Two key features found in all programming languages are the concepts of looping and branching.

- ❖ Branching is the process of determining which code block to execute based on a set of criteria.
- ❖ Looping refers to the process of executing the same block of code a finite number of times.

Java contains several mechanisms for both looping and branching. These mechanisms will be addressed in detail in this chapter.

The examples in this chapter will all execute directly in the `main` method of a class. If you would like to follow these examples in Eclipse, create a new project called `LoopsAndBranching` and add a class with a `main` method.

Branching

Branching allows a program to determine a path to follow based on the evaluation of a `boolean` expression. This chapter will introduce three different language features that support branching.

If-then-else

The most fundamental branching mechanism in Java is the `if-then-else` block. In its simplest form, the `if-then-else` block consists only of an `if`-statement, and the code inside the block executes if the expression inside the `if`-statement evaluates to `true`. The code below contains two `if`-blocks: one of these will print a statement, and the other will not:

```
package branching;
public class IfThenElse {
```

```java
public static void main(String[] args) {
    int i = 10;
    if (i > 5) {
        System.out.println("This will print");
    }
    if (i < 10) {
        System.out.println("This will not print");
    }
}
}
```

The first `if`-block will execute, because 10 is greater than 5. The second `if`-block will not execute because 10 is not less than 10. If the 2nd expression had been specified as `i <= 10` then this block would have also executed.

Notice that I am declaring the code block to execute via the familiar curly brackets - { }. Because this program now has three levels of nested brackets, it is important that you adhere to the formatting convention seen here – each new block should be indented – typically either with tabs or 4 spaces. Indentation ensures that it is easy to determine where each block starts and finishes.

> Eclipse can help find matching brackets. If you place the cursor after a closing bracket, the editor will highlight its matching opening bracket (and vice versa).
>
> Eclipse can also help you format a source file. This can be achieved by right-clicking inside the editor and choosing `Source -> Format`.

Technically the brackets could have been omitted in this case, and the code rewritten as follows:

```java
public static void main(String[] args) {
    int i = 10;
    if (i > 5)
        System.out.println("This will print");
    if (i < 10)
        System.out.println("This will not print");
}
```

If the `if`-block consists of a single statement, the curly brackets are optional: Java will automatically assume that the next statement is the one that should be executed if the `if`-block evaluates to `true`.

It is not recommended to ever use this approach. It is a common source of bugs, especially when an extra line is added to the `if`-block without realizing that the curly brackets are missing. It also tends to make code more difficult to read.

In the previous examples a block of code executed when an expression evaluated to true. It is also common to execute an alternative block of code when the expression evaluates to false. This can be achieved by adding an else-block:

```java
public static void main(String[] args) {
    int i = 10;
    if (i > 10) {
        System.out.println("The number is greater than 10");
    } else {
        System.out.println("The number is NOT greater than 10");
    }
}
```

This example will print the following:

```
The number is NOT greater than 10
```

With an if-else construct, either the if-block or the else-block are guaranteed to be executed (but they can never both execute).

Finally, there are often cases where you may want one of many branches to execute. For instance, the following is a method that prints out one of 4 values depending on whether the number is

⇒ A positive even number
⇒ A positive odd number
⇒ A negative even number
⇒ A negative odd number

In order to achieve this, the code takes advantage of the else if construct:

```java
public static void main(String[] args) {
    int i = -10;
    if (i >= 0 && i % 2 == 0) {
        System.out.println("Positive even number");
    } else if (i >= 0) {
        System.out.println("Odd even number");
    } else if (i < 0 && i % 2 == 0) {
        System.out.println("Negative even number");
    } else {
        System.out.println("Negative odd number");
    }
}
```

There are a number of important points to note here:

⇒ This code uses the modulus (%) operator to determine if a number is odd or even: if dividing a number by 2 produces a remainder of 1, the number is odd.
⇒ Only one of the four blocks will execute. If the first and second if-statements both evaluated to true, only the first of them will be executed.
⇒ You can guarantee that one of these four blocks will execute, because the last block is an else block. If all the blocks were else-if blocks, it would be conceivable that none of the blocks would execute.

⇒ The first if-statement joins together two `boolean` expressions with the `&&` (and) operator. Both expressions must be `true` in order for the code in this block to execute.

⇒ The second statement can assume that if the number is `>= 0` then it is odd, and therefore only needs to check that the number is greater or equal to 0.

⇒ Technically the third block could be written `else if (i % 2 == 0)`, because you know it is a negative number (or one of the other blocks would have evaluated to `true`). Sometimes it is still worth adding extra code for clarity however.

⇒ The final block is an `else` block: this is possible because any number that has not evaluated to `true` in one of the other statements must be an odd, negative number.

It is also possible to nest `if`-blocks inside one another. The previous example could easily be rewritten as a nested expression: the outer block would determine whether the number is even/odd, while the inner expression would determine whether the number is positive or negative:

```
public static void main(String[] args) {
    int i = -10;
    if ( i % 2 == 0) {
        if (i >= 0) {
            System.out.println("Positive even number");
        } else {
            System.out.println("Negative even number");
        }
    } else {
        if (i >= 0) {
            System.out.println("Positive odd number");
        } else {
            System.out.println("Negative odd number");
        }
    }
}
```

Switch statement

The second way to perform branching is via the `switch` statement. The `switch` statement is different from the `if`-statement: it accepts a single variable, and then provides a set of blocks that execute when the value of the variable equals the value specified. Here is a basic example:

```
public static void main(String[] args) {
    int i = 2;
    switch (i) {
        case 1 :
            System.out.println("The number is 1");
            break;
        case 2 :
            System.out.println("The number is 2");
            break;
        case 3 :
            System.out.println("The number is 3");
            break;
```

```
        default :
            System.out.println("The number is greater than 3");
            break;
        }
    }
}
```

A `switch` block is introduced with the following statement:

```
switch (i) {
```

This specifies the variable that will be switched on (which happens to have the value of 2).

Inside the `switch` block are a series of statements such as:

```
case 1 :
```

These are equivalent to `if (i == 1)`: they evaluate to `true` when the value on the right hand side of the `case` statement equals the value of the variable being switched on. The `switch` statement can only evaluate to `true` based on equality; there is no way to use expressions such as greater than or less than.

If a `case` statement evaluates to `true`, all the code below it executes (except the `case` statements), until a `break` statement is reached. This is somewhat surprising, and means that if you remove the break statements from this code:

```
switch (i) {
    case 1 :
        System.out.println("The number is 1");
    case 2 :
        System.out.println("The number is 2");
    case 3 :
        System.out.println("The number is 3");
    default :
        System.out.println("The number is greater than 3");
}
```

This result will be:

```
The number is 2
The number is 3
The number is greater than 3
```

This is one of those classic cases where a language does not behave as you would intuitively expect. The reason for this is historical: the syntax of Java is based on the C language, and the C language used this convention. It has since become a major source of bugs, because even experienced programmers forget to add `break` statements sometimes.

There is a reason that this convention was originally adopted: imagine you want the same block to execute if the number is 1, 2 or 3, and another block to execute otherwise. You can write this as follows:

```
switch (i) {
    case 1 :
    case 2 :
```

```
    case 3 :
        System.out.println("The number is 1, 2 or 3");
        break;
    default :
        System.out.println("The number is greater than 3");
        break;
}
```

There are a number of other points to note about switch statements. The first is the default block that can optionally exist as the end of the switch statement: this will evaluate if none of the other case statements has matched. If this block is omitted, and none of the case statements match, no code will execute within the switch block.

The next point to understand is the data-types that can be passed to the switch statement. Originally the switch statement only supported integers (specifically byte, short, char and int). The switch statement does not support floating-point numbers, or even the long data-type.

Support was added for enums in Java 5 (these will be covered later in the book), and then, in Java 7, support was added for Strings. The following is an example of a switch statement using Strings:

```
public static void main(String[] args) {
    String s = "one";
        switch (s) {
            case "zero" :
                System.out.println("The number is 0");
                break;
            case "one" :
                System.out.println("The number is 1");
                break;
            case "two" :
                System.out.println("The number is 2");
                break;
            default :
                System.out.println("The number is greater than 2");
                break;
        }
    }
}
```

Ternary operator

The final way to implement branching is via a special type of operator that accepts three parameters (and is therefore called the ternary operator). This operator essentially provides a version of if-then-else in a single expression. The following is an example of the ternary operator in action:

```
public static void main(String[] args) {
    int i = 22;
    String s = i % 2 == 0 ? "even" : "odd";
    System.out.println("The number is "+s);
}
```

The key line to look at is this one:

```
String s = i % 2 == 0 ? "even" : "odd";
```

This is setting the variable `s` to be the result of

```
i % 2 == 0 ? "even" : "odd"
```

Although this line looks somewhat daunting, it is manageable if broken into its three constituent parts.

The first part is a `boolean` expression: in this case `i % 2 == 0`. In this particular case the expression will evaluate to `true`, because `i` is an even number.

The next part of the expression (following the question mark) is `"even"`. This is the statement that will be returned by the overall expression if the `boolean` expression evaluates to `true`. In this case the statement is a `String` literal, but it can be any statement supported by the language, such as an assignment statement.

The third part of the expression (following the colon) is returned by the overall expression if the `boolean` expression evaluates to `false`.

The ternary operator therefore always returns one of two values.

Looping

There are many cases in a computer program where a task needs to be performed repetitively. For instance, you may need to loop through as array and perform an operation on each member in turn.

For-loops

The first type of loop you will look at is the `for`-loop. The `for`-loop is probably the most common form of loop used in Java programs. The following is a very basic example of a `for`-loop. This prints out 10 lines to the console:

```
public static void main(String[] args) {
    for (int i = 0; i < 10; i++) {
        System.out.println("The number is "+i);
    }
}
```

If you run this, the output should be as follows:

```
The number is 0
The number is 1
The number is 2
The number is 3
The number is 4
The number is 5
The number is 6
The number is 7
The number is 8
The number is 9
```

The key to understanding `for`-loops is the following declaration:

```
for (int i = 0; i < 10; i++) {
```

This line can look daunting, but it is straightforward if you break it up into its three constituent parts (each of which are separated by a semi-colon).

The first part `int i = 0` declares a variable that will act as a counter. This variable will be used to keep track of how many times the loop has executed.

In this particular case I am using a variable called `i`, and because it has not already been declared I am telling the compiler what type it is. If the variable had already been declared I would omit the data-type.

I am also specifying a starting value for the variable. It is traditional to start counting from 0 rather than 1, but this is entirely up to the programmer. It is also traditional to use `i` as the variable name (short for "index"), but again, any valid variable name can be used.

The second part of the statement `i < 10` declares the condition that must hold `true` for the loop to continue. In this case, the loop will continue as long as the variable `i` is less than 10. This expression will be evaluated on every iteration of the loop.

The third part of the statement `i++` declares how the variable `i` should be modified at the *conclusion* of each iteration of the loop. In most cases you want the loop counter variable to be increased by 1. If the value of `i` did not change after each iteration of the loop, there would be no way the loop would ever end (it would be an *infinite loop*).

If you put all this together you have a loop that will execute 10 times (starting at 0, and ending at 9). Each time the loop executes it will execute the block of code between the brackets, which in this case is a single line of code printing out the current value of `i`.

Although you can refer to the variable `i` inside the loop, you may be wondering what happens to this variable when the loop finishes. Because the variable `i` was declared inside the `for`-loop declaration, its scope is limited to the `for`-loop. If you attempt to use this variable after the loop finishes you will receive a compilation error, because the compiler knows the variable no longer exists.

It is also possible to declare other variables inside the loop itself. In the next example I declare a variable called `squared` inside the loop. Because this is defined inside the loop, it is initialized on every iteration of the loop (and therefore has no knowledge of the value it had on the previous iteration). Naturally it is not possible to access this variable outside the loop.

```
public static void main(String[] args) {
    for (int i = 0; i < 10; i++) {
        int squared = i * i;
        System.out.println("The number is "+i);
        System.out.println("Squared is "+squared);
    }
}
```

The previous example was reasonably straightforward, but the three parts of the loop can be used in quite creative ways. For instance, suppose you wanted to write code that reversed the value of a `String`. This can be achieved as follows:

```
public static void main(String[] args) {
    String s = "Welcome to Java";
    for (int i = s.length(); i > 0; i--) {
        System.out.print(s.charAt(i-1));
    }
}
```

This particular example will reverse the `String` `"Welcome to Java"`. The three parts of the for-loop declaration are as follows:

⇒ The variable `i` is set to be the length of the `String` (15)
⇒ The loop should continue as long as the variable `i` is greater than 0
⇒ The value of `i` should be reduced by 1 each time the loop iterates

Inside the `for`-loop the code obtains the character in the `String` at the position `i-1`, and prints that to the console using `System.out.print`. The code block uses `i-1`, because if the length of a `String` is 15 characters, the last character is available at position 14 (because counting starts at 0).

The next example of a `for`-loop will add up all the numbers in a multi-dimensional array. In this example, the outer array will have 4 members, and each of its members will consist of an array containing 3 numbers. In order to process this array a `for`-loop needs to be nested inside a `for`-loop. The outer `for`-loop will iterate over the 4 elements in the outer array, while the inner loop will iterate over the 3 elements inside each inner array:

```
public static void main(String[] args) {
    int[][] numbers = {{1,2,3},{4,5,6},{7,8,9},{10,11,12}};
    int result = 0;
    for (int i = 0; i < numbers.length; i++) {
        for (int j = 0; j < 3; j++) {
            result += numbers[i][j];
        }
    }
    System.out.println(result);
}
```

Notice that the variable used to control the inner loop is `j` rather than `i`: This allows the code to keep track of two counts at the same time. The variable `j` is reset to 0 every-time the outer loop starts a new iteration.

The final point worth noting about `for`-loops is that all three parts of the loop declaration are optional. If the second part is omitted, however, the loop body must contain a `break` statement (as explained in the next section) to allow the loop to finally exit.

The following is a valid `for`-loop declaration, and will create a loop that loops indefinitely until something in the body of the loop causes it to halt:

```
for (;;) {
```

Break and continue

There are often cases with loops where it is useful to halt a loop even though the loop has not finished. Consider a loop that is responsible for determining whether all the elements in an array collectively add up to 100 or more:

```
public static void main(String[] args) {
    int[] numbers = {3,5,43,2,5,33,2,45,5,3};
    int checkGreaterThan = 100;
    int sumOfNumbers = 0;
    for (int i = 0; i < numbers.length; i++) {
        sumOfNumbers += numbers[i];
    }
    if (sumOfNumbers > checkGreaterThan) {
        System.out.println("It is greater");
    }
}
```

This code is perfectly valid, but it is also slightly wasteful in terms of processing. It may make more sense to check whether the sumOfNumbers is greater than checkGreaterThan inside the for-loop, and stop processing as soon as it is. In order to achieve this, you need some way of telling the for-loop that you do not need it to continue processing: this can be achieved with the break keyword:

```
for (int i = 0; i < numbers.length; i++) {
    sumOfNumbers += numbers[i];
    if (sumOfNumbers > checkGreaterThan) {
        System.out.println("It is greater");
        break;
    }
}
```

As soon as the break statement is encountered the loop immediately terminates.

The break keyword always breaks out of the current loop, so if you are using nested for-loops the break will relate to the specific loop it is executed within. Imagine the same code processing a multi-dimensional array however: it may be desirable to break out of all the loops when a specified condition is met. This can be achieved via a concept called labels:

```
public static void main(String[] args) {
    int[][] numbers = {{11,12,3},{14,15,16},{17,18,19},{10,11,12}};
    int checkGreaterThan = 100;
    int sumOfNumbers = 0;
    outer: for (int i = 0; i < numbers.length; i++) {
        for (int j = 0; j < 3; j++) {
            sumOfNumbers += numbers[i][j];
            if (sumOfNumbers > checkGreaterThan) {
                System.out.println("It is greater");
                break outer;
            }
        }
    }
}
```

Notice that the outer loop has been tagged with the label `outer`. A label is just an arbitrary tag, followed by a colon. The `break` statement then specifies the label of the loop it wishes the `break` to apply to, thereby allowing you to break out of the outer-most loop, rather than the loop that the `break` statement is executed within.

Labels are not widely used in Java, and are discouraged by many due to their similarity to the dreaded `goto` statement that appears in many older languages. The `goto` statement allowed any line of code to jump to any other line of code, and was notorious for creating *spaghetti code* that could not be understood.

Labels were introduced as a *controlled* form of the `goto` statement. The creators of Java did not wish to introduce the `goto` statement, but they also acknowledged the `goto` statement was useful in the specific case of nested loops.

The `continue` keyword is syntactically similar to the `break` keyword, except it provides a way of ending the current iteration of the loop, and immediately jumping to the next iteration.

Consider a revised version of the adder program. This example will only count even numbers; therefore if it encounters an odd number it needs to immediately jump to the next number (and the next iteration of the loop). This can be achieved as follows:

```
public static void main(String[] args) {
    int[] numbers = {3,5,44,2,5,33,2,45,5,3,44,22,26,7,9,11};
    int checkGreaterThan = 100;
    int sumOfNumbers = 0;
    for (int i = 0; i < numbers.length; i++) {
        if (numbers[i] % 2 != 0) {
            continue;
        }
        sumOfNumbers += numbers[i];
        if (sumOfNumbers > checkGreaterThan) {
            System.out.println("It is greater");
            break;
        }
    }
}
```

The `continue` statement is effectively stating that there is no reason to process the remainder of this iteration of the loop, so the loop should immediately begin processing the next iteration of the loop.

As with the `break` keyword, `continue` can also use labels.

While loop

The next form of loop is the `while`-loop. The `while`-loop declaration is syntactically simpler than the `for`-loop: it specifies a condition than must remain `true` for the loop to continue processing:

```
public static void main(String[] args) {
    int i = 0;
    while (i < 10) {
```

```
        System.out.println("The number is "+i);
        i++;
    }
}
```

In many ways `while`-loops are similar to `for`-loops. The three parts of the `for`-loop definition still exist, but two of the parts are declared outside the loop declaration:

- ⇒ The declaration of the variable that will control iteration needs to occur before the loop is declared. In this example the variable `i` is declared on the first line of the method.
- ⇒ The `boolean` expression to determine whether the loop should continue occurs inside the loop declaration. In this case the expression is `i < 10`.
- ⇒ The modification of the counter variable must occur inside the loop. In this case the variable is modified with the following statement: `i++`.

If the body of the loop did not augment the `i` variable, the loop could never stop (an infinite loop would be created). The Java compiler cannot detect infinite loops, and therefore they are a common source of run-time bugs.

Most other features of `while`-loops are the same as `for`-loops. They execute a block of code with each iteration, they can use the `continue` and `break` keywords to control execution, and they can be nested inside one another.

Do-while loops

With `while` loops it is possible that the code inside the while loop will never execute. This will occur when the initial evaluation of the `boolean` expression is `false`, for instance:

```
while (i > 0) {
```

This leads on to the final type of loop, the `do-while` loop.

The only difference between a `do-while` loop and a `while` loop is that a `do-while` loop is guaranteed to execute at least once, even if the `boolean` expression evaluates to `false` the first time it is evaluated. For this reason, the `boolean` expression appears after the body of the loop:

```
public static void main(String[] args) {
    int i = 0;
    do {
        System.out.println("The number is "+i);
        i++;
    } while (i < 10);
}
```

If you try changing both this loop, and the `while`-loop, to use the expression `i < 0`, you will notice that the `do-while` loop still executes once.

In honesty, I can count on one hand the number of times I have used a `do-while` loop, but it is important to know they exist, and occasionally you will find a use for them.

10 DEBUGGING

Debugging is one of the most important concepts for a software engineer. It provides a mechanism to examine a program as it executes, and therefore allows any bugs to be diagnosed and resolved. Without debugging you would need to resort to logging information to the console, and piecing together the state of the program from that logging.

The Eclipse IDE provides a built-in debugger, which will be the focus of this chapter.

Before beginning to look at debugging it is useful to introduce a new Eclipse concept called the *perspective*. Up until this point you have been using the Java perspective. This perspective includes a number of views, most notably the package explorer view, the editor view, and the console view.

Eclipse allows you to customize the display of a perspective. You can drag the views around the screen, change their size, or add new views to a perspective (using the `Window -> Show view` option).

The basic idea of a perspective is that it is a way of collecting a set of views together to aid you with performing a specific task. Your task up until this point has been writing and executing Java code, therefore the Java perspective has met your needs. When you start debugging a program you will use another perspective called the Debug perspective. This also contains a number of views, but these will differ to some extent from those seen in the Java perspective.

You can choose the perspective you wish to use via this toolbar in the top right hand corner of Eclipse, as seen in figure 10-1:

FIGURE 10-1

As you can see, the Java perspective is selected, while the Debug perspective is available. Clicking the left-most button (with the gold star) provides access to a number of other perspectives that will not be examined in this book.

As you will see, Eclipse automatically opens the Debug perspective when you start debugging code, but you will need to switch back to the Java perspective at the end using this toolbar.

Getting Started

In order to get started you need to choose a program that you want to debug. The program you will debug is the `ArrayAdder` program from the Loops and Branching chapter. The class should look as follows:

```java
package loops;
public class ArrayAdder {
    public static void main(String[] args) {
        int[] numbers = {3,5,43,2,5,33,2,45,5,3};
        int checkGreaterThan = 100;
        int sumOfNumbers = 0;
        for (int i = 0; i < numbers.length; i++) {
            sumOfNumbers += numbers[i];
            if (sumOfNumbers > checkGreaterThan) {
                System.out.println("It is greater");
                break;
            }
        }
    }
}
```

This class prints `It is greater` if the sum of all the numbers in the array is greater than 100.

Open this class in the Java editor and double click in the left-most margin against the line:

```
sumOfNumbers += numbers[i];
```

A blue dot should appear in the margin. If you do not see a blue dot, ensure you are clicking where the dot displays in figure 10-2:

```
for (int i = 0; i < numbers.length; i++) {
    sumOfNumbers += numbers[i];
    if (sumOfNumbers > checkGreaterThan) {
        System.out.println("It is greater");
```

FIGURE 10-2

This dot is called a breakpoint. When the program is run in debug mode, the execution will pause when it reaches this line and allow you to interact with the program in real time.

Now, right-click on the `ArrayAdder` class in the Package Explorer and choose to debug it as a Java Application, as seen in figure 10-3:

FIGURE 10-3

The program will immediately start executing. When the breakpoint is reached, the prompt seen in figure 10-4 will be displayed asking if you would like to launch the Debug perspective. I recommend ticking the "Remember my decision" option and choosing "Yes".

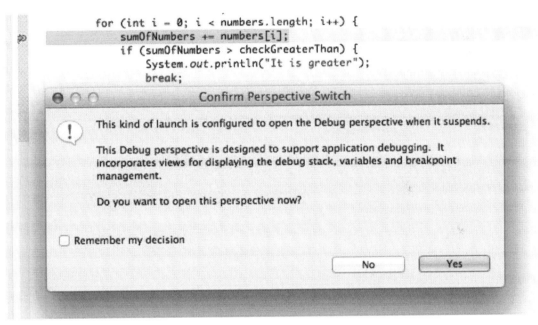

FIGURE 10-4

There are a number of useful views in the debugger. As you can see, the editor is still the main view of the perspective, but the editor contains addition features: for instance, it highlights the line of code that the debugger is currently paused on.

Another important view is the "Variables" view, as seen in figure 10-5:

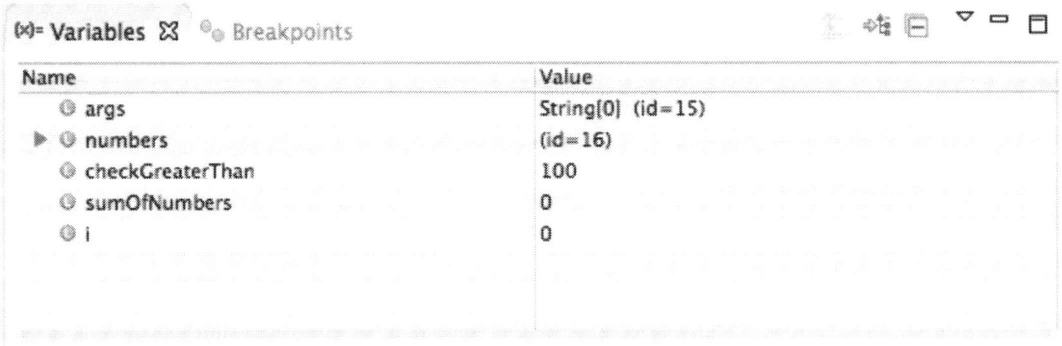

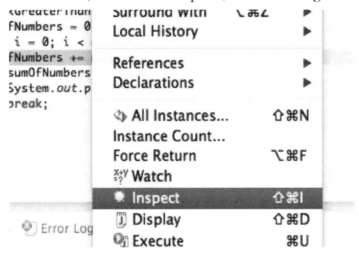

FIGURE 10-5

This shows the current value of all variables that are currently *in-scope*. For instance, you can see that `i` and `sumOfNumbers` are both set to 0, which you would expect at this stage in the program execution. You can also find the value of any variable by hovering over it in the editor with the cursor.

Now that the program is paused, you can begin to interact with it as it executes. For a start, you may wonder what will be the value of the expression `numbers[i]`. In order to find out, you can highlight this piece of code (not including the semi-colon), right click on the selected text, and choose "Inspect", as shown in figure 10-6:

FIGURE 10-6

This will cause the statement to be executed, and the result (3) to be displayed.

You can now begin stepping through the program line by line and watch it as it executes. The main debugging controls can be found in the top menu, as shown in figure 10-7. Hovering over each button will tell you its purpose:

FIGURE 10-7

The feature you will use initially is "Step over". This is the second of the yellow arrows (fifth from the left). If you press this, the debugger will move to the next line of code, and therefore execute the line that the debugger had been paused on. As a result of this the value of the sumOfNumbers variable will be set to 3.

You can now select the code sumOfNumbers > checkGreaterThan and choose "Inspect" on the right-click menu: this will inform you that the expression evaluates to false. You can also confirm this by choosing "Step over" one more time: execution will then continue back to the top of the for-loop.

The button beside "Step over" is "Step into". This button is useful if the current line involves method calls, because it allows the debugger to enter those method calls rather than just step over them.

If you press "Step over" a few more times you will see the code executing, and the values of the in-scope variables change as the execution progresses. You can also press the green button on the left hand side of the debug menu if you would like to progress to the next break point in the program (i.e. the next iteration of the loop in this case).

After seeing the program execute for a couple of iterations of the loop you may decide you only want the program to pause if it is going to print out It is greater. With the program paused you can therefore double click the margin beside the line:

```
System.out.println("It is greater");
```

This will add a breakpoint to this line. You can then and double click on the blue dot next to the line:

```
sumOfNumbers += numbers[i];
```

This will remove the breakpoint from this line.

If you now press the green "Continue" button, execution will continue until it stops on the new breakpoint. You will now be able to confirm that the condition was met on the 8th iteration through the loop (i= 7, because counting started at 0), and that the value of sumOfNumbers is 138 - as shown in figure 10-8:

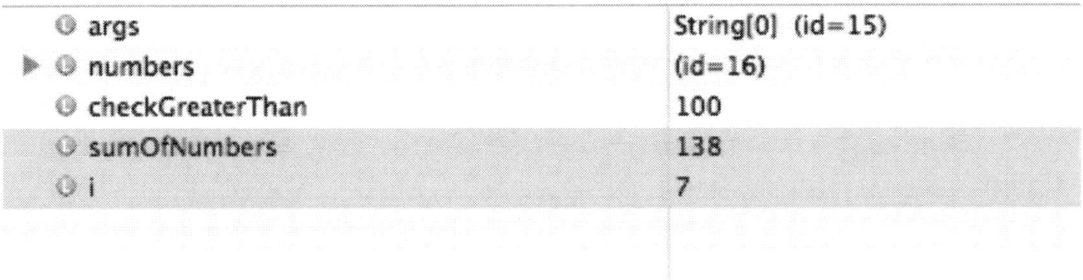

⊙ args	String[0] (id=15)
▶ ⊙ numbers	(id=16)
⊙ checkGreaterThan	100
⊙ sumOfNumbers	138
⊙ i	7

FIGURE 10-8

The highlighting over these variables indicates that their values have changed.

11 OBJECT REFERENCES

The previous few chapters have introduced the concepts of objects and classes. This chapter will look at objects in more detail, specifically; you will look at the difference between objects, and the variables that hold references to these objects. Up until now I have not necessarily distinguished these two concepts, but learning to distinguish them is an essential aspect of learning Java.

Consider the following line of code:

```
StringBuffer sb1 = new StringBuffer("Hello World");
```

This line looks simple enough: it has instantiated a `StringBuffer` object, and assigned it the text `"Hello World"`. Additionally, after this line of code executes, a variable called `sb1` can be used for accessing that object.

It may be tempting to assume that `sb1` and the object created are one and the same thing: for instance, that `sb1` is simply the name assigned to the newly created object. This is not, however, an accurate interpretation of this line of code: `sb1` is a *reference* to the object.

In order to make the distinction clear, consider the impact of adding the following 2 lines immediately after the line above:

```
StringBuffer sb2 = sb1;
sb2.append("!!!");
```

`sb1` and `sb2` are now both referring to the same object. Only a single object has been created (an object can only be created via the `new` keyword), but both these variables are referring (or pointing) to this object.

For this reason, when I append "!!!" to the `StringBuffer` referenced by `sb2`, the extra text will be seen when I print out the value of `sb1` *or* `sb2`:

```
System.out.println(sb1);
System.out.println(sb2);
```

Both of these lines will print the same value because they are both printing the value of the *same* object.

It is possible to use the == operator to determine if two references refer to the same object, for instance, the following expression will return `true`:

```
sb1 == sb2;
```

The best way to visualize the previous example is via the drawing in figure 11-1:

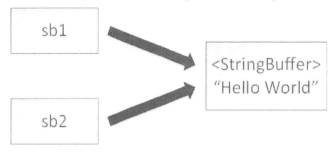

FIGURE 11-1

With this understood it is now possible to explain the default behavior of the `equals` method defined on the `Object` class; this method returns `true` if two references are compared that refer to the same underlying object:

```
sb1.equals(sb2);
```

The default `equals` method, therefore, is the same as using ==. In later chapters you will look at how you can provide your own implementation of this method.

In some programming languages the distinction between objects and the references to them is made explicit, and it is possible to access either the reference or the underlying object. In Java this is not possible: you can only access objects via their references.

Confusingly primitives do not act in this manner. Consider the following lines:

```
int num1 = 2;
int num2 = num1;
num2 = 5;
System.out.println(num1);
System.out.println(num2);
```

If primitives behaved like objects you would expect that this example would print out the number 5 twice. In fact it prints out the following:

```
2
5
```

When you declare a variable as a primitive type, the variable (e.g. `num1`) is not a reference to the primitive; the variable and the value are one and the same thing. It is not therefore possible for two variables to refer to the same primitive value (although, obviously, they can have the same value).

Another way to think about the distinction between objects and references is that both the object and the reference are occupying independent areas of computer memory. The reference stores the memory address of the referenced object in its memory: therefore if two references hold the same memory address, they are referring to the same object.

In the case of a primitive, the only memory that is allocated is the memory required by the primitive type (for instance, 64 bits for a `long`), and any time the primitive variable is accessed, this memory is accessed directly.

Garbage Collection

Once you understand object references it is also possible to understand an important Java concept called *garbage collection*. In order to understand the need for garbage collection, consider the fact that a computer program has a finite amount of memory that it can utilize. It is possible for a Java program to specify the amount of memory that it wishes to utilize, but there will always be limits.

Whenever a Java program instantiates an object, that object will use memory. The object is allocated space in an area of memory called the *heap*: this is a general-purpose area of memory where space can be allocated as required.

> In some programming languages it is necessary to request a specific amount of space on the heap when instantiating objects; in Java this is always automatic. It is entirely up to the Java Runtime Environment to determine how space is allocated on the heap, and to ensure sufficient space is allocated when objects require extra space (for instance, if you append text to a `StringBuffer`).

Although the allocation of space on the heap is automatic, it is also important that you de-allocate the space when an object is no longer needed. An object is no longer needed when there are no references to it. Remember, an object can only be accessed via its references, therefore, if there are no references to the object, the program can never access the object.

Some languages include explicit mechanisms for de-allocating memory. These mechanisms place the burden on the programmer to know when an object is no longer needed, and to de-allocate its memory. This tends to be error prone, and can lead to "memory-leaks" when objects are left on the heap when they are no longer referenced.

Java uses a process called garbage collection to de-allocate the memory used by unreferenced objects. Whenever a Java program is running, a process periodically runs automatically that determines whether objects are still referenced: If they are not, their space is automatically de-allocated.

Consider the following three lines of code:

```
StringBuffer sb1 = new StringBuffer("hello");
```

```
StringBuffer sb2 = sb1;
sb2 = null;
```

The first two lines are familiar: you create a single `StringBuffer` object with two references to it. At this point the `StringBuffer` object would not be available for garbage collections because there are two references referring to it.

On the third line one of these references is set to `null`, indicating that `sb2` is no longer referring to the `StringBuffer` object (it is now not referring to anything). The object still has one reference referring to it however (`sb1`), therefore it still isn't available for garbage collection.

Another way to de-reference an object is to declare that a reference now refers to a different object. A variable such as `sb2` can only refer to one object at a time; therefore if you change the object that the reference is referring to, it can no longer be used to access the original object, for instance:

```
sb2 = new StringBuffer("new object");
```

Image now that you added a fourth line to this code:

```
sb1 = null;
```

Once this is executed, the program no longer has any references referring to the original `StringBuffer` object. Because the `StringBuffer` object can no longer be referenced by any code (now or in the future), it is available for garbage collection.

The garbage collection process will not necessarily happen immediately, it occurs periodically as the program executes. The JVM has complete control over when it decides to run garbage collection, although it is possible to pass parameters to the Java program when it starts to tell it which garbage collection strategy to use.

> There tends to be a trade-off with garbage collection. The more memory that is allocated to a program, the longer the garbage collection process can take. This is why it is common to cluster multiple Java application servers on a machine, rather than have a single Java application server use all the available memory on a machine.
>
> This subject is not important for the programs you are writing in this book, but if you would like to learn more about configuring garbage collection, the following site provides a wealth of information:
>
> http://www.oracle.com/technetwork/java/javase/tech/vmoptions-jsp-140102.html
>
> Garbage collection also makes it difficult (but not impossible) to implement real-time systems with Java – because the garbage collection process essentially halts the program (at least some of the

> time). You would not want your car's airbag to be controlled by Java if it meant it might not be able to respond in the split second you needed it.

There is no way to force garbage collection to run. It is possible to request the JVM to run garbage collection, however, by invoking:

```
System.gc();
```

Even this is only a request to the JVM, and it generally should not be necessary to invoke this.

When the garbage collector detects an object that has no references it first calls a method called `finalize` on the object: this is one of the methods provided by the `Object` class itself, but you can provide your own implementation. This method was intended to provide an opportunity to clean up any resources used by the object, such as open files, although it tends not to be used in modern Java programming, because generally you will not de-reference an object with open resources.

If you would like to see finalize in action, try executing the following program. It creates 1 million objects, and immediately dereferences them (for reasons that will be explained shortly), making them available for garbage collection:

```
package finalize;
public class FinalizeExample {
   @Override
    protected void finalize() throws Throwable {
        System.out.println("Finalize called");
    }

    public static void main(String[] args) {
        for (int i = 0; i < 10000000; i++) {
            FinalizeExample f = new FinalizeExample();
        }
    }
}
```

After `finalize` is invoked, the JVM reclaims the space that was occupied by the object, and makes it available for use elsewhere in the program.

> Garbage collection does not guarantee that your program will not contain memory leaks. If you hold unnecessary references to objects, your program will utilize more memory than required.

Reassigning a reference, or setting a reference to `null` are two ways to remove the association between a reference and an object, but often it is not necessary to even do this. This can be seen by looking at a more complex scenario:

```java
public class GC {
    public static void main(String[] args) {
        GC gc = new GC();
        StringBuffer sb = gc.createStrings();
    }

    public StringBuffer createStrings() {
        StringBuffer sb1 = new StringBuffer("hello");
        StringBuffer sb2 = new StringBuffer("world");
        return sb2;
    }
}
```

In this example the `createStrings` method declares two `StringBuffers` – each with a single reference referring to them (`sb1` and `sb2`). This method is called by the `main` method, and when the method ends, it returns one of these references to the caller. The `main` method then retains this reference.

When objects are instantiated inside a method they are placed on the heap (as mentioned earlier), but the references to them (which, remember, also consume memory) are placed in a different area of memory called the stack. The stack and the heap are two distinct areas of memory inside the JVM.

Figure 11-2 demonstrates the state of the stack and heap as the program executes.

> Primitive variables declared inside a method are also placed on the stack.

The stack operates slightly differently from the heap. As its name suggests, as variables are declared in a method they are placed on the top of the stack, just like plates being placed on top of one another. When the method finishes, all the variables declared inside the method are popped off the top of the stack and destroyed. This means they are no longer referencing any object.

When `createStrings` completes, therefore, the references `sb1` and `sb2` are destroyed, and therefore no longer refer to any objects. This means that one of the objects (the one referred to by `sb1`), is available for garbage collection. This exact same process occurs every time a loop completes as well – explaining how the finalize example worked.

The object referred to by `sb2` is more complex. Because this is returned from the method, the reference `sb` in the `main` method now refers to this object, and therefore this object is not available for garbage collection until the `main` method ends: which only happens when the program ends.

One way to think about this is that the `createStrings` method has returned the memory location of an object to the `main` method (x1110, as seen in figure 11-2), and the `main` method stores this location inside the variable `sb`.

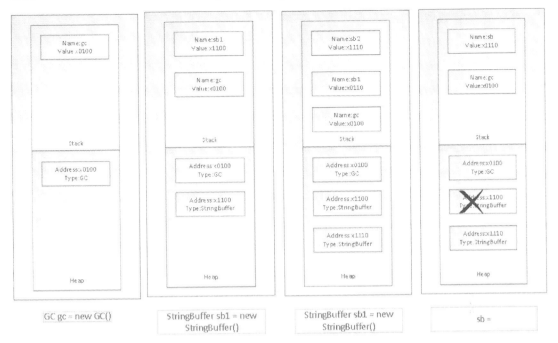

FIGURE 11-2

Although figure 11-2 implies objects are allocated at sequential addresses on the heap, this should not be taken literally. The JVM can place objects at any memory location it sees fit.

Method arguments

With an understanding of the difference between references and objects it is possible to understand how arguments are passed to methods, and more importantly, what happens when a method modifies one of these arguments. For instance, if a `StringBuffer` is passed to a method, and that method modifies it, does the caller of the method see the change to that `StringBuffer`, or does it retain a view to the `StringBuffer`'s original value?

Programming languages handle this possibility in two different ways, neither of which is inherently right or wrong:

⇒ **Pass by value**: with this approach any changes made to an argument **will not** be seen by the caller. In the example mentioned, the caller would retain a view to the original `StringBuffer`, and the method would work with a copy of that object.

⇒ **Pass by reference**: with this approach the caller **will** see any changes made to an argument inside a method when the method completes. With pass by reference, a reference to the object is passed, and therefore both parties are modifying the same underlying object when they use that reference.

Java does not easily fit into either of these categories.

When primitives are passed as arguments to a method, Java uses a **pass by value** approach. This means that the caller does not see any changes the method makes. This can be seen in the following example:

```
package parameters;
public class Primatives {
    public static void main(String[] args) {
        int num1 = 5;
        System.out.println("Value at point 1 is "+num1);
        changeMe(num1);
        System.out.println("Value at point 3 is "+num1);
    }

    private static void changeMe(int num) {
        num += 5;
        System.out.println("Value at point 2 is "+num);
    }
}
```

In this case, the method `changeMe` receives the value held by `num1` (5). This is actually a copy of the value held by of `num1`, however, therefore any modification to this value inside `changeMe` will not be seen by the `main` method. This program therefore produces the following output:

```
Value at point 1 is 5
Value at point 2 is 10
Value at point 3 is 5
```

When a program passes an object reference to a method, however, things become more complex. Arguments are still passed by value, but to complicate matters, it is the reference to the object that is passed by value. This is an important distinction that even many experienced Java programmers do not fully understand. In order to understand the implications, consider the following example:

```
package parameters;
public class PassObject1 {
    public static void main(String[] args) {
        StringBuffer sb = new StringBuffer("Hello");
        System.out.println("Value at point 1 is "+sb);
        changeMe(sb);
        System.out.println("Value at point 3 is "+sb);
    }

    private static void changeMe(StringBuffer sb1) {
        sb1 = new StringBuffer("Hello World");
        System.out.println("Value at point 2 is "+sb1);
    }
}
```

This example behaves the same as the primitive-based example. A copy of the `sb` reference is passed to the `changeMe` method: the `changeMe` method then modifies which object on the heap this reference is referring to. Naturally, changing the value of this new object does not impact the original object. This can be seen in figure 11-3:

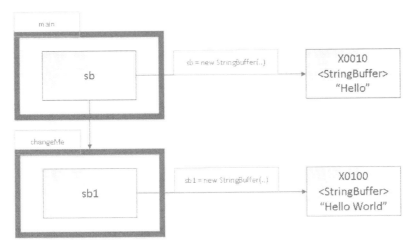

FIGURE 11-3

This program therefore prints:

```
Value at point 1 is Hello
Value at point 2 is Hello World
Value at point 3 is Hello
```

Make sure you fully understand this distinction. When the method is invoked, a copy of the original reference is created, and this copy refers to the same underlying object. Therefore, the memory addresses held by the two references are the same when changeMe is invoked.

Inside changeMe, the memory address of the copied references is changed so that it points to another object. This has absolutely no impact on the original reference held by the main method.

Compare this with the following program:

```
package parameters;
public class PassObject2 {
    public static void main(String[] args) {
        StringBuffer sb = new StringBuffer("Hello");
        System.out.println("Value at point 1 is "+sb);
        changeMe(sb);
        System.out.println("Value at point 3 is "+sb);
    }

    private static void changeMe(StringBuffer sb1) {
        sb1.append(" World");
        System.out.println("Value at point 2 is "+sb1);
    }
}
```

Rather than modifying the reference, the changeMe method is modifying the object that the sb1 parameter refers to, and this makes a big difference to the behavior of the program.

Remember, a copy of the sb reference from the main method has been passed to the changeMe method, but both the original and the copy are referring to the same object on the heap. As a result, the changeMe method now directly affects the value of the object created by the main method. As a result, the program prints the following:

```
Value at point 1 is Hello
Value at point 2 is Hello World
Value at point 3 is Hello World
```

This can be visualized as seen in figure 11-4:

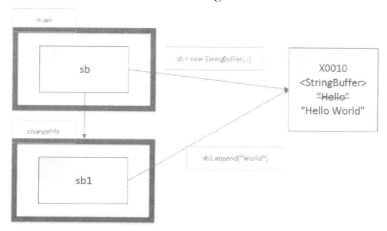

FIGURE 11-4

I cannot stress enough how important it is that you understand these distinctions if you want to work effectively with Java. Take these examples and play around with them in Eclipse so you can assure yourself you understand what is happening in each case.

One final point worth emphasizing is the behavior of immutable objects such as Strings. Because there is no way that a method can modify the underlying value of an immutable object, this has an impact on the way argument passing works: specifically, it is not possible for the called method to alter the value of the object in a manner that will be reflected to the calling method:

```java
package parameters;
public class PassObject3 {
    public static void main(String[] args) {
        String s = "Hello";
        System.out.println("Value at point 1 is "+s);
        changeMe(s);
        System.out.println("Value at point 3 is "+s);
    }

    private static void changeMe(String s) {
        s += " World";
        System.out.println("Value at point 2 is "+s);
    }
}
```

This produces the following result:

```
Value at point 1 is Hello
Value at point 2 is Hello World
Value at point 3 is Hello
```

The key to understanding this program is the following line:

```
s += " World";
```

Due to the fact that `Strings` are immutable, this line causes a new `String` object to be created: it does not change the value of the `String` originally created in the `main` method.

Final keyword

It is possible to specify that a field on an object, or a variable, cannot be changed once it has been assigned a value using the `final` keyword. Consider the following example, which will not compile:

```
package parameters;
public class FinalFields {
    private final StringBuffer sb;

    public FinalFields() {
        sb = new StringBuffer("Hello World");
    }

    public void run() {
        sb.append("!!!");
        sb = new StringBuffer("Hello World");
    }
}
```

The `sb` field is defined as `final`, therefore it can only ever refer to a single object throughout its lifetime. This reference must either be defined inline:

```
private final StringBuffer sb = new StringBuffer("Hello World");
```

or, as in this case, inside the constructor.

The example above is invalid because the second line of the `run` method attempts to change the object that `sb` refers to:

```
sb = new StringBuffer("Hello World");
```

You may be wondering about the first line of the `run` method. This also changes the object by appending text to it. As it happens, this line is valid. Even though the field has been declared as `final`, it is possible to change the internal contents of the object referred to, it just is not possible to change which object is referred to.

For this reason, `final` should not be thought of as a mechanism for making objects read-only (unfortunately). If you want an object to be read-only (or immutable) you need to implement this yourself and make sure its internal state cannot be changed. The `final` keyword is simply intended to ensure that an object reference cannot be changed.

The exception to this is primitives of course. With primitives there is no distinction between the field and the value. Declaring a primitive field as `final`, therefore, does exactly what you would expect: it prevents any code from changing its value.

Null references

Now that you understand the difference between an object and a reference to an object, it is easier to understand the concept of `null`. You have already seen that object references can be set to `null` to make the objects they refer to eligible for garbage collection. Object references can also be set to `null` when they are declared:

```
String s = null;
```

When a reference is `null` it does not refer to an object on the heap. Although a reference can be declared as `null`, it still has a type, and this dictates the type of object that the reference can eventually refer to.

A common issue in Java programs is invoking methods on an object reference that is `null`. For instance, consider the following example:

```
package nullexample;
public class NullString {
    public static void main(String[] args) {
        StringBuffer sb = null;
        sb.append("Hello");
    }
}
```

This program will compile, but obviously there is a problem on the second line of the `main` method. Even Eclipse has spotted this error: that is why the `sb` reference is underlined in yellow on the second line of the method

When line 2 of the `main` method is executed it will generate a type of exception called a `NullPointerException`. You will look at exceptions in detail in the coming chapters, but `NullPointerException`s are probably the most common type of exception you will come across with Java.

It is interesting to note that the following program is functionally equivalent, but does not compile:

```
package nullexample;
public class NullString {
    public static void main(String[] args) {
        StringBuffer sb;
        sb.append("Hello");
    }
}
```

In this case the compiler is smart enough to realize that `sb` has never been initialized. Because object references default to `null`, the two programs are functionally equivalent, but the compiler guards against one scenario and not the other.

12 INHERITANCE

Inheritance is another of the key concepts associated with Object Orientated Programming, and is one of the most important mechanisms for achieving code-reuse. Inheritance allows you to take an existing class, and create a new class that uses it as its base.

Code reuse is an important subject in software engineering. Each line of code written not only creates overhead during development, it adds expense to ongoing maintenance. Code duplication can also lead to inconsistencies in software, because making a change in one place may not apply to the whole program.

You have actually already used inheritance in your programs: as mentioned earlier, all classes in Java inherit from the `Object` class, and therefore, all classes automatically inherit the methods `equals`, `toString`, amongst others.

It turns out that this inheritance is identical to the inheritance I will discuss in this chapter, with the exception that all classes *automatically* extend the `Object` class – in all other cases, inheritance must be explicitly declared.

Understanding difficult subjects like inheritance starts with forming the correct mental model of the subject. There are a couple of different ways to think about inheritance:

⇒ **As a parent/child relationship.** In this case the base class is the parent, and the classes extending it can be thought of as its children. The child class can be thought of as adding functionality to the parent. As an example, you could think of a Vehicle as the parent of Car and Truck.

⇒ **As a specialization relationship.** In this case the base class has a large amount of functionality that you require, but you need this functionality to be specialized in some way to meet the requirements of your task at hand. You therefore create a specialized class, that modifies functionality in the base class where required. As an example, you could think of a Race Horse as a specialization of a Horse.

These are not necessarily competing views of inheritance. In some cases inheritance will simultaneously perform both these tasks: a sub-class will both augment functionality in its parent, and add new functionality.

As an example of inheritance, consider a drawing program that allows the user to draw shapes on a canvas. The program may allow the user to draw several types of shape, for instance, squares, triangles and octagons.

In this program you may decide to represent every type of shape as a distinct class, so you would create three classes (`Square`, `Triangle` and `Octagon`), as seen below. This seems to make sense, because each type of shape is different in some way:

```java
package shapes;
public class Square {
    private final int sides = 4;
    private String fillColor;
    private String lineColor;

    public Square() {}

    public void draw() {
        System.out.println("I am drawing a square");
        System.out.printf("I have %d sides", sides);
    }
    public int getSides() {
        return sides;
    }
    public String getFillColor() {
        return fillColor;
    }
    public void setFillColor(String fillColor) {
        this.fillColor = fillColor;
    }
    public String getLineColor() {
        return lineColor;
    }
    public void setLineColor(String lineColor) {
        this.lineColor = lineColor;
    }
}

package shapes;
public class Triangle {
    private final int sides = 3;
    private String fillColor;
    private String lineColor;

    public Triangle() {}

    public void draw() {
        System.out.println("I am drawing a triangle");
        System.out.printf("I have %d sides", sides);
    }
```

```java
    public int getSides() {
        return sides;
    }
    public String getFillColor() {
        return fillColor;
    }
    public void setFillColor(String fillColor) {
        this.fillColor = fillColor;
    }
    public String getLineColor() {
        return lineColor;
    }
    public void setLineColor(String lineColor) {
        this.lineColor = lineColor;
    }
}

package shapes;
public class Octagon {
    private final int sides = 8;
    private String fillColor;
    private String lineColor;

    public Octagon() {}

    public void draw() {
        System.out.println("I am drawing a octagon");
        System.out.printf("I have %d sides", sides);
    }
    public int getSides() {
        return sides;
    }
    public String getFillColor() {
        return fillColor;
    }
    public void setFillColor(String fillColor) {
        this.fillColor = fillColor;
    }
    public String getLineColor() {
        return lineColor;
    }
    public void setLineColor(String lineColor) {
        this.lineColor = lineColor;
    }
}
```

If you read through this code you will notice a large amount of duplication. Each of these classes has identical fields called `fillColor` and `lineColor`, along with the relevant getters and setters.

Anytime you see code being duplicated like this you should ask yourself if there is a way to remove the duplication (or *refactor* the code). One of the key ways of reducing duplication is through inheritance.

In order to introduce inheritance you need to think of a name for a class that *generalizes* what all these classes have in common. Ask yourself "Squares, triangles and octagons are all

_____ ".

In this case the most obvious name to fill in the blank would be "Shapes". I will refer to Shape as the super-class (this is sometimes also referred to as the parent-class), and Square, Triangle and Octagon as sub-classes.

The second step is to identify the functionality that can be extracted from the sub-classes into the super-class. For now I will limit myself to the fillColor and lineColor fields and methods:

```java
package shapes;
public class Shape {
    private String fillColor;
    private String lineColor;

    public Shape() {}

    public String getFillColor() {
        return fillColor;
    }
    public void setFillColor(String fillColor) {
        this.fillColor = fillColor;
    }
    public String getLineColor() {
        return lineColor;
    }
    public void setLineColor(String lineColor) {
        this.lineColor = lineColor;
    }
}
```

Next, I will remove this functionality from each of the subclasses, and most importantly, state that these sub-classes extend Shape (only the Square class is shown below for brevity, but make the same changes to Triangle and Octagon if you are coding this yourself). I have also changed the draw method so that it prints out the fill and line color:

```java
package shapes;
public class Square extends Shape {
    private final int sides = 4;

    public Square() {}

    public void draw() {
        System.out.println("I am drawing a square");
        System.out.printf("I have %d sides\n", sides);
        System.out.printf("My fill color is %s\n", getFillColor());
        System.out.printf("My line color is %s\n", getLineColor());
    }
    public int getSides() {
        return sides;
    }
}
```

Notice that the Square class is able to access properties on Shape via their getter methods. Square is not able to access the fillColor and lineColor fields directly, however, because they are declared `private`.

As it happens, you can make fields, constructors and methods accessible to subclasses without making them `public` (and therefore available to external classes). This can be achieved by using the `protected` access modifier. In order to demonstrate this, change the `getFillColor` and `getLineColor` methods on Shape to be `protected`:

```
protected String getFillColor() {
    return fillColor;
}
protected String getLineColor() {
    return lineColor;
}
```

The code will still compile, but you will see in a moment that external classes cannot call these methods.

Once the inheritance hierarchy is in place you can begin using the classes:

```
package shapes;
public class Main {
    public static void main(String[] args) {
        Square s = new Square();
        s.setFillColor("Blue");
        s.setLineColor("Red");
        s.draw();
    }
}
```

This will print the following:

```
I am drawing a square
I have 4 sides
My fill color is Blue
My line color is Red
```

Although the variable s is a reference to a Square, it is possible to invoke `public` methods defined on the Shape class exactly as if they were declared on Square itself: this therefore allows them to be reused by any class that extends Shape.

When you construct a Square, you are still only constructing a single object, but this object has access to the functionality defined in 2 classes (plus, of course, the functionality defined in Object).

If you think of this from the point-of-view of the main method: it is not aware whether the methods it is invoking are defined on Square, or whether they are inherited from Shape. Not only does it not know, it does not care. All that the main method cares about is that it can invoke the draw method on an instance of Square, and this will produce the appropriate output.

You can also see at this point that if you attempt to invoke the `protected` methods from the Main class you will receive a compilation error, for instance:

```
s.getFillColor();
```

Overriding methods

The implementation so far has made some progress towards eliminating duplicate code, but clearly the `draw` method is another candidate for reuse.

As a start, you may notice that the final two lines of the `draw` method could easily be placed in the `Shape` class. These are accessing fields defined on `Shape`, and therefore any class that extends `Shape` will have access to these fields.

You can therefore create a `draw` method on `Shape`, and provide it with the following implementation:

```
public void draw() {
    System.out.printf("My fill color is %s\n", getFillColor());
    System.out.printf("My line color is %s\n", getLineColor());
}
```

You can then change the implementation in the subclasses as follows:

```
public void draw() {
    System.out.println("I am drawing a square");
    System.out.printf("I have %d sides\n", sides);
    super.draw();
}
```

If you execute the program again, it should produce identical output to the original example. The `draw` method in `Square` is now said to be *overriding* the `draw` method on `Shape`. Subclasses can override methods on their parent classes if they wish to provide an alternative implementation. They do this by providing a method with the exact same signature as the one defined on the parent class.

Notice also the following line in the `draw` method of the `Square` class:

```
super.draw();
```

The use of `super` allows the `Square` class to invoke the `draw` method on its parent (`Shape`), thereby ensuring that both methods are executed when `draw` is invoked on `Square`. Both `Square` and `Shape` are therefore working together to provide the implementation of the `draw` method that the caller will see.

The `super` keyword is similar to the `this` keyword seen previously. Just as `this` allows an object to refer to itself, `super` allows an object to refer to its parent. You only need to use the `super` keyword where both the parent and child implement the same method: if the child class wants to call any other method on its parent then the `super` keyword is optional.

If you had not used the `super` keyword in this case, the `draw` method would be invoked on `Square` itself. This would be bad news, because this invocation of the `draw` method would also invoke itself, and so on, for infinity – or more precisely – until the JVM crashed from a `StackOverflowException`.

It is important to realize that there is no way for external code with a reference to a `Square` to invoke the `draw` method on `Shape` directly. This goes back to my earlier point: any code using my classes should not care how I have implemented specific functionality, or which underlying class actually contains the methods they are invoking: all they need to concern themselves with is the public API exposed by my classes.

Just because one sub-class overrides a method does not mean that all sub-classes must override the method. For instance, the `Circle` class may decide not to override the `draw` method, but instead utilize the version defined on `Shape`. In this case, invoking `draw` on a `Circle` would produce the output:

```
My fill color is Blue
My line color is Red
```

Final keyword

There are some cases where a super-class may determine that a method should never be overridden by a sub-class. In order to prevent a method being overridden it can be defined as `final`. For instance, if the `draw` method on `Shape` was defined as follows, the `Square` class would not be allowed to override it:

```
public final void draw() {
```

Notice that the use of the `final` keyword in this context differs from the one we have seen in relation to fields.

It is also possible to stop classes being extended completely through the use of the `final` keyword. For instance, if `Square` did not want any other class to be able to extend it, it could be defined as follows:

```
public final class Square extends Shape {
```

It is good practice to define classes as `final` if you have any reason for thinking other code should not ever extend them. As an example, consider the `String` class in Java. This has been declared as `final` because if any class was able to extend it, they would be able to make changes to the internal string it held, and thereby make it mutable.

The `final` keyword is one of many in Java that changes it meaning based on where it is used. You have now seen all three ways the `final` keyword can be used in Java: in the context of fields, methods and classes.

Abstract Classes

The `draw` method now involves a degree of reuse, but clearly the first two lines of the `draw` method look very similar from sub-class to sub-class. It would be nice to remove `draw` from the sub-classes entirely, and provide a generic implementation in `Shape`.

Before working out how to achieve this, you will deal with another issue that will turn out to be related. It is possible for external classes to create instances of the `Shape` class:

```
Shape s1 = new Shape();
```

This clearly makes no sense: `Shape`s cannot exist in their own right, they are an *abstract* concept, and need to be realized as squares, circles, triangles etc. In order to prevent

Shapes being instantiated they can therefore be declared as `abstract`:

```
public abstract class Shape {
```

If you try to instantiate the `Shape` class using the `new` keyword you will now receive a compilation error.

The `abstract` keyword is the mirror opposite of the `final` keyword. When the `final` keyword is used on a class definition, the class *cannot* be extended. When the `abstract` keyword is used on a class definition, the class *must* be extended. For this reason it is not possible to declare a class both `abstract` and `final`.

You will now move the remainder of the `draw` method from the sub-classes to the parent class. Therefore, change the `draw` method on `Shape` as follows:

```
public void draw() {
    System.out.println("I am drawing a square");
    System.out.printf("I have %d sides\n", sides);
    System.out.printf("My fill color is %s\n", getFillColor());
    System.out.printf("My line color is %s\n", getLineColor());
}
```

This will result in a compilation error due to the fact that the `sides` field is not visible to `Shape`. Don't worry about the compilation errors for now; you will deal with this shortly.

After changing this code, remove the `draw` method entirely from the sub-classes such as `Square`.

You will first deal with the compilation error in this method. This stems from the fact that the parent class is attempting to access a field called `sides`: this is only defined on sub-classes, so is not available to the parent-class.

This is nothing to do with the fact that the `sides` field is `private`: a parent-class cannot access any fields or methods on its sub-classes; inheritance only works in one direction.

The way around this is for the `Shape` class to declare that any class that extends it must provide a method called `getSides`. The `Shape` class does not need to define the code for this method; it only needs to define its *signature*. Therefore, add the following line to `Shape`:

```
public abstract int getSides();
```

Notice the use of the `abstract` keyword: when a method is defined as `abstract`, only its signature needs to be provided (in fact it is not possible to define an implementation).

As soon as this line is added to `Shape`, all sub-classes of `Shape` must implement this method, otherwise the program will not compile.

Notice that `Shape` does not care how its sub-classes implement this method, or what the implementation does: it only cares that an implementation is provided, and that this implementation returns an `int`.

You can now change the `draw` method in `Shape` as follows:

```
public void draw() {
    System.out.println("I am drawing a square");
    System.out.printf("I have %d sides\n", getSides());
    System.out.printf("My fill color is %s\n", getFillColor());
    System.out.printf("My line color is %s\n", getLineColor());
}
```

The `Shape` class is able to invoke the `getSides` method because it has certainty that any sub-class will provide an implementation of this method. Because the sub-classes do already implement this there is nothing for you to do.

It is only possible to define `abstract` methods in `abstract` classes.

> Any class with an `abstract` method must be declared `abstract`, although it is possible for a class to be `abstract` even though it has no `abstract` methods.
>
> There would obviously be problems if it were possible for a non-abstract class to include `abstract` methods. When the class was instantiated it would contain undefined methods.

The whole purpose of the `abstract` keyword is to pass the buck. It is a way of saying I need this particular method implemented, although I myself do not know how to implement it.

It is also possible to have multiple levels of `abstract` classes. For instance, if `Square` declared itself as `abstract` it would not need to provide an implementation of `getSides` (although it could if it chose to). The only rule is that all `abstract` methods must be implemented by the time you reach the first non-`abstract` class in the class hierarchy.

The `draw` method still has one remaining problem: it always prints out "I am drawing a square", even if the class that is instantiated is a `Triangle`. In order to solve this I will add another `abstract` method to `Shape` called `getType`, and then use it in the `draw` method: the full implementation of `Shape` will be as follows:

```
package shapes;
public abstract class Shape {
    private String fillColor;
    private String lineColor;

    public Shape() {}

    public abstract int getSides();

    public abstract String getType();

    public void draw() {
        System.out.printf("I am drawing a %s\n", getType());
```

```
        System.out.printf("I have %d sides\n", getSides());
        System.out.printf("My fill color is %s\n", getFillColor());
        System.out.printf("My line color is %s\n", getLineColor());
    }
    protected String getFillColor() {
        return fillColor;
    }
    public void setFillColor(String fillColor) {
        this.fillColor = fillColor;
    }
    protected String getLineColor() {
        return lineColor;
    }
    public void setLineColor(String lineColor) {
        this.lineColor = lineColor;
    }
}
```

As soon as the `getType` method is added to `Shape`, any sub-classes extending it will fail to compile. The easiest way to solve this is to click on the error beside the class definition of each sub-class and choose "Add unimplemented methods", as seen in figure 12-1:

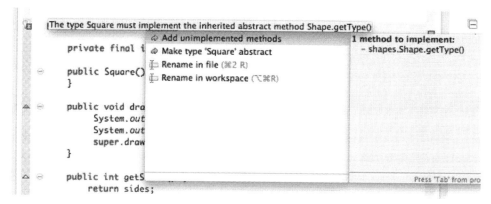

FIGURE 12-1

Simply change the stub it creates to return an appropriate value for each sub-class:

```
@Override
public String getType() {
    return "Square";
}
```

Notice how Eclipse has added a piece of text above the method:

```
@Override
```

This is called an *annotation*, and is optional in this context. I will cover annotations in more detail later in the book, but for now think of them as tags that can add extra meaning to a piece of code. In this particular case the annotation is telling the compiler "I think I am overriding a method called `getType`, so please check that there really is a method with this signature on my super-class".

Annotations are used for a wide variety of tasks in Java at compile time, build time and run-time. If you choose to remove this annotation nothing will change in the functionality of the class, but it won't have the extra compile-time check to ensure this method really is overriding a method in its parent.

The `Square` class can now been reduced to this:

```
package shapes;
public final class Square extends Shape {
    private final int sides = 4;

    public Square() {}
    @Override
    public int getSides() {
        return sides;
    }
    @Override
    public String getType() {
        return "Square";
    }
}
```

Once `getType` is implemented in all sub-classes, you can change the `Main` program as follows:

```
package shapes;

public class Main {

    public static void main(String[] args) {
        Square s = new Square();
        s.setFillColor("Blue");
        s.setLineColor("Red");
        s.draw();
        Triangle t = new Triangle();
        t.setFillColor("Green");
        t.setLineColor("Orange");
        t.draw();
    }
}
```

When executed, this will print out the following:

```
I am drawing a square
I have 4 sides
I am drawing a Square
I have 4 sides
My fill color is Blue
My line color is Red
I am drawing a triangle
I have 3 sides
```

Polymorphism

Now that you understand the basics of inheritance, you can move to the related (and slightly daunting) subject of *polymorphism*. Polymorphism is one of the most important concepts in object-orientated programming, in fact it could be argued it is the most important concept; therefore it is essential for you to gain a good understanding of what it is, and how it works.

Polymorphism can be a difficult concept to grasp – even its name is somewhat challenging. I don't think it is as complex as it is sometimes deemed to be, however, so rather than starting with an explanation you will work through some examples.

Imagine you wanted to add a method to the `Main` class that assigned a random fill color to any `Shape` that it was passed. You can add this as follows:

```
package shapes;
public class Main {
    public static void main(String[] args) {
        Square s = new Square();
        assignFillColor(s);
        s.setLineColor("Red");
        s.draw();
        Triangle t = new Triangle();
        assignFillColor(t);
        t.setLineColor("Orange");
        t.draw();
    }

    private static String[] colors = {"Red", "Blue",
        "Green", "Black", "Orange", "Pink"};

    private static void assignFillColor(Shape shape) {
        int num = (int)(Math.random() * colors.length);
        shape.setFillColor(colors[num]);
    }
}
```

The `assignFillColor` method uses the `Math.random` utility provided by Java to return a random `double` value greater than 0 and less than 1. This is then multiplied by the length of the `colors` array (6), and cast to an `int`. This will ensure that `num` contains a random number between 0 and 5 (because casting causes a number to be round down).

The most interesting aspect of `assignFillColor`, however, is that it accepts a parameter of type `Shape`. This is interesting, because `Shape` is an `abstract` class, so there can never be instances of `Shape`.

If a method accepts parameters of a specific type, it can actually be passed an instance of this type, or an instance of its sub-types.

Due to the fact that `assignFillColor` does not know which implementation of `Shape` it will be passed, it can only invoke methods that are common to all instances of `Shape`, that is, those defined on `Shape` itself. For instance, if `Square` had implemented a method called `getArea`, this could not be invoked without first casting the parameter passed to a `Square`.

This possibly does not seem very interesting: the `Shape` class defines a method `setFillColor`, therefore it is perhaps not surprising that `assignFillColor` is able to invoke this method on it. In order to see the true power of this functionality, however, you will override `setFillColor` on `Square` as follows:

```
public void setFillColor(String fillColor) {
    System.out.println("setFillColor called on Square");
    super.setFillColor(fillColor);
}
```

And override the method on `Triangle` as follows:

```
public void setFillColor(String fillColor) {
    System.out.println("setFillColor called on Triangle");
    super.setFillColor(fillColor);
}
```

These methods print out the class they are being invoked on, and then invokes the `setFillColor` method on their parent.

If you run the program again it will produce the following output:

```
setFillColor called on Square
I am drawing a Square
I have 4 sides
My fill color is Green
My line color is Red
setFillColor called on Triangle
I am drawing a Triangle
I have 3 sides
My fill color is Pink
My line color is Orange
```

Notice the lines in bold: even though the `assignFillColor` method only knows it has been passed a `Shape` at compile-time, when it invokes a method on the object it has been passed at run-time, it invokes the method declared on the sub-class it has been passed.

There is clearly some magic going on here: at compile-time the `assignFillColor` method does not know which sub-class of `Shape` is going to be passed to it. For instance, you could have used the random number generator to decide whether to create triangles or squares. Despite this, at run-time, Java is still able to invoke the appropriate method.

Understanding this is the key to understanding polymorphism, and is why polymorphism is also referred to as *late-binding*. Java is able to determine the specific implementation it has been passed at run-time, and determine "on the fly" which is the correct method to call. Historically compilers have mapped out the entire program execution flow at compile time, making this behavior impossible.

Another way to think about polymorphism is that any time you refer to the type of a variable, parameter or field; there are two distinct types involved. This stems from the fact that objects are distinct from object-references, as seen multiple times already in this book.

The first is the type of the object reference (for instance `Shape`). The compiler will ensure that the object reference always refers to an object of this type *or one of its sub-classes*.

The second type is the type of object. This will either be the same type as the reference to it, or a sub-class of this type. Any method executed will be executed on the object that the reference refers to, therefore allowing polymorphism to work its magic.

A consequence of polymorphism is that you are able to change the type of object a reference refers to midway through a program. Consider the following program:

```java
package shapes;
public class ChangingShape {
    public static void main(String[] args) {
        Shape s = null;
        s = new Square();
        s.setLineColor("Red");
        s.setFillColor("Red");
        s.draw();
        s = new Triangle();
        s.setLineColor("Orange");
        s.draw();
    }
}
```

This will produce the following output:

```
setFillColor called on Square
I am drawing a Square
I have 4 sides
My fill color is Red
My line color is Red
I am drawing a Triangle
I have 3 sides
My fill color is null
My line color is Orange
```

Notice that the variable s is defined as a Shape, but set to null when it is first declared. This means that s is capable of referring to any object constructed from a sub-type of the Shape class.

On the second line of the main method s is set to refer to an instance of Square, therefore when draw is invoked on line 5, it is the definition found on Square that is invoked.

The sixth line of the program then declares that s now refers to an instance of Triangle:

```java
s = new Triangle();
```

This is allowed because Triangle is a sub-class of Shape: so the object reference declared as a Shape is still referring to a valid object. When draw is invoked on s on the final line of the method, the implementation executed is that found on Triangle.

In a sense, therefore, the variable s has changed its type during the execution of this method, but it has done so within the bounds of its defined type (Shape).

You can take this idea even further. You will remember from earlier in the book that every class descends from Object, therefore it is possible to write code like this:

```
public static void main(String[] args) {
    Object o1 = "Hello world";
    System.out.println(o1);
    o1 = new Square();
    System.out.println(o1);
}
```

Notice that the variable `o1` is defined to refer to any object that is of the type `Object` – therefore, because every class descends from `Object`, this reference can refer to any type of object. Notice in this case, however, you can only invoke the methods that are declared on `Object`: printing an `Object` causes its `toString` method to be invoked, which is defined on `Object`.

It is also possible to define methods that accept instances of `Object` – these methods can then be passed references to any type of object. The method in the next example, called `receiveObject`, accepts a parameter of type `Object`, but then determines what type it has actually been passed at runtime using the `instanceof` operator.

If it has been passed an instance of `Shape`, it defines a new variable called `s`, and assigns a *cast* version of the parameter to it. Once it has redefined the parameter as a `Shape`, it calls the `draw` method on it. Remember in this case that you are simply constructing a new object reference of the appropriate type: there is still only one actual object on the heap that both `o` and `s` are referring to.

Any parameters that are not `Shapes` are simply printed using `System.out.println`.

```
package shapes;
public class Main2 {
    public static void main(String[] args) {
        Object o1 = "Hello world";
        receiveObject(o1);
        o1 = new Square();
        ((Shape)o1).setFillColor("Red");
        ((Shape)o1).setLineColor("Blue");
        receiveObject(o1);
    }
    public static void receiveObject(Object o) {
        if (o instanceof Shape) {
            Shape s = (Shape)o;
            s.draw();
        } else {
            System.out.println(o);
        }
    }
}
```

This program demonstrates two different approaches for casting objects. The first mechanism involves a new reference being created:

```
Shape s = (Shape)o;
```

The second mechanism can be seen in the `main` method, and involves casting the object to type `Shape`, and invoking a method on it, all in the same expression.

```
((Shape)o1).setFillColor("Red");
```

The brackets are important in this expression. The first part of the expression evaluated is:

```
(Shape)o1
```

The result of this is a `Shape`. The result of this expression has the `setFillColor` method invoked on it. These two approaches to casting are equivalent, and it is simply a matter of preference.

It is important to mention, however, that casting in this manner does bring dangers if you are not sure of the underlying type. Remember, casting is your way of telling the compiler to trust you: you know what type the underlying object is, even though it doesn't. For instance, this program compiles with no errors:

```
package shapes;
public class Main3 {

    public static void main(String[] args) {
        Object o1 = "Hello world";
        ((Shape)o1).setFillColor("Red");
    }
}
```

The compiler knows that `o1` refers to an object that extends `Object`, but takes your word for it when you state on the second line that it can be cast as a `Shape` (when obviously it is a `String`). If you attempt to run this program you will receive an exception stating:

```
Exception in thread "main" java.lang.ClassCastException: java.lang.String cannot be cast to shapes.Shape
```

Interfaces

In the previous examples you defined an `abstract` class called `Shape` that could not exist in its own right: it could only be instantiated via its sub-classes. Despite this, the `Shape` class was able to implement methods.

If you image how `Shape` might be used in a drawing program (and drawing real shapes rather than printing text), you may discover that there were other types of object that you wanted to draw that are not `Shapes`, and that really have nothing in common with `Shapes` other than the fact they could be drawn on screen. For instance, many drawing programs allow text to be drawn on the canvas, but text is not a shape.

Interfaces provide a mechanism for defining how different types are similar without defining any concrete details. For instance, in a drawing program you may want to state that anything that can be drawn on screen must implement a method called `draw`, even though you have no way of providing a generic implementation of the `draw` method.

> It is worth to mentioning at this point a major change that has occurred in Java 8. Up until Java 8 it has not been possible to provide implementation details in interfaces.
>
> Starting with Java 8 it is possible, with certain restrictions. I am going to pretend that Java 8 never happened in this chapter to provide you a classical view of how interfaces work. Later in the book you will look at how interfaces can provide implementation details – and why this may occasionally be useful.

You can declare an interface that all *drawable* objects can implement as follows:

```
package shapes;

public interface Drawable {
    public void draw();
}
```

Rather than declaring `Drawable` as a `class`, it has been declared as an `interface`. It then defines the signature of the methods that must be defined by any class implementing this interface. In this case the interface only has a single method, but interfaces can declare as many methods as you need.

Interfaces are commonly thought of as contracts. For instance, if a class wants to produce objects that can be drawn on screen, it must adhere to the contract set out in `Drawable`.

The way methods are defined on an interface is almost identical to the way `abstract` methods are declared on `abstract` classes, but omits the keyword `abstract`. As it happens it is also possible to omit the `public` access modifier in interfaces, because all methods in an interface are assumed to be `public`, and it is not possible to use any other access modifiers.

> It is also possible to define `static` fields inside an interface, but non-static fields can only be declared in classes.

Once you have defined an interface, you can declare that classes implement it. For instance, you may define a new class called `Text` that can be used to draw text on the screen:

```
package shapes;
public class Text implements Drawable {
    public String text;
    public String color;
    public Text(String text, String color) {
        this.text = text;
```

```
        this.color = color;
    }
    @Override
    public void draw() {
        System.out.printf("I am drawing a %s text string with the value %s\n",
color, text);
    }
}
```

Notice that the `Text` class declares that it `implements Drawable` rather than `extends` it. This turns out to be an important detail, and requires that we backtrack a little and look at inheritance again.

> Interfaces can actually extend other interfaces. For instance, you may have an existing interface, and wish to add more method definitions to it. In this case, the second interface `extends` rather than `implements` the first interface.

In Java, a class can only `extend` one other class: this is called single inheritance. For instance, if a class extends `Shape` it cannot extend another class. `Shape`, of course, could extend another class itself, so it is possible to have a chain of classes inheriting from one another, but each individual class can only extend, at most, one other. Put another way, a child class can only have one parent.

As mentioned earlier, if a class does not extend another class it implicitly extends `Object`. Therefore all Java classes, except `Object`, extend one, and only one, other class.

Some other programming languages support multiple inheritance (most notably C++), but the designers of Java decided early on that multiple inheritance was a bad idea. As will be shown later in the book, the Java language designers have somewhat changed their minds on this in Java 8 – but those complications can be left for later.

Rather than allow multiple inheritance, the designers of Java introduced the concept of interfaces, and made it possible to implement as many interfaces as required, while still extending only one other class.

In order to demonstrate this, I will first state that the `Shape` class implements `Drawable`:

```
public abstract class Shape implements Drawable {
```

Notice that `Shape` can implement `Drawable` even though its implementation of the `draw` method is `abstract`. This is because the compiler can be sure all concrete sub-classes will implement this method. I could have also declared that the individual `Shape` sub-classes implemented `Drawable`:

```
public final class Square extends Shape implements Drawable {
```

Notice in this case that the `implements` clause comes after the `extends` clause.

I can now add a second interface to the program. This interface will indicate that an implementing class has color, and will return the primary color of the object.

```
package shapes;
public interface Colorable {
    public String getColor();
}
```

I can now declare that both `Shape` and `Text` implement `Colorable` as well as `Drawable`, for instance:

```
package shapes;
public class Text implements Drawable, Colorable {
    public String text;
    public String color;
    public Text(String text, String color) {
        this.text = text;
        this.color = color;
    }

    @Override
    public void draw() {
        System.out.printf("I am drawing a %s text string with the value %s\n",
color, text);
    }

    @Override
    public String getColor() {
        return color;
    }
}
```

In the case of `Shape` you may decide that the fill color is the best representation of the Shape's color. This highlights another important characteristic of interfaces: it is up to the implementers to decide on the implementation of the method, and the implementation will vary from implementer to implementer.

You can declare references to use interface-based types anywhere you can use class-based types. The following code demonstrates that a method can be declared that receives instances of an interface – they can then be passed instances of any class that implements that interface:

```
package shapes;
public class UsingInterfaces {
    public static void main(String[] args) {
        Shape s = new Square();
        receiveDrawable(s);
        receiveColorable(s);
        Text t = new Text("Hello World", "Red");
        receiveDrawable(t);
        receiveColorable(t);
    }

    public static void receiveDrawable(Drawable d) {
        System.out.printf("I have been passed a Drawable: it is really a %s\n",
d.getClass().getSimpleName());
```

```
        d.draw();
    }

    public static void receiveColorable(Colorable d) {
        System.out.printf("I have been passed a Colorable that is %s: it is
really a %s\n", d.getColor(), d.getClass().getSimpleName());
    }
}
```

This produces the following output:

```
I have been passed a Drawable: it is really a Square
I am drawing a Square
I have 4 sides
My fill color is null
My line color is null
I have been passed a Colorable that is null: it is really a Square
I have been passed a Drawable: it is really a Text
I am drawing a Red text string with the value Hello World
I have been passed a Colorable that is Red: it is really a Text
```

Notice that it is possible to use `getClass` (which is defined on `Object`) to determine the actual type of an object. This method returns an instance of `Class`, which itself supports a set of utility methods, including `getSimpleName` and `getName`.

> Later in the book you will look at the other methods defined on `Class`. As you will see, these allow you to examine the structure of a class at run-time through a process called *reflection*.

As the next example shows, it is also possible to declare variables via the interface their referenced objects implement:

```
public static void main(String[] args) {
    Drawable d = new Square();
    receiveDrawable(d);
    receiveColorable((Colorable)d);
    d = new Text("Hello", "Red");
    receiveDrawable(d);
    receiveColorable((Colorable)d);
}
```

In this example d is declared of type `Drawable`. This means it can reference instances of `Square` and `Text`, because both these classes implement `Drawable`.

You can naturally pass d to any method that accepts a `Drawable` as a parameter. Notice, however, that if you wish to pass d to a method that accepts a `Colorable` you need to cast d to `Colorable`.

Remember, the compiler only knows that d is referring to an object that conforms to the `Drawable` interface; it has no idea whether this object also conforms to the `Colorable` interface. It is your job to tell the compiler that d does conform to the `Colorable` interface via a cast.

Many Java programmers use interfaces extensively, and define all their APIs in terms of interfaces. The benefit of this approach is that it is possible to change the concrete implementation of a program (the classes) without modifying the APIs – and therefore the underlying structure of the program. This tends to make programs both more maintainable, and more extendible.

Design Patterns

Inheritance lends itself to a number of useful *design patterns*. A design pattern is a reusable approach for a common problem. Most professional programmers use design patterns extensively, and the fact that all programmers understand these patterns helps make code more maintainable and comprehensible to others.

The beauty of design patterns is that they represent proven approaches to generic problems. For instance, if an object needs to notify one or more other objects when its state changes, you could choose to implement this in many different ways. Most professional programmers, however, would be familiar with the Observer pattern that describes a well-understood approach, and would base their implementation on this pattern.

This section will introduce you to two of the patterns I use extensively in my coding that take advantage of inheritance.

Template Pattern

The template pattern starts from the assumption that you often wish to implement multiple related algorithms that are different in some of their details, but generic in many other details.

Consider a program that processes different type of files. Regardless of the type of file, many of the steps in the algorithm will be the same:

⇒ Open the file
⇒ Iterate through the lines of the file
⇒ Close the file

Some steps however will be different depending on the type of file, most notably, processing each line in the file.

In this section you will create two algorithms that both process files with currency exchange rate information.

⇒ The first algorithm will process a comma-separated file, and will also be responsible for stripping extraneous quotes from each token and capitalizing the currency codes.
⇒ The second implementation will be responsible for processing a pipe-separated file. This file format will contain a header line that should be ignored.

In either case, the output of the program should be the same; a set of lines formatted as follows:

```
The exchange rate from USD to EUR is 0.741410, you will get $74.14 for each
$100
```

The first file (which should be named `file1.csv`) is as follows:

```
"usd","eur",0.74141
"usd","gbp",0.60833
"usd","cad",1.11329
"usd","nzd",1.23678
```

The second file (which should be named `file2.csv`) is as follows:

```
from currency,to currency,rate
USD,EUR,0.74141
USD,GBP,0.60833
USD,CAD,1.11329
USD,NZD,1.23678
```

> These files are available on the book's website, along with a variety of other resources: www.cisdal.com/java.html

You will start by writing a class that can hold the information pertaining to a single exchange rate. This is a simple JavaBean:

```java
package template;
public class ExchangeRate {
    private String fromCurrency;
    private String toCurrency;
    private Double rate;

    public ExchangeRate(String fromCurrency, String toCurrency, Double rate) {
        this.fromCurrency = fromCurrency;
        this.toCurrency = toCurrency;
        this.rate = rate;
    }

    public String getFromCurrency() {
        return fromCurrency;
    }
    public String getToCurrency() {
        return toCurrency;
    }
    public Double getRate() {
        return rate;
    }
}
```

Next, you will write a class that performs the generic processing, but leaves placeholders (`abstract` methods) for the implementation specific portions of the algorithm:

> This implementation uses the Java File APIs that will only be introduced in later chapters. You can ignore the details of these APIs for now.
>
> This implementation also uses exception-handling approaches that will be introduced in later chapters: these take advantage of the `try` and `catch` keywords.
>
> You can download this code from the book's website rather than typing it yourself.

```java
package template;
import java.io.BufferedReader;
import java.io.FileNotFoundException;
import java.io.FileReader;
import java.io.IOException;

public abstract class FileProcessor {
    private String file;
    private int lineNumber = 0;
    BufferedReader br = null;
    public FileProcessor(String file) {
        this.file = file;
    }

    public final void process() {
        try {
            openFile();
            processLines();
            closeFile();
        } catch (IOException e ) {
            e.printStackTrace(System.out);
        }
    }

    protected void openFile() throws FileNotFoundException {
        br = new BufferedReader(new FileReader(file));
    }

    private void processLines() throws IOException {
        String line;
        while ((line = br.readLine()) != null) {
            ExchangeRate result = processLine(lineNumber, line);
            if (result != null) {
                printLine(result);
            }
            lineNumber++;
        }
    }

    protected void closeFile() throws IOException {
```

```
        br.close();
    }

    protected abstract ExchangeRate processLine
        (int lineNumber, String line);

    protected void printLine(ExchangeRate rate) {
        System.out.printf("The exchange rate from %s to %s is %f, you will get $%f for each $100\n",
                rate.getFromCurrency(), rate.getToCurrency(),
                rate.getRate(), rate.getRate()*100);
    }
}
```

The heart of this implementation is the `process` method: this method orchestrates the algorithm by calling all the methods in their appropriate order. For instance, it knows to open a file first, then process the lines, and then close the file.

The `process` method has been declared as `final` because you don't want sub-classes changing the overall logic of the algorithm, only specific steps in the algorithm.

The other important thing to notice is that this class defines an `abstract` method as follows:

`protected abstract ExchangeRate processLine(int lineNumber, String line);`

Each sub-class is expected to override this. They may optionally also override any of the other `protected` methods if required (for instance, they may wish to read files from the network instead of the file system).

The following implementation can be used to process the comma-separated file. Notice that this class extends `FileProcessor`:

```
package template;
import java.util.StringTokenizer;

public class CSVFileProcessor extends FileProcessor {
    public CSVFileProcessor(String file) {
        super(file);
    }

    @Override
    protected ExchangeRate processLine(int lineNumber, String line) {
        StringTokenizer st = new StringTokenizer(line, ",");
        int i = 0;
        String fromCurrency = null;
        String toCurrency = null;
        Double rate = null;
        while (st.hasMoreTokens()) {
            String s = st.nextToken();
            s = s.replaceAll("\"", "");
            switch (i) {
                case 0 :
                    fromCurrency = s;
                    break;
```

```
            case 1 :
                toCurrency = s;
                break;
            case 2 :
                rate = Double.valueOf(s);
                break;
            }
            i++;
        }
        return new ExchangeRate(fromCurrency, toCurrency, rate);
    }
}
```

This implementation uses a useful utility class called a `StringTokenizer`. This accepts a `String` and a delimiter, and splits the `String` into sub-strings each time that delimiter is encountered. You can then use a `while`-loop to iterate through all the tokens found.

Finally, add a main class for executing the program using the `CSVFileProcessor`:

```
package template;
public class Main {
    public static void main(String[] args) {
        CSVFileProcessor csv1 = new CSVFileProcessor("file1.csv");
        csv1.process();
    }
}
```

Before running this, ensure that `file1.csv` is copied into the parent directory of the Eclipse project (i.e. the same folder containing the `src` folder, rather than inside the `src` folder itself).

> Notice that the public API exposed by `CSVFileProcessor` contains a single method called `process`. This ensures that any code that uses this class must use it as intended.

It is now trivial to add a second implementation for the pipe-separated file:

```
package template;
import java.util.StringTokenizer;
public class PipeFileProcessor extends FileProcessor {
    public PipeFileProcessor(String file) {
        super(file);
    }

    @Override
    protected ExchangeRate processLine(int lineNumber, String line) {
        if (lineNumber == 0) {
            return null;
        }
        String fromCurrency = null;
        String toCurrency = null;
        Double rate = null;
```

```
        String[] tokens = line.split("\\|");
        for (int i = 0; i < tokens.length; i++) {
            String s = tokens[i];
            s = s.replaceAll("\"", "");
                switch (i) {
                    case 0 :
                        fromCurrency = s;
                        break;
                    case 1 :
                        toCurrency = s;
                        break;
                    case 2 :
                        rate = Double.valueOf(s);
                        break;
                }
            i++;
        }
        return new ExchangeRate(fromCurrency, toCurrency, rate);
    }
}
```

Notice that this implementation ignores the first line by returning `null`. This is because the pipe-separated file contains a header line that should be ignored.

In this case I have used a different approach to split each line based on a delimiter: I have used the `split` method on `String`. You will notice that the delimiter passed to `split` contains two backslashes before the actual delimiter:

```
String[] tokens = line.split("\\|");
```

This is because `split` accepts a regular expression, and the pipe character has special meaning in regular expressions. The double backslash creates a regular expression that denotes I want to split on the literal pipe character.

Now change the `Main` class as follows:

```
package template;
public class Main {

    public static void main(String[] args) {
        FileProcessor csv1 = new CSVFileProcessor("file1.csv");
        csv1.process();
        csv1 = new PipeFileProcessor("file2.csv");
        csv1.process();
    }
}
```

Before running this program, ensure that `file2.csv` is copied to the same directory as `file1.csv`.

As you can see, a single variable declared to be of type `FileProcessor` can be used for both processors.

It is easy to imagine how you could now extend this program to determine the correct processor to use based on the contents of the file provided at run-time. It is also easy to see how quick it would be to add new processors for new file formats.

Abstract Factory

The abstract factory design pattern supports the creation of families of objects, but where the concrete implementation created will depend on the factory used at run-time. As usual, an example helps to understand this pattern.

The abstract factory pattern is classified as a *creational pattern*, because it is responsible for instantiating objects.

Imagine a library that is capable of creating UI components such as text fields, labels and combo boxes. This library may wish to provide different concrete implementations of these components for different operating systems: on a Windows systems the components would be styled to match Windows standards, while on OSX systems the components would be styled to match OSX standards.

You could leave the responsibility for creating these components up to the program: this would mean that each time the program needed a text field it would need to determine which system it was running on, and construct the appropriate component.

The problem with this approach is that you would be tying large amounts of code to the relevant operating system, which makes it harder to repurpose the code for a different platform. Additionally, if you wanted to support a new operating system, you would need to change the code in many different places.

With the abstract factory pattern you create an abstract class that defines the API the program can use for creating objects of specific types, and then implement this for each concrete family of objects.

Before starting you will create three different types of components. Each will contain an interface and two classes implementing the interface. For brevity sake, these classes will not actually do anything.

TextField:

```
package abstractfactory;
public interface TextField {
}

class WindowsTextField implements TextField {
}

class OSXTextField implements TextField {
}
```

Label:

```
package abstractfactory;
```

```
public interface Label {
}

class WindowsLabel implements Label {
}

class OSXLabel implements Label {
}
```

ComboBox:

```
package abstractfactory;
public interface ComboBox {
}

class WindowsComboBox implements ComboBox {
}

class OSXComboBox implements ComboBox {
}
```

> You can place the interface declaration and the two class definitions in a single source file, provided that there is only a single `public` interface or class. The name of the underlying file must conform to the name of the `public` class or interface defined.
>
> I generally avoid this approach, but the approach has been used here to make it quicker to create these structures.

You can now create the generic factory for creating components. All methods in this class will be `abstract`:

```
package abstractfactory;
public abstract class UIFactory {
    public abstract TextField createTextField();
    public abstract Label createLabel();
    public abstract ComboBox createComboBox();
}
```

> This could have also been defined as an interface rather than an abstract class.

You can now provide two concrete implementations of the `UIFactory`: one for each operating system supported:

```java
package abstractfactory;
public class WindowsUIFactory extends UIFactory {
    public TextField createTextField() {
        return new WindowsTextField();
    }
    public Label createLabel() {
        return new WindowsLabel();
    }
    public ComboBox createComboBox() {
        return new WindowsComboBox();
    }
}
```

And:

```java
package abstractfactory;
public class OSXUIFactory extends UIFactory {
    public TextField createTextField() {
        return new OSXTextField();
    }
    public Label createLabel() {
        return new OSXLabel();
    }
    public ComboBox createComboBox() {
        return new OSXComboBox();
    }
}
```

Once this inheritance structure is in place, using the abstract factory is as simple as *injecting* the appropriate implementation into the program at run-time:

```java
package abstractfactory;
public class Main {
    public static void main(String[] args) {
        UIFactory factory = getUIFactory();
        TextField tf = factory.createTextField();
        Label l = factory.createLabel();
        ComboBox cb = factory.createComboBox();
        System.out.println(tf.getClass().getSimpleName());
        System.out.println(l.getClass().getSimpleName());
        System.out.println(cb.getClass().getSimpleName());
    }

    public static UIFactory getUIFactory() {
        if (System.getProperty("os.name").equals("Mac OS X")) {
            return new OSXUIFactory();
        } else {
            return new WindowsUIFactory();
        }
    }
}
```

> The concept of *injecting* dependencies has become a very important paradigm in the Java world, and is supported by a wide variety of frameworks (most notably the Spring framework). Although it is beyond the scope of this book, I highly recommend learning more about *dependency injection*.
>
> http://en.wikipedia.org/wiki/Dependency_injection

Notice that the `main` method is oblivious to the concrete implementation of the factory provided to it, or the components created from that factory. If the code is run on an OSX machine this will print:

```
OSXTextField
OSXLabel
OSXComboBox
```

Otherwise it will print:

```
WindowsTextField
WindowsLabel
WindowsComboBox
```

Writing code in this manner is highly adaptable to change. If you decide in the future that you would like to change the `UIFactory` used by a particular Operating System, this can be changed without affecting any of the code that uses these implementations.

The abstract factory pattern emphasizes an important trait in object-orientated programming mentioned earlier in this chapter: programming to an interface. It is generally best practice to declare interfaces for all the types in a program, and have the programs use these types. This ensures the concrete implementations can be easily changed over time without needing to change the rest of the program.

13 COMPOSITION

Inheritance provides one mechanism for reusing code. An alternative mechanism supported by Object Orientated Programming is *composition*.

Inheritance is best used in cases where a class "is-a" instance of something else:

⇒ A circle is-a shape
⇒ A car is-a vehicle
⇒ A cat is-an animal

Composition, by comparison, is best used for modeling "has-a" relationships:

⇒ A circle has-a border
⇒ A car has-a door
⇒ A cat has-an owner

It is commonly said that composition should be favored over inheritance, especially in programming languages that only support single inheritance. I don't believe this is necessarily true: inheritance should be used when modeling an "is-a" relationship, while composition should be used when modeling a "has-a" relationship. Generally you will come across more "has-a" cases than "is-a" cases, and therefore composition is generally more common.

Composition is a very simple subject in Java: any time an object encapsulates a field that refers to an object you are using composition. Typically composition is broken down into three sub-categories:

⇒ **Composition**: this refers to cases where the lifecycle of the composed object is implicitly linked to the lifecycle of the composing object. This is the case with the circle and the border: the lifecycle of the border is presumably linked to the lifecycle of the circle: if the circle is destroyed, the border will also be destroyed. Composition therefore implies ownership.

⇒ **Aggregation**: this refers to cases where there is a "has-a" relationship between two objects, but they can both exist independent of each other. For instance, a cat's owner can still exists independent of the cat.
⇒ **Association**: this refers to cases where one object uses another object, but there is not a strong relationship between the two objects. As an example, a cat may use a cat door.

The term *composition* will refer to any one of these categories.

As an example, consider a case where you want to represent a color as three `int` values representing the ratio of red, green and blue in the color. The class will also capture a name for the color, and provide a method to return a hex encoded `String` for the color (as used by HTML/CSS). The `Color` class may look as follows:

```
package colors;
public class Color {
    private int red, green, blue;
    private String name;
    public Color(int red, int green, int blue, String name) {
        assert(red < 256 && red >= 0);
        assert(green < 256 && green >= 0);
        assert(blue < 256 && blue >= 0);
        this.red = red;
        this.green = green;
        this.blue = blue;
        this.name = name;
    }
    String getName() {
        return name;
    }
    public String getHexValue() {
        return "#"+getHexValue(red)+getHexValue(green)+
            getHexValue(blue).toUpperCase();
    }
    private String getHexValue(int intValue) {
        String s = Integer.toHexString(intValue);
        if (s.length() == 1) {
            return "0"+s;
        } else {
            return s;
        }
    }
}
```

This class introduces a number of new concepts you have not seen up until now. These are not implicitly linked to the concept of composition, but I will begin by discussing these.

The `Color` class declares three `int` fields. Where multiple fields are declared of the same type, the declaration can be performed in a single line:

```
private int red, green, blue;
```

This is the direct equivalent of declaring the fields on three separate lines. The only disadvantage with this approach is that it is not possible to initialize the fields to different values.

You will also notice that the `getHexValue` method takes advantage of a helper on the `Integer` class for converting a number into a hexadecimal `String`. In this particular case, I want to ensure that the hex value for each color is always two characters long, because this is the convention used by HTML, therefore I prepend a `"0"` if necessary.

Finally, notice that I have used the `assert` keyword in the constructor of `Color` to validate the numeric parameters are between 0 and 255 inclusive. This keyword provides a mechanism for asserting (or insisting) that a specific condition holds true. This is very useful for validating the arguments passed to a method.

If an assertion fails at runtime it will throw an `AssertionError`, which prevents the method or constructor from completing. It should be noted, however, that assertions are disabled by default at runtime: this means that by default Java will not check the assertion, and will not raise an exception.

You can specifically enable assertions at runtime by providing the VM argument `-ea`. It is typically to enable assertions during development, and disable them in production.

> VM arguments are distinct from program arguments. Rather than providing values to the program, they provide information to the JVM telling it how to run the program. This may include options such as how much memory it needs to allocate.
>
> Eclipse provides a separate input field for JVM arguments on the Arguments tab when "Run Configurations…" is selected.

Now that I have created a `Color` class, I can compose it within other classes; for instance, I may rewrite a `Shape` class as follows:

```
package colors;

public abstract class Shape {
    private Color fillColor;
    private Color lineColor;
    . . .
```

Each instance of a `Shape` now composes two instances of `Color`.

The beauty of composition is that once the `Color` class has been written and tested, it can be composed onto as many classes as we wish, and therefore all these classes benefit by reusing of the same code.

When designing and implemented classes, it is important to think about how they will be used by other classes, and design robust APIs that meet these needs. This ensures that your classes will be reusable by other code, and will prevent code duplication.

14 CONSTRUCTORS

You have already encountered constructors in earlier chapters, and learned how they can be used to initialize objects. This chapter is intended to enhance and consolidate your understanding of constructors, and look at a number of important rules that may not be obvious.

Multiple Constructors

You may have noticed that you have not added constructors to all your classes. If you omit constructors from your class, Java automatically generates a *no arguments* constructor for you: this is called the default constructor. The default constructor does not do anything, but it is the reason why you can instantiate a class with no constructors, for instance:

```
A a = new A();
```

As soon as you add your own constructor to a class, or extend a class that has a constructor defined, the default constructor disappears and can no longer be invoked. Java assumes that because you have added a constructor you want all code to use this constructor.

It is, however, possible to add a no arguments constructor alongside another constructor: the following class has two constructors:

```
package constructors;
public class Person {
    private String firstName;
    private String lastName;

    public Person() {}
    public Person(String firstName, String lastName) {
        this.firstName = firstName;
        this.lastName = lastName;
    }
}
```

In fact, a class can have as many constructors as you need, as long as each constructor is unique in terms of the number and/or type of parameters.

I will now create a slightly more complex example. I want to add a `yearRegistered` field to the `Person` class. This needs to be populated with the current year when a `Person` is instantiated, and can never be changed after that point.

In order to create a field that can never be changed I can mark it as `final`. As mentioned earlier in the book, a `final` field can only be initialized on the line that declares it, or inside a constructor.

Inside this program I want to initialize the field from a `Calendar` so that it is always assigned the current year. This introduces a problem, however, because I don't want to add the same code to both constructors. I can overcome this problem as follows:

```
package constructors;
import java.util.Calendar;
import java.util.GregorianCalendar;

public class Person {
    private String firstName;
    private String lastName;
    private final int yearRegistered;

    public Person() {
        Calendar c = new GregorianCalendar();
        yearRegistered = c.get(Calendar.YEAR);
    }

    public Person(String firstName, String lastName) {
        this();
        this.firstName = firstName;
        this.lastName = lastName;
    }
}
```

> This example takes advantage of the `GregorianCalendar` class. This will be examined in detail later in the book, along with a better way of encapsulating years.

I have placed the code for initializing `yearRegistered` in the no-arguments constructor. I then invoke the no-arguments constructor from the second constructor by calling `this()`. The call to `this()` must be the first line in the constructor, and ensures that the code in the no-arguments constructor is executed regardless of which constructor is invoked.

This is a very common pattern with constructors, and can include several levels of invocation. For instance, a three arguments constructor may invoke a two arguments constructor, which in turn invokes a no arguments constructor. The only thing you need to guard against is creating a loop – for instance if the no-arguments constructor invoked the three arguments constructor.

If you ever find yourself writing the same code in multiple constructors, think back to this example and try to structure your code to remove the duplication.

Constructors and Inheritance

It is also important to understand how constructors work in inheritance hierarchies.

In order to demonstrate this, I will start by creating a simple class called A. This class will contain two constructors, a no arguments constructor and a constructor accepting an `int` parameter. These constructors will simply print out the fact they have been called.

```
package constructors;
public class A {
    public A() {
        System.out.println("This is the A constructor");
    }

    public A(int num) {
        System.out.println("This is the A constructor with an int parameter");
    }
}
```

I will now create a new class called B that extends A. This will contain the same two constructors. This class will also contain a `main` method that instantiates two instances of B, one using each constructor:

```
package constructors;
public class B extends A {
    public B() {
        System.out.println("This is constructor B");
    }

    public B(int num) {
        System.out.println("This is constructor B with an int parameter");
    }

    public static void main(String[] args) {
        B b = new B();
        B b2 = new B(1);
    }
}
```

If you run this program you may be surprised by the output:

```
This is the A constructor
This is constructor B
This is the A constructor
This is constructor B with an int parameter
```

In both cases there has been an implicit call to the no-arguments constructor on A before the code in the B constructor executes. This ensures that A gets a chance to initialize itself.

Notice that there was nothing explicit in the B constructors that caused the A constructor to be invoked: it happened automatically. Also notice that the constructor on A that is invoked does not relate to the arguments passed to B: in both cases the no arguments constructor is invoked on A.

It is also possible for B to dictate the constructor that should be used to initialize A. This can be achieved with the `super` keyword, which also must appear as the first statement in the constructor:

```
package constructors;
public class B extends A {
    public B() {
        super(1);
        System.out.println("This is constructor B");
    }

    public B(int num) {
        super(num);
        System.out.println("This is constructor B with an int parameter");
    }

    public static void main(String[] args) {
        B b = new B();
        B b2 = new B(1);
    }
}
```

The use of `super` here is essentially the same use you saw in the inheritance chapter when a sub-class invoked methods on its super-class.

> If present, calls to `super` and `this` must be on the first line of the constructor. This means it is not possible for the same constructor to invoke both `this` and `super`.

This produces the following output:

```
This is the A constructor with an int parameter
This is constructor B
This is the A constructor with an int parameter
This is constructor B with an int parameter
```

Things get slightly more interesting if A does not have a no-arguments constructor. Remember, when an instance of B is created, by default the no-arguments constructor of A is being called. What should happen, therefore, if that constructor does not exist?

In order to demonstrate this, change A as follows:

```
package constructors;
public class A {
    public A(int num) {
```

```
        System.out.println("This is the A constructor with an int parameter");
    }
}
```

And change B to have no constructor:

```
package constructors;
public class B extends A {
    public static void main(String[] args) {
        B b = new B();
    }
}
```

You will notice that a compilation error occurs:

```
Implicit super constructor A() is undefined for default constructor. Must
define an explicit constructor
```

This is telling you that the compiler does not know how to initialize A when an instance of B is created. Due to the fact that A only has a single argument constructor, this needs to be invoked directly, which can only be achieved by adding a constructor to B and invoking `super`.

The default constructor does take some getting used to – and the fact that it suddenly disappears when an explicit constructor is added can lead to some head scratching.

Static initializers

Constructors are used for initializing objects. There is a related concept called *static initializers* that can be used for initializing the `static` fields on a class. I have never found many uses for static initializers, mainly because `static` fields can usually be given a value when they are defined. You may occasionally find uses for them however.

The following is an example:

```
package staticinit;
public class A {
    public static final int STATIC_FIELD;
    static {
        STATIC_FIELD = 22;
    }
}
```

The declaration of a `final static` field without initializing it would normally result in a compilation error: however, the `static` initialization block takes care of the initialization, and therefore the code is valid.

On a separate note, you will notice that the field STATIC_FIELD is defined in capital letters. This is the convention for `final static` fields because they are *constants*.

A constant is a value that never changes for the life of the program. Some languages have a built-in concept of a constant, and in those languages it is customary to use capital letters to name them. Most Java programmers continue to follow this convention when naming `final static` fields.

It is good practice to use constants such as this in place of literal values, especially where the value will be used in more than one place. This ensures that if the constant value needs to change, it can be changed in one place and reflected everywhere.

Alternatives to constructors

Constructors are the most common way to construct objects in Java, but there are two alternative approaches that are also worth understanding. Both of these approaches are based on design-patterns familiar in many programming languages. Both approaches do ultimately use constructors (because every object must be created via a constructor), but the pattern takes care of invoking the constructor.

Factory method

Factory methods are a pattern for creating objects without specifying the exact implementation that will be constructed. The factory method pattern uses a `static` method to construct objects rather than a constructor. The object created is usually based on an interface; therefore the factory method can determine the appropriate implementation of that interface to instantiate.

The following is an example:

```
package factorymethod;
public class A {

    private A() {
    }

    public static A getInstance() {
        return new A();
    }
}
```

If any code wishes to create an instance of class A, it must do so by invoking the following:

```
A a = A.getInstance();
```

In order to force code to use the factory method, the constructor on A has been made `private`. This means it is possible for the `static` method defined in A to invoke this constructor, but no other code in the program can create an instance of A by invoking:

```
A a = new A();
```

In this particular case the factory method is always instantiating an instance of A, which may lead you to wonder why I don't just use the constructor.

There are two main reasons I may want to use a factory method in this case. The first is that I may want the flexibility to return a sub-class of A in the future, without trying to find all the code that constructs instances of A. Remember, because the factory method returns an instance of A, it could return an instance of any class that extended A.

The other main reason for using factory methods in cases such as this is that I may want to control some aspect of the object instantiation process that cannot be controlled with constructors: the most common example is that I may want to control how many instances of a class are created.

Imagine a scenario where you only ever want a single instance of a class to be created, but for this to be available to any code in the program. For instance, the class may not define any state, it may simply consist of a set of methods: therefore it would be wasteful on memory to ever instantiate more than a single instance.

This requirement is supported by another design pattern called the *Singleton* design pattern. This can be implemented as follows:

```
package factorymethod;
public class Single {
    private static Single single;

    private Single() {
    }

    public static Single getInstance() {
        if (single == null) {
            single = new Single();
        }
        return single;
    }
}
```

> There is a deficiency in this implementation that will be overlooked for now. This is a non-thread safe implementation of a singleton, and multiple instances of Single could conceivably be created in a multi-threaded program.
>
> If you need to create singletons in multi-threaded environments the Internet provides plenty of examples.

If I write a client to use this class, you will see that only one Single object is ever created:

```
package factorymethod;
public class Client {
    public static void main(String[] args) {
        Single s = Single.getInstance();
        Single s2 = Single.getInstance();
        assert(s == s2);
    }
}
```

On the first invocation of getInstance, the single static field will be null, and therefore an instance of Single will be created and stored in this field. On subsequent invocations, `single` will not be `null`, so it will be returned directly.

Cloning

Another way to instantiate objects is via *cloning*. As its name suggests, cloning involves creating a new object as a copy of an existing object.

You may have already noticed the `Object` class, from which all other objects are derived, supports a `clone` method:

```
protected native Object clone() throws CloneNotSupportedException;
```

This method throws a `CloneNotSupportedException` if the object in question cannot be cloned.

In order to make an object *cloneable* it is necessary to add the `Cloneable` interface to the class definition, or extend from a class or interface that implements this interface. This interface does not contain any methods; it is simply a *tagging interface*.

There are two poorly thought through features in the way Java has implemented cloning. The first is that the `clone` method should arguably have be declared on the `Cloneable` interface itself. The second is that the `clone` method is protected; therefore it is often necessary to override the method and make it `public`. The following is an example of a clone-able class:

```
package cloning;
public class A implements Cloneable {
    private StringBuffer sb = new StringBuffer("hello");
    private int num = 10;

    public A() {}

    public StringBuffer getSb() {
        return sb;
    }
    public void setSb(StringBuffer sb) {
        this.sb = sb;
    }
    public int getNum() {
        return num;
    }
    public void setNum(int num) {
        this.num = num;
    }

    @Override
    public Object clone() throws CloneNotSupportedException {
        return super.clone();
    }
}
```

Notice that it is perfectly valid to override a method and make it more accessible: in this case I have overridden a `protected` method and made it `public`.

It is not however possible to override a method and make it less accessible: you cannot override a `public` method and make it `protected`. The reason for this is that an external class may not know it is using a sub-type rather than the super-type: therefore anything it can do to the super-type, it needs to be able to do to the sub-type.

The following is a simple program that creates an initial instance of A via its constructor, and then a second instance of A via the clone method:

```
package cloning;
public class Main {
    public static void main(String[] args) {
        try {
            A a1 = new A();
            A a2 = (A) a1.clone();
            a2.setNum(100);
            System.out.println(a1.getNum());
            System.out.println(a2.getNum());
            a2.getSb().append(" World");
            System.out.println(a1.getSb());
            System.out.println(a2.getSb());
        } catch (CloneNotSupportedException e) {
            e.printStackTrace();
        }
    }
}
```

When an object is cloned, all fields are given copies of the fields in the original object. This code is intended to demonstrate a specific point about cloning, however, and is directly related to the lessons learned in Chapter 11 when you looked at object references.

The primitive value stored in the num field is changed on the cloned instance:

`a2.setNum(100);`

Because a2 had a copy of this value, changing this does not affect instance a in any way. It retains its original value.

If you modify the `StringBuffer` on a2, however, you get a very different result. The final two `println` statements print the following:

```
hello World
hello World
```

You can see that the `StringBuffer` referred to by a has also been changed.

The reason for this is that when the `clone` operation was executed, a copy was made of the sb object reference, but this copy still referred to the same object.

The `clone` method provided by Java performs what is known as a "shallow clone". It creates a new instance of the top-level object, and creates a copy of any primitives and object references, but it does not create a copy of any composite objects.

If you want any composite objects to also be cloned, you need to perform a "deep clone".

The simplest way to implement deep cloning is through a process called *serialization*. Serialization converts an object into a series of bytes, and is commonly used when sending an object over the network, or when saving an object to disk. A side effect of serialization is that when the object is de-serialized, the new object contains new instances of all composite objects, and therefore fulfills the deep cloning requirements.

In order to make an object serializable, its class must implement `java.io.Serializable`. This is another tagging interface, and does not have any methods that need implementing. The `clone` method can then be implemented as follows:

```java
@Override
public Object clone() throws CloneNotSupportedException {
    try {
        ByteArrayOutputStream baos = new ByteArrayOutputStream();
        ObjectOutputStream oos = new ObjectOutputStream(baos);
        oos.writeObject(this);
        ByteArrayInputStream bais =
            new ByteArrayInputStream(baos.toByteArray());
        ObjectInputStream ois = new ObjectInputStream(bais);
        return ois.readObject();
    } catch (IOException e) {
        return null;
    } catch (ClassNotFoundException e) {
        return null;
    }
}
```

> You will need to include the following `import` for this class to compile:
>
> `import java.io.*;`

I will not describe this implementation in detail, because it uses features that are the subject of future chapters. If you run the `Main` program now, however, it should produce the correct results:

```
10
100
hello
hello World
```

15 EXCEPTION HANDLING

During the execution of a program, unexpected events can occur. For instance:

⇒ The program may try to access an index in an array greater than the length of an array
⇒ The program may attempt to invoke a method on a `null` reference
⇒ The program may attempt to open a file that does not exist

When these events occur an exception is generated, and either:

⇒ Some other code in the program will handle the exception, allowing the program to recover, or
⇒ The program will halt

Exception handling is one of the most important subjects to understand with the Java language, and defining effective approaches to exception handling is one of the key ways to build stable and robust software.

Types of Exception

Before looking at any code, it is important to understand that there are three fundamental types of exceptions in Java, and each has a very distinct purpose. In addition, the way you handle these three types of exception will be very different.

Runtime (or unchecked) **exceptions**: these are caused at runtime by bugs in the program, for instance, using an object before it is instantiated, dividing an integer by 0 or accessing an array index that is outside the bounds of the array.

It is useful to think of runtime exceptions as coding bugs that could not be detected by the compiler, and therefore only become evident at run-time.

Runtime exceptions should not generally be handled; instead the code should be fixed to ensure these exceptions do not occur.

Checked exceptions: these exceptions represent abnormal events that can be handled by the program. For example, opening a file on the file-system that does not exist will generate an exception, but this exception can be alleviated by creating the file, or telling the user that the file does not exist. In Java, the compiler insists that you handle checked exceptions in some way.

Errors: these are different from other exceptions, because it is generally not possible for the program to handle these exceptions even if it wants to, and they are not necessarily related to coding bugs. Examples of errors are out of memory errors and stack overflow errors. Errors will not be examined in this chapter, because there is generally nothing you can do about them.

> Errors typically imply that the JVM has exhausted its resources (such as memory). Because it has exhausted its resources, resources are not available to the JVM to handle the issue.

In general, the way you determine the type of exception that has occurred in Java is by inspecting its type. All types of exception in Java are just simple objects, although they can contain any state required to provide further information about the exception. Figure 15-1 shows the class diagram for the Exception hierarchy in Java.

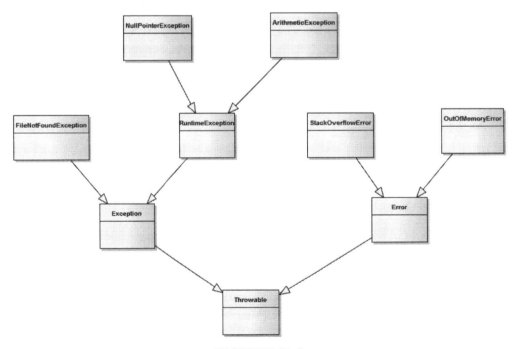

FIGURE 15-1

As you can see, all classes in the hierarchy extend a class called `Throwable`.

> This diagram is a UML class diagram. In class diagrams, the arrows shown here indicate that the pointing class extends the class it points to. As such, `Throwable` is the base class all other classes are extending.

`Errors` are placed in a separate tree of the hierarchy to indicate that they cannot be handled, and therefore are not technically "exceptions" in Java. Two subclasses of `Error` are shown (`OutOfMemoryError` and `StackOverflowError`), but several other sub-types are supported by Java.

Any exception that is a sub-class of, `RuntimeException` is considered a runtime exception, while all other classes that extend `Exception` are checked exception. Again, although some examples are shown, many other sub-types are supported by Java, and it is possible to create your own sub-types.

Checked Exceptions

You will begin by looking at checked exceptions. Checked exceptions are typically used to enforce business rules in a program. They represent events that can be expected to occur at runtime, but which are invalid, and therefore must be explicitly handled.

Checked exceptions are best thought of as a way of moving responsibility for handling a specific problem to some other block of code that knows how to handle the problem.

Consider as an example an object that must be initialized before it is used, but which can only be initialized once. This object could throw an exception if it is initialized a second time, and could also throw an exception if it was used before being initialized.

In order to demonstrate this, you will start by defining two sub-classes of `Exception` to represent exceptions to these two business rules.

Technically you can represent an exception with an instance of `Exception`, but this is not very useful for the receiving party, because it does not provide them sufficient context to understand what has gone wrong, and what they should do to compensate. The following are the exception definitions (these need to be placed in two separate classes):

```
package exceptions;
public class UninitializedException extends Exception {
    public UninitializedException(String message) {
        super(message);
    }
}
```

And

```
package exceptions;
public class ReinitializationException extends Exception {
    public ReinitializationException(String message) {
        super(message);
    }
}
```

Notice that these both extend Exception – which in turn extends Throwable.

Also notice that both these classes accept a message. It is customary for exceptions to carry additional contextual information about the exception that has occurred, and often this is in the form of a String of text.

You will now write the code for the object that will *throw* these exceptions:

```
package exceptions;
public class CheckedExample {

    private boolean initialized = false;

    public void initialize() throws ReinitializationException {
        if (initialized) {
            throw new ReinitializationException
                ("Object is already initialized");
        }
        initialized = true;
        System.out.println("I am initialized");
    }

    public void execute() throws UninitializedException {
        if (!initialized) {
            throw new UninitializedException
                ("Object is already initialized");
        }
        System.out.println("I am executing");
    }
}
```

Notice that the method signatures declare the fact that they throw exceptions of a specific type. This is not optional: if a method throws a checked exception it must declare the fact. This ensures that any method calling this method knows it has to handle this eventuality.

Remember, it is not necessarily a coding bug for code to attempt to re-initialize this object. The object may have been originally initialized from a completely independent piece of code, therefore our code does not know if it needs to invoke initialize or not.

You can now write the code that uses this object. The compiler forces you to handle the exceptions that may occur in one of two ways, both of which will be shown in the next two examples.

The first example invokes initialize and then handles the exception by enclosing the invocation in a try/catch bloc:

```
package exceptions;
public class Main {
    public static void main(String[] args) {
        CheckedExample ce = new CheckedExample();
        try {
            ce.initialize();
        } catch (ReinitializationException e) {
            System.out.println("ReinitializationException occurred");
        }
    }
}
```

Notice that the compiler does not care how you handle the exception - and this example simply prints a `String` of text to the console. The `try/catch` block is simply your mechanism to assure the compiler you have thought about the exception that can occur, and done what is necessary to handle it.

The second way to deal with the exception is to specify that the invoking method `throws` the exception. This will cause the exception to be propagated one level further up the call chain, where it can also be handled or thrown. This is shown in the following example:

```
package exceptions;

public class Main {
    public static void main(String[] args) throws ReinitializationException {
        CheckedExample ce = new CheckedExample();
        ce.initialize();
    }
}
```

> If the `main` method `throws` an exception, no other methods are available in the call chain to handle the exception, and therefore the program will immediately terminate.

The `try/catch` block can surround as many lines of code as required, not just the single line that will generate the exception. The only thing you need to bear in mind, however, is that any code between the exception being raised, and the exception being handled, will not be executed. For instance, the `println` statement in the next example will not be executed when an exception is raised on the previous line:

```
public static void main(String[] args) {
    CheckedExample ce = new CheckedExample();
    try {
        ce.initialize();
        System.out.println("Not called");
    } catch (ReinitializationException e) {
    }
}
```

Just to prove the exception handling does work, change the `Main` class as follows:

```
package exceptions;
public class Main {
    public static void main(String[] args) {
        CheckedExample ce = new CheckedExample();
        try {
            ce.initialize();
        } catch (ReinitializationException e) {
            System.out.println("This will not be called.");
        }
        try {
            ce.initialize();
        } catch (ReinitializationException e) {
            System.out.println("This will be called.");
        }
    }
}
```

This code attempts to re-initialize the object, therefore when the program runs it will produce the following output:

```
I am initialized
This will be called.
```

In the case of a `ReinitializationException` the program probably does not need to do anything inside the `catch` block – and in a real program I would not even `throw` this exception: if the object was already initialized I would just return immediately without performing the initialization routine – all the caller really cares about is that after invoking `initialize`, the object is initialized.

You can now add the code for invoking the `execute` method, but with a slight twist that will simulate the behavior of a client that does not know whether the object needs to be initialized:

⇒ The code will first attempt to invoke `execute`: if the object is not initialized, an exception will be thrown.

⇒ If an exception is thrown in step 1, the `initialize` method will be invoked, followed by `execute` one more time

This can be implemented as follows:

```
package exceptions;
public class Main {
    public static void main(String[] args) {
        CheckedExample ce = new CheckedExample();
        try {
            ce.execute();
        } catch (UninitializedException e) {
            try {
                ce.initialize();
                ce.execute();
            } catch (ReinitializationException e1) {}
              catch (UninitializedException e1) {}
        }
    }
}
```

> This example has been chosen to highlight specific exception handling features; it is not necessarily the best way to write this specific functionality.

You will notice is that the first call to execute is surrounded by a `try/catch` block that catches `UninitializedException`. If this exception is caught, the object is not initialized, and therefore you need to invoke `initialize` and then call `execute` again.

Notice that due to the fact that `initialize` and `execute` can generate new exceptions, it is necessary to nest another `try/catch` block inside the first `catch` block.

Another interesting feature of this second catch block is that it needs to catch two types of exception. In this case, the two types of exception have been caught in two separate `catch` blocks associated with a single `try` statement:

```
catch (ReinitializationException e1) {}
catch (UninitializedException e1) {}
```

As of Java 7, it is also possible to write this as follows:

```
catch (ReinitializationException | UninitializedException ex) {}
```

This approach allows you to provide a single `catch` block for multiple types of exception.

Because both types of exception extend `Exception`, it would also be possible to provide the following `catch` block:

```
catch (Exception ex) {}
```

This is generally bad practice, however, because if `initialize` or `execute` were modified to throw any new types of exception, this `catch` block would implicitly handle these exception types, despite the fact that the new types of exception may need to be handled differently. This `catch` block would also catch any `RuntimeExceptions` generated (because these also `extend Exception`), which typically should be avoided.

> Technically an exception could match two catch blocks, for instance:
> ```
> catch (ReinitializationException e1) {}
> catch (Exception e1) {}
> ```
> In this case, only the first `catch` block that matches the exception will be executed.

The `try/catch` construct can also contain an optional block at the end called a `finally` block: this will be executed regardless of whether an exception occurred. For instance, if you wanted to print a line after `execute` is invoked, you could add the following:

```
try {
    ce.execute();
} catch (UninitializedException e) {
    System.out.println("An exception has occurred");
} finally {
    System.out.println("Code has completed");
}
```

In this case, `"Code has completed"` will be printed regardless of whether the call to `execute` results in an exception or not.

> There are much better ways of logging contextual information to the console when an error occurs, these will be examined later in the book when you look at Logging in general.

One final point worth mentioning about `try/catch` blocks is that the `catch` block can re-throw the exception, for example:

```
catch (UninitializedException e) {
    throw e;
}
```

The catch block can even throw an exception of a different type, including a `RuntimeException`. Naturally, if the exception is re-thrown, and not handled elsewhere in the method, the method must declare that it `throws` the exception type.

It is common to re-throw exceptions if your method needs to perform some processing when an exception occurs (such as closing files), but cannot fully handle the scenario – for instance it may not know how to provide feedback to the user.

Runtime Exceptions

Runtime exceptions generally occur as a result of coding bugs. By far the most common type of runtime exception you will encounter is the `NullPointerException`. This occurs when you attempt to access a field or method on an object reference that has a `null` value, i.e. it is not a reference to an object on the heap.

The following is a simple program that generates a `NullPointerException`:

```
package exceptions;
public class Runtime {
    public static void main(String[] args) {
        StringBuffer sb = new StringBuffer("Hello");
        StringBuffer sb2 = null;
```

```
        appendWorld(sb);
        appendWorld(sb2);
    }

    private static void appendWorld(StringBuffer sb) {
        sb.append(" World");
    }
}
```

If you run this program it will generate the following output:

```
Exception in thread "main" java.lang.NullPointerException
    at exceptions.Runtime.appendWorld(Runtime.java:11)
    at exceptions.Runtime.main(Runtime.java:7)
```

This is referred to as a stack trace – it is a dump of the call stack of the program when the exception occurred. Stack traces are the most common mechanism available for diagnosing an exception after the fact.

> All exceptions contain stack traces, not just `RuntimeException`.

The first line of the stack trace tells you the type of exception that has occurred and the thread that it occurred in. This is a single threaded program, but when I introduce multi-threading you will see why this is important.

The remaining lines of the stack trace show the call-stack of the program at the point the error occurred. You always read stack traces from top to bottom. The first line of the stack-trace is the line that the exception occurred on (line 11 of the `Runtime` class). The next line tells you the line in the program that called this method (line 7 in the `Runtime` class).

In real-world programs stack traces can become very long, sometimes 20 or 30 levels deep, but usually the first couple of lines are sufficient to understand what was happening when the exception occurred.

Once you understand the context of the exception you can quickly determine what has happened. If you look at line 11 of `Runtime`, the only reason that this exception could have occurred would be if `sb` was `null`. You can therefore determine that at line 7 of the `Runtime` class you are passing a `null StringBuffer` to `appendWorld`.

You will notice that methods do not need to declare the fact that they `throw` runtime exceptions. The reason for this is that the list of possible runtime exceptions that could conceivably be thrown by a method could be large (virtually all methods could generate a `NullPointerException`).

The fact that you do not have to handle runtime exceptions leads some programmers to favor them over checked exceptions – even in cases where checked exceptions are more appropriate. Try not to fall into this trap – if an exception represents a business rule violation, rather than a coding bug, it should not be a `RuntimeException`.

I mentioned earlier that `RuntimeExceptions` such as `NullPointerExeption` should not be handled. The reason for this is that they are bugs: you never should have passed a `null` `StringBuffer` to the `appendHello` method. Instead of adding exception-handling logic, therefore, you should change your code. For instance, you may decide that the best way to handle this exception is for `appendWorld` to check whether it has been passed a `null` reference:

```
private static void appendWorld(StringBuffer sb) {
    if (sb != null) {
        sb.append(" World");
    }
}
```

The following are the most common `RuntimeExceptions` you will encounter in Java:

`IllegalArgumentException`: this occurs when an invalid value is passed to a method. For instance, if the method only accepts positive numbers, it may throw an `IllegalArgumentException` if it is passed a negative number.

`IllegalStateException`: this indicates that the method has been invoked at an illegal time. I could have used this exception instead of `UninitializedException` earlier, because I was essentially stating that an invocation had occurred at the wrong time (before the object was initialized).

`ArrayIndexOutOfBoundsException`: this occurs when you access an index in an array that is greater than the length of the array.

`ClassCastException`: this occurs when you cast an object to be an invalid type: for instance if you cast a `String` to a `StringBuffer`.

`UnsupportedOperationException`: as its name suggests, this is thrown when an operation is not supported. For instance, if a method required by an interface has not been implemented yet it could throw an `UnsupportedOperationException`.

`ArithmeticException`: this most commonly occurs when you divide an integer by 0.

There is nothing to stop you throwing these exceptions in your own code. In fact, before creating your own specific exception types it always makes sense to find out if an existing exception type exists in Java.

16 METHODS

It may seem rather late in the book for a chapter called "Methods", after all you have been using methods since the very first examples. There are however a number of interesting subjects and features that you have not covered up until this point

As you have already seen, methods provide Java objects with their behavior. Methods operate on a set of data (either the state of the object, local variables or arguments passed to them) and (optionally) return a result.

Overloading

Java allows methods to be overloaded. This means a class can define multiple methods with the same name, as long as they accept different parameters (either in type or the number of parameters).

For instance, the following is a valid class, containing two methods called `printDate`:

```java
package overloading;
import java.text.DateFormat;
import java.text.SimpleDateFormat;
import java.util.Date;
public class OverLoaded {
    public void printDate(Date date) {
        DateFormat sd = new SimpleDateFormat("yyyy-MM-dd");
        System.out.printf("The date is %s", sd.format(date));
    }

    public void printDate() {
        printDate(new Date());
    }
}
```

This class is valid because the method signatures of the two methods are different: one accepts a `Date` parameter while the other accepts no parameters. If the no-arguments method is invoked, the current date is passed to the `printDate` method that accepts a `Date`.

It is never possible to overload methods where the signature differs only by return type. For instance, it is not be possible to add an additional method to `OverLoaded` with the following signature:

```
public Date printDate() {
```

This is because the compiler would not be able to determine which method you were invoked, because even when a method returns a value, the invoker has no obligation to assign this to a variable (you are calling a method for *its side effects*). For instance, which method would be invoked by the following of code?

```
OverLoaded ol = new OverLoaded();
ol.printDate();
```

Similarly it is not possible to overload methods where only the parameter names differ:

```
public void printDate(Date date2) {
```

This is because the parameter names are irrelevant to the compiler when determining which method to call: it is the data types that are important.

Finally, it is not possible to overload methods where their signatures are the same, but their `throws` clause differs. For instance, I could not add the following method to this class:

```
public void printDate(Date date) throws RuntimeException {
```

Overloading is a reasonably simple technique, but does become more complex when inheritance is involved.

In order to demonstrate this, start by adding a simple inheritance hierarchy in the `overloading` package by creating a new class called `Shape`. Next, add `Circle` and `Square` classes that extend `Shape`:

```
package overloading;

public class Shape {
}

class Circle extends Shape {
}

class Square extends Shape {
}
```

> You can also use the objects defined earlier in the book if you like.

You will now create a class with three overloaded methods for accepting these three different classes. The method implementations will simply print out the method that has been called:

```java
package overloading;
public class ShapePrinter {
    public void acceptShape(Shape s) {
        System.out.printf("Method called with shape of type %s\n",
            s.getClass().getSimpleName());
    }

    public void acceptShape(Circle s) {
        System.out.printf("Method called with circle of type %s\n",
            s.getClass().getSimpleName());
    }

    public void acceptShape(Square s) {
        System.out.printf("Method called with square of type %s\n",
            s.getClass().getSimpleName());
    }
}
```

Notice that the three method names are the same, but each method accepts a different class in the hierarchy. The methods simply print out that they have been called, and the type that they have been passed.

You can now write the following program to call these methods. Before running this program try to figure out what the result will be:

```java
package overloading;
public class Main {
    public static void main(String[] args) {
        ShapePrinter sp = new ShapePrinter();
        Circle c = new Circle();
        sp.acceptShape(c);
        Shape sq = new Square();
        sp.acceptShape(sq);
    }
}
```

A reasonable assumption would be that this example would print:

```
Method called with circle of type Circle
Method called with square of type Square
```

This is due to the fact that a `Circle` and `Square` are passed in turn. In fact it prints:

```
Method called with circle of type Circle
Method called with shape of type Square
```

This second line here is likely to come as a surprise. The final line of the `main` method passes an instance of `Square` to `acceptShape`, but the version of the method invoked is the one accepting `Shape`.

Even many experienced Java programmers do not understand this feature of the language. After learning about polymorphism in the previous chapters it would be reasonable to assume that method overloading worked in the same way: Java would call the appropriate method, based on the type of the object at runtime.

In fact Java determines the overloaded method that will be invoked at compile time, and therefore it uses the type of the reference, rather than the type of the object they reference at runtime, when determining which method to invoke.

Because c was declared as type `Circle`, it is passed to the method declaring a `Circle` parameter. This is because the compiler knows that at run-time, c will either refer to an instance of `Circle` or a sub-type of `Circle`.

The variable sq, by comparison, has been defined as a reference to a `Shape`. The compiler, therefore, can only guarantee that this reference will refer to an instance of `Shape` (or one of its sub-types). As a result, the version of `acceptShape` invoked is the one accepting a parameter of type `Shape`.

The key to understanding this functionality, and how it differs from polymorphism, is to understand that the decision of which method to invoke is being determined at compile time, while with polymorphism the decision is being made at run-time.

You could argue in this case that it is obvious to the compiler that sq refers to a `Square`. Although this is true in this particular case, as a general rule the compiler is not able to determine the specific type references refer to.

Some programming languages do determine the method to invoke at runtime, and therefore exhibit the more expected behavior. Given that these languages also support polymorphism, this feature is referred to as double-dispatch: the method called at runtime depends on both:

⇒ The runtime type of the object the method is invoked on, and
⇒ The runtime type of the objects passed to the method

It is easy enough to change the behavior of this program to behave in the expected manner: you can move the `printShape` method to the shapes themselves:

```
package overloading;
public class Shape {
    public void printShape() {
        System.out.printf("Method called with shape of type %s\n",
            this.getClass().getSimpleName());
    }
}

class Circle extends Shape {
    public void printShape() {
        System.out.printf("Method called with circle of type %s\n",
            this.getClass().getSimpleName());
    }
```

```
}

class Square extends Shape {
    public void printShape() {
        System.out.printf("Method called with square of type %s\n",
            this.getClass().getSimpleName());
    }
}
```

And then rewrite the `Main` class as follows:

```
package overloading;
public class Main2 {
    public static void main(String[] args) {
        Circle c = new Circle();
        c.printShape();
        Shape sq = new Square();
        sq.printShape();
    }
}
```

Due to the magic of polymorphism, this produces the following result:

```
Method called with circle of type Circle
Method called with square of type Square
```

Visitor Pattern

Rewriting the method in this manner shown in the previous example is not always possible. Consider the following example:

⇒ You have an inheritance hierarchy of shapes.

⇒ You have an inheritance hierarchy of document types (e.g. PDF documents, Word documents).

⇒ Shapes can be passed to document types, but the way they print will depend on the run-time type of the shape and the run-time type of the document. For instance, a `Square` on a PDF document will print differently to a `Square` in a Word document and a `Circle` on a PDF document will print differently from a `Circle` on a Word document.

In order to implement this feature you need to simulate double-dispatch in Java. This can be achieved via another design pattern called the *Visitor* pattern.

> This can be one of the most difficult patterns to get your head around.
>
> The first key to understanding the solution the visitor pattern provides is understanding the problem it is solving. Therefore, you may choose to attempt to implement this functionality using an alternative implementation first.

To begin, you need to alter the shape classes to specify the types of document they can work with (or "visit"). You also need to specify the behavior of these shapes when they visit the various document types:

```
package visitor;
public interface Shape {
    public void visit(WordDocument wd);
    public void visit(PDFDocument pdf);
}

class Circle implements Shape {
    @Override
    public void visit(WordDocument wd) {
        System.out.println("Printing a circle on a Word Document");
    }

    @Override
    public void visit(PDFDocument pdf) {
        System.out.println("Printing a circle on a PDF Document");
    }
}

class Square implements Shape {
    @Override
    public void visit(WordDocument wd) {
        System.out.println("Printing a square on a Word Document");
    }

    @Override
    public void visit(PDFDocument pdf) {
        System.out.println("Printing a square on a PDF Document");
    }
}
```

In this case, when a `Shape` visits a `Document` it simply prints the fact that it has done so. In a real program, the `Shape` would implement the necessary functionality to draw itself into the specific type of document

The document type hierarchy can then be added as follows:

```
package visitor;
public interface DocumentType {
    void accept(Shape s);
}

class PDFDocument implements DocumentType {
    @Override
    public void accept(Shape s) {
        s.visit(this);
    }
}
class WordDocument implements DocumentType {
    @Override
    public void accept(Shape s) {
        s.visit(this);
    }
}
```

Each concrete type of document is capable of accepting a `Shape`. When it accepts the `Shape` it calls the `visit` method on the `Shape`, and passes itself as the parameter (`this`). This is the key to the pattern, so I will investigate this in more detail once you are satisfied that the pattern works.

Finally, create a `Main` program as follows:

```
package visitor;
public class Main {
    public static void main(String[] args) {
        DocumentType dt = new WordDocument();
        Shape s = new Square();
        dt.accept(s);
        dt = new PDFDocument();
        s = new Circle();
        dt.accept(s);
    }
}
```

Even though all object references refer to the parent type, this produces the desired result, and prints the following:

```
Printing a square on a Word Document
Printing a circle on a PDF Document
```

The key to understanding this pattern is to realize that you have relied on the power of polymorphism twice. The first time you rely on polymorphism is on these lines in the `main` method:

```
dt.accept(s);
```

As explained earlier in the book, the method that is invoked will depend on the run-time type of the `Document`, and therefore, on line 3 the `accept` method on `WordDocument` will be invoked, passing a `Square` as a parameter:

```
public void accept(Shape s) {
    s.visit(this);
}
```

When the `accept` method accepts the `Square`, it calls `visit` on it:

```
s.visit(this);
```

Again, because you are invoking a method on an object reference, the method invoked depends on the run-time type of the `Shape` (which is a `Square`), and therefore the following method is invoked:

```
class Square implements Shape {
    @Override
    public void visit(WordDocument wd) {
        System.out.println("Printing a square on a Word Document");
    }
```

The visitor pattern is useful anytime you have two hierarchies of object that interact, and you do not know the specific types of objects that will be used at compile time.

Recursion

Java methods can invoke themselves: a technique referred to as recursion.

Recursion is an alternative to iteration: any algorithm that can be implemented iteratively can also be implemented recursively, and vice versa.

There are, however, a number of problems that can be more concisely expressed as recursive algorithms. This is particularly true when a large problem can be broken into a number of simpler sub-problems – an approach commonly termed divide and conqueror.

Recursion is very similar to iteration: each time a method invokes itself it must progress towards an answer, otherwise the algorithm will not ever end and a `StackOverflowException` will occur – this is the recursive equivalent to an infinite loop.

As a very simple example, consider the following class that computes the factorial of a number supplied:

```java
package recusion;
public class Factorial {
    public int compute(int value) {
        if (value == 1) {
            return 1;
        }
        return value * compute(value-1);
    }
}
```

If the `value` passed to `compute` is 1, the method simply returns 1. This is the end of the recursion. If the value is greater than 1, the `value` is multiplied by the result of calling `compute` with a number 1 smaller.

As you can see, each call to `compute` takes us one step closer to the end of the recursion. Additionally, a complex problem of calculating the factorial of a number is replaced by a series of simpler problems – multiplying two numbers together.

In order to understand the behavior of this method, add the following `println` statements:

```java
package recusion;
public class Factorial {
    public int compute(int value) {
        System.out.println("compute called with "+value);
        if (value == 1) {
            System.out.println("returning 1");
            return 1;
        }
        int returnVal =  value * compute(value-1);
        System.out.println("returning "+returnVal);
        return returnVal;
    }
}
```

You can now create the following `Main` class to invoke this:

```
package recusion;
public class Main {
    public static void main(String[] args) {
        Factorial f = new Factorial();
        int result = f.compute(6);
        System.out.println("The result is "+ result);
    }
}
```

If you run this program it will print the following:

```
compute called with 6
compute called with 5
compute called with 4
compute called with 3
compute called with 2
compute called with 1
returning 1
returning 2
returning 6
returning 24
returning 120
returning 720
The result is 720
```

As you can see, the algorithm is solving the complex problem by determining the factorial of every number from 1 to the number provided. It begins by descending down a set of method calls until it reaches a specified value (1 in this case). The algorithm then effectively works its way up, out of the method calls, multiplying the result of one method call with the result of the next.

Arguments

The methods you have seen up until this point accept a defined list of parameters. Although this suits many needs, it does sometimes pose a limitation. Consider a method that wishes to accept an arbitrary number of parameters, add them together, and return the result.

You could achieve this by declaring an array of `int`:

```
package arguments;
public class Adder {

    public static void main(String[] args) {
        int[] vals = {4,7,5,1,8};
        System.out.print(add(vals));
    }

    private static int add(int[] vals) {
        int result = 0;
        for (int i = 0; i < vals.length; i++) {
            result+= vals[i];
        }
        return result;
```

        }
}

Although there is nothing wrong with this code, it would be potentially more convenient to just be able to pass an arbitrary number of parameters to the add method. This can be achieved as follows:

```
package arguments;
public class Adder {

    public static void main(String[] args) {
        System.out.print(add(4,7,5,1,8));
    }

    private static int add(int...vals) {
        int result = 0;
        for (int i = 0; i < vals.length; i++) {
            result+= vals[i];
        }
        return result;
    }
}
```

Notice that the parameter has been declared as follows int...vals. This means that the method will accept 1 or more int values. The parameter still behaves like it is an array (just like the previous example), but this approach means that the arguments passed in do not need to be encapsulated in an array: they are simply defined as (4,7,5,1,8).

This technique can be used even in cases where multiple named parameters are defined by a method, but only the last parameter in the method signature can use the ... notation.

17 COLLECTIONS

The Java Collections API is one of the most extensively used APIs in Java. It provides a set of classes and interfaces that are similar to arrays (they encapsulate a group of objects), but provide far more features than are found with traditional arrays.

There are three main types of `Collection` in the Collections API, all of which are defined via interfaces:

⇒ **List**: a list is an ordered collection of objects, and allows duplicate elements
⇒ **Set**: a set is a collection of unique elements that may or may not be sorted
⇒ **Map**: a map is set of key/value pairs, and allows fast lookup of values via their key

Java also supports an additional related class called `Vector`. This predated the Collections API, but was retrofitted into the API as a `List`. `Vectors` will not be discussed in this chapter because they are seldom the best option for solving a problem.

Unlike arrays, Collections can only hold objects (not primitives), but unlike arrays their size does not need to be specified in advance: they will happily grow as new data is added to them.

> Collections can of course hold primitive wrappers such as `Integer` and `Long`, therefore the restriction against primitives has no real impact on programmers.

By default the methods on Collections are defined to work with instances of `Object` – therefore, because every class extends `Object`, any object can be stored in them. This creates a highly flexible API, but is somewhat error prone - because objects retrieved from a

`Collection` must be cast to their appropriate type – this can lead to `ClassCastExceptions`.

In order to make the Collections API more *type-safe*, a concept was added to Java called *generics*. Generics were introduced in Java 5, and allows the programmer to specify the types another class will use at compile time. This gives you the benefits of compile-time type-checking, with the flexibility of an API that can operate on any type of object.

For instance, it is possible to specify that a `List` will contain objects of the type `Address`; the compiler will then ensure all elements added to the list are instances of this class, and will allow `Address` instances to be retrieved from the `List` without casting.

You will initially explore the Collections API without generics: in this mode any type can be added to a Collection. You will then gain an understanding of how generics can be used to enhance the Collections API, and how they can be used more generally in Java code.

The Collections API has also changed significantly in Java 8 with the introduction of the Streams API. These are exciting developments in the Java world, and will be covered later in the book.

Object Equality and Hash Keys

The three distinct types of `Collection` outlined earlier require objects to provide the following three features:

⇒ The ability to determine if an object is equal to another object: this allows sets to maintain uniqueness.
⇒ The ability to determine whether an object should be sorted higher or lower than another object: this allows lists to be sorted.
⇒ The ability to provide a key to represent themselves: this allows certain optimizations, such as determining if a particular object is unique. Although the need for this feature is not immediately obvious, it will be explained shortly.

This section will examine how objects provide these capabilities in a generic manner.

Equality

In previous chapters you have encountered the equality operator (==), and the `equals` method (that uses the equality operator by default). This allowed you to determine whether two references referred to the same underlying object.

This is a very strict definition of equality, and is not always the definition you will wish to use. In many cases two objects can be considered equal if their fields (or sometimes a subset of their fields) contain the same values. For instance, in a pay-role system, two `Employee` objects may be considered equal if they have the same Social Security Number.

Objects typically represent physical entities in the real world (e.g. cars, people, hotels). As discussed earlier, these objects are abstractions of physical entities, and contain the information derived from these entities that is relevant to the program using them. In this sense, if two objects have the same values for these fields, they represent the same physical entity, and are therefore equal.

As an example, create the following `Address` class:

```
package addresses;
public class Address implements Comparable {
    private int streetNumber;
    private String street;
    private String city;
    private int postCode;
    private String country;

    public Address(int streetNumber, String street, String city,
            int postCode, String country) {
        this.streetNumber = streetNumber;
        this.street = street;
        this.city = city;
        this.postCode = postCode;
        this.country = country;
    }
}
```

> Getters and setters have been omitted for brevity, but should be added to all fields.

If two addresses have the same values for all these fields, you can say that they are equal (at least within this program). For instance, if two different users entered exactly the same address details you may determine that the two address objects represent the same physical location.

It may turn out that this abstraction of an address is insufficient: for instance it may not handle apartments, but, again, it will depend on the nature of the program using these `Address` objects.

In order to enforce this definition of equality, you need to override the `equals` method from the `Object` class. The easiest way to implement the `equals` method is to right click on the class and choose `Source -> Generate hashCode() and equals()`. This will present the dialog box shown in figure 17-1

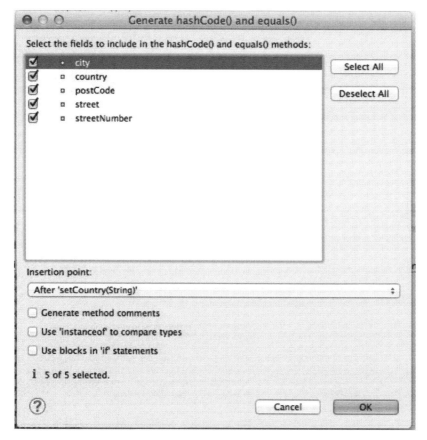

FIGURE 17-1

This dialog asks you which fields should be used to determine whether two objects are equals. In some cases you could just use a single field, or subset of fields, but in this case you should select all fields.

When you click "OK" two methods will be created for you: `equals` and `hashCode`. You will initially focus on the `equals` method:

```
@Override
public boolean equals(Object obj) {
    if (this == obj)
        return true;
    if (obj == null)
        return false;
    if (getClass() != obj.getClass())
        return false;
    Address other = (Address) obj;
    if (city == null) {
        if (other.city != null)
            return false;
    } else if (!city.equals(other.city))
        return false;
    if (country == null) {
        if (other.country != null)
```

```
            return false;
    } else if (!country.equals(other.country))
        return false;
    if (postCode != other.postCode)
        return false;
    if (street == null) {
        if (other.street != null)
            return false;
    } else if (!street.equals(other.street))
        return false;
    if (streetNumber != other.streetNumber)
        return false;
    return true;
}
```

> Notice that Eclipse has omitted brackets when `if` or `else` statements only contain a single line of code. The dialog for creating `equals` methods does contain an option that can be checked to add brackets.

Although this method is reasonably long, it is fairly simple to understand what it is doing. This method is passed an object, and asked to return `true` or `false` depending on whether it considers itself equal to that object:

⇒ It starts by checking if the two object references refer to the same object on the heap (==): if they do it does not bother doing any more checks, because they must be equal. This is added for efficiency, the two objects would still return true based on the additional checks below.

⇒ It next checks it is not being compared to a `null` reference: if it is, it is not equal to this reference.

⇒ It then checks that the object it is being compared to is an instance of the same class – if not, there is no way they can be equal.

⇒ Finally, it goes through all the relevant fields and checks that it has the same values as the object passed in. You will notice that this uses the `equals` method provided by `String` when two `Strings` are being compared. This is necessary, because, as you have seen, two `Strings` can have the same value, but not be equal when compared with the == operator.

As a general rule all Java classes should implement the `equals` method. Although the concept has been introduced in relation to the Collections API, the `equals` method is far more widely used in Java programs, and is an important component in many APIs.

Hash Code

The second method added in the previous example is called `hashCode`. You will examine the need for hash codes in more detail shortly, but this section will briefly introduce the subject.

In essence, a hash code is a number that can be generated from the data held by an object. There are, however, a number of rules and best practices that apply when producing hash codes:

- ⇒ If two objects are equal they must generate the same hash code. The language does not enforce this rule, but failure to follow it is likely to result in difficult to find bugs.
- ⇒ If two objects produce the same hash code they do not have to be equal – **read that again because it is important, and not entirely obvious.** The reason for this is that the range of int values is potentially smaller than the number of distinct objects that can be created for a particular type. For instance, there are an infinite number of unique Strings, but only a finite number of int values to represent them.
- ⇒ Where objects are not equal it should be uncommon for them to produce the same hash code. This is not an explicit rule, but as you will see, there are good reasons for following this best practice advice.

If you are familiar with hashing algorithms such as MD5 and SHA1 this process probably sounds familiar. These algorithms produce a *hash* for a sequence of bytes. Hashing algorithms are far more advanced, however, because they must mathematically prove that collisions are very uncommon, i.e. situations where two different byte sequences produce the same hash.

As with the equals method, hashCode is defined on the Object class, but can be overridden. Technically it is possible to add an equals method without adding a hashCode method. This is not recommended because it will result in the default implementation being used, and therefore two objects may be equal, but produce different hash codes.

The following hashCode has been generated for the Address class:

```
@Override
public int hashCode() {
    final int prime = 31;
    int result = 1;
    result = prime * result + ((city == null) ? 0 :
        city.hashCode());
    result = prime * result + ((country == null) ? 0 :
        country.hashCode());
    result = prime * result + postCode;
    result = prime * result + ((street == null) ? 0 :
        street.hashCode());
    result = prime * result + streetNumber;
    return result;
}
```

The main thing to note about this method is that it is utilizing the same fields as the `equals` method to produce its answer, and as a result, if two objects are equal they will produce the same hash code.

You will also notice that this method is making heavy use of a prime number (31). This ensures that the result generated by the method is more widely distributed than it would have been if this were omitted. If Eclipse had not used a prime number as a factor, or had used a non-prime factor, you could easily have cases where two distinct objects would create the same hash code.

For instance, consider an object that had the following fields:

```
int a = 10;
int b = 20;
```

A naïve implementation of `hashCode` may simply add these values together. This would easily cause collisions in cases where the values were flipped however:

```
int a = 20;
int b = 10;
```

This is because `(10+20) = (20 + 10)`

By introducing a prime factor, however, the hash codes produced are different:

`(10 + 31) * 31 + 20 = 1291`

`(20 + 31) * 31 + 10 = 1591`

Also notice that this method invokes the `hashCode` method `Strings` inherently provide when including a `String` value in the hash code result. This implementation has been well thought out; therefore it is likely to produce better results than a custom implementation.

The method produced by Eclipse is very unlikely to produce the same `hashCode` for two objects unless they are equals. Technically it is still possible, (for instance, there will be two different `Strings` that return the same `hashCode`), but this will be very rare.

Comparing Objects

The next method you need to add to the class is a mechanism for comparing instances of an object to another object so that they can be sorted. The `Object` class does not provide a method you can override to provide this functionality, but there is an interface you can implement called `Comparable`. This interface requires you to implement a method with the following signature:

```
public int compareTo(Object o)
```

The decision of how you would like to sort objects is really up to you. Even in simple cases such as people's names, the approach to sorting is not black and white: you may sort by first name or last name.

The decision of how to sort addresses would need to be made when specifying the requirements for the program that was using addresses. For instance, in a postal delivery system they may be sorted according to the order in which delivery will occur, whereas in other systems they may be sorted by street name and number.

You will create a comparator that simply sorts addresses alphabetically based on their city. If the object that is being compared with an `Address` is not an `Address` itself, the two objects will be considered equal from a sorting perspective – i.e. you have no way of comparing them.

You may have noticed that the `compareTo` method returns an `int`. Despite this, there are only three distinct value that can be returned from the method:

⇒ **A positive number**, to indicate that this object is greater than the one it is being compared to.
⇒ **A negative number**, to indicate that this object is less than the one it is being compared to.
⇒ **Zero** to indicate that the objects are equal in terms of sort order.

I still continually forget which way round these numbers operate.

It is also important to ensure that the algorithm used to compare objects is *transitive*. For instance if A > B and B > C then it must be the case that A > C: if this principle does not hold the sorting algorithm will fail at run-time.

Start by declaring that the `Address` class implements `Comparable`:

```
public class Address implements Comparable {
```

`Comparable` is in the `java.lang` package, therefore no `import` is required.

Next, add an implementation for the `compareTo` method:

```
@Override
public int compareTo(Object o) {
    if (o instanceof Address) {
        Address other = (Address)o;
        return city.compareTo(other.getCity());
    } else {
        return 0;
    }
}
```

Notice that this implementation takes advantage of the `compareTo` implementation that already exists on `String`s in order to perform the comparison. If required, you could have invoked `toLowerCase` on both `String` instances before comparison to perform a case-insensitive comparison.

To String

Finally, you will add a `toString` implementation to `Address`. This is not technically needed, but will turn out to be useful. A native implementation of this method exists on

Object, but does not produce very meaningful output. Adding your own implementation will allow you to print a `Collection` of `Address` objects and receive sensible output.

> Whenever an object needs to be represented as a String, the `toString` method is invoked. For instance, if an object is included in string concatenation (using the + operator), `toString` is invoked on the object to produce a textual version of the object, and this is appended to the String.
>
> Unfortunately, the default implementation of `toString` is essentially meaningless.

The following `toString` implementation should be added:

```
@Override
public String toString() {
    return streetNumber + " " + street +
        ", " + city + ", " + country + "\n";
}
```

With these four methods in place you can start using the Collections API.

Lists

`Lists` are probably the most common type of `Collection` encountered in Java programs. As mentioned earlier, a `List` is an ordered collection of objects, and does not require its elements to be unique.

Lists are often used even if sorting is not required, because the Collections API does not support a general-purpose `Collection` (sometimes called a "bag") that does not care about sorting *or* uniqueness.

Rather than calling `Lists` *ordered*, it is perhaps best to think of them as *maintaining order*. By default they are ordered based on the sequence in which elements are added to them. You can change this ordering by sorting a `List`.

Because `List` is an interface, it cannot be used directly. Java provides several implementations of `List` in the Collections API; this section will focus on two: `ArrayList` and `LinkedList`.

As its name suggests, `ArrayList` provides many of the features of arrays, but can dynamically grow as elements are added. The following program adds five addresses to an `ArrayList` and then prints out the list:

```
package addresses;
import java.util.ArrayList;
import java.util.List;
```

```
public class ListsMain {
    public static void main(String[] args) {
        List addresses = new ArrayList();
        Address a1 = new Address(799, "E Dragham",
            "Tucson", 85705, "USA");
        Address a2 = new Address(200, "Main Street",
            "Phoenix", 85123, "USA");
        Address a3 = new Address(100, "Main Street",
            "Seattle", 98104, "USA");
        Address a4 = new Address(8400 , "London Place",
            "Washington", 20521, "USA");
        Address a5 = new Address(8400 , "London Place",
            "Washington", 20521, "USA");
        addresses.add(a1);
        addresses.add(a2);
        addresses.add(a3);
        addresses.add(a4);
        addresses.add(a5);
        System.out.println(addresses);
    }
}
```

Notice that the `addresses` variable has been defined as a `List`, but holds a reference to an `ArrayList`. This is best practice because it allows you to change the concrete implementation in the future (e.g. to a `LinkedList`) without impacting any other code. This approach is possible because the `List` interface supports most of the key methods for interacting with `ArrayLists`.

This program will produce the following output:

```
[799 E Dragham, Tucson, USA
, 200 Main Street, Phoenix, USA
, 100 Main Street, Seattle, USA
, 8400 London Place, Washington, USA
, 8400 London Place, Washington, USA
]
```

This demonstrates that the `List` has preserved the order of the items as they were added, and also demonstrates that the `toString` method is invoked on each element when the `List` is printed.

If you need to sort the contents of the `List` using the `compareTo` method added earlier, you must explicitly sort the contents of the `List` before printing it using the following line of code:

```
Collections.sort(addresses);
```

> The `Collections` class contains a set of static helpers for working with Collections, just as the `Arrays` class does for arrays.

With that line added immediately before the `List` is printed, the program will now output the following:

```
[200 Main Street, Phoenix, USA
, 100 Main Street, Seattle, USA
, 799 E Dragham, Tucson, USA
, 8400 London Place, Washington, USA
, 8400 London Place, Washington, USA
]
```

> I will introduce an alternative mechanism for sorting `Lists` later in the book. This is based on the `sort` method implemented directly on `Lists`.
>
> Before learning about this approach it is necessary to understand some other features added to Java 8.

The `List` interface contains the following methods for performing operations. These methods can therefore be performed on any implementation of `List`:

⇒ `add`: in addition to the `add` method seen in the code earlier, `add` can specify the index for the element. When adding an element at a specific index, all elements with a greater index have their index increased by 1

⇒ `addAll`: this can be used to add a `Collection` of elements to the `List`, thereby merging the two collections

⇒ `clear`: removes all elements from the `List`

⇒ `contains`: checks whether a specified object appears in the `List` based on the `equals` method

⇒ `get`: return the object at a specified index

⇒ `indexOf`: return the first index of a specified object (identified using the equals method)

⇒ `remove`: removes a specified object, or (if passed an `int`) the object at a specified index

⇒ `size`: returns the length of the `List`

Changing the implementation outlined earlier to use the `LinkedList` implementation is as simple as changing a single line of code:

```
List addresses = new LinkedList();
```

You may be wondering why Java provides multiple implementations of the `List` interface? The main reason is that some implementations perform better in some scenarios than others.

For instance, it is very efficient to insert an element into the middle of a large `LinkedList`, whereas it is inefficient to perform this operation on an `ArrayList`. Conversely, it is very efficient to locate an element in an `ArrayList` by its index, while this is inefficient with `LinkedLists`.

As a general rule I use `ArrayLists` for most situations. If you are writing a program that adds, sorts or searches very large lists it may be worth benchmarking which implementation provides the best performance.

Sets

As mentioned earlier, the defining characteristic of `Sets` is that all the elements must be unique (based on the implementation of the `equals` method). If you add a duplicate element to a `Set` it will replace the existing element that it is equal to.

`Set` is also an interface: the two main implementation of `Set` are `HashSet` and the `TreeSet`.

Deciding which implementation to use is somewhat simpler than with `Lists`: if the order of elements in the `Set` is not important use `HashSet`, otherwise use `TreeSet`. Operations such as `add`, `remove`, `contains` and `size` are typically far faster with `HashSet` than `TreeSet`, but `HashSets` cannot be ordered.

The performance of `Sets` is conditional on providing a good implementation of the `hashKey` method, because this provides a critical mechanism for quickly detecting duplicate elements.

For instance, when objects are added to a `Set`, they are indexed based on the value of their `hashKey`. All objects with the same `hashKey` are grouped together in *buckets*. As mentioned earlier, `hashKey` will not necessarily produce unique results, so buckets may contain more than one object, but typically the buckets will be very small.

When you add an object to a `Set`, the `Set` need to find out if there are any other elements in the `Set` that are equal to the new object.

One way of implementing this would be to iterate through all the elements in the `Set` and call `equals` on them with the new object. A far faster mechanism, however, is to find the `hashCode` of the object being added, and then locate the bucket of objects for this value (which is extremely quick, because the lookup is based on a numeric index). Once the bucket is found, the new object can be compared for equality with the objects in the bucket.

Because buckets will typically contain 0 or 1 objects, the `equals` method will probably only be invoked (at most)once per `add`.

Consider, however, what would happen if you provided the following `hashKey` implementation:

```
public int hashCode() {
    return 1;
}
```

This is actually a valid implementation of `hashKey`: if two objects are equal they will return the same `hashKey`.

Despite being valid, it would result in very poor performance when adding a new element to a Set, because it would result in the following logic:

⇒ Find the hashKey of the object passed as a parameter (1)
⇒ Find the bucket with this hashKey (the bucket would contain all objects in the Set)
⇒ Loop through these objects and check if they are equal to the object passed in.

As you can see, you have completely negated the performance optimizations associated with hashCodes and indexing.

The following program demonstrates the use of a HashSet:

```
public static void main(String[] args) {
    Set addresses = new HashSet();
    Address a1 = new Address(799, "E Dragham",
        "Tucson", 85705, "USA");
    Address a2 = new Address(200, "Main Street",
        "Phoenix", 85123, "USA");
    Address a3 = new Address(100, "Main Street",
        "Seattle", 98104, "USA");
    Address a4 = new Address(8400 , "London Place",
        "Washington", 20521, "USA");
    Address a5 = new Address(8400 , "London Place",
        "Washington", 20521, "USA");
    addresses.add(a1);
    addresses.add(a2);
    addresses.add(a3);
    addresses.add(a4);
    addresses.add(a5);
    System.out.println("Size = " + addresses.size());
    System.out.println(addresses);
}
```

This produces the following output:

```
Size = 4
[799 E Dragham, Tucson, USA
, 8400 London Place, Washington, USA
, 200 Main Street, Phoenix, USA
, 100 Main Street, Seattle, USA
]
```

Notice that even though you have added 5 elements to the Set, the Set only contains 4 elements: this is because the final two addresses added to the Set meet the definition of equality defined by Address, and therefore the second instance overwrites the first.

Also notice that the order in which the addresses are printed out does not match the order they were added; HashSet makes no attempts to maintain any order.

An example using TreeSet would look identical; except the output would adhere to the order the elements were added. I will leave you to implement that yourself.

Maps

The Map interface is part of the Collections API, but unlike List and Set it does not extend the `Collection` interface. The primary reason for this is that each entry in a `Map` consists of two parts: a key and a value. This means that adding an element to a `Map` requires two values to be provided rather than one.

In some ways `Maps` are like `HashSets`: both data structures use indexed keys to facilitate fast lookup. The main difference is that with `HashSets` the key is implicitly generated from the `hashKey` method, whereas with `Maps` the key is explicitly provided, and therefore allows two otherwise unrelated objects to be associated with one another.

The two most common implementations of `Map` are `HashMap` and `TreeMap`. The main difference between these implementations is that `TreeMaps` sort elements based on their key, while `HashMaps` do not. `HashMap` should be your preferred option unless you have a specific reason for needing sorting, because it generally provides superior performance.

Consider a case where you want to quickly retrieve the `Address` of a particular person. You will start by defining a very simple `Person` class and adding `hashCode` and `equals` methods:

```java
package addresses;
public class Person {
    String firstName;
    String lastName;

    public Person(String firstName, String lastName ) {
        this.firstName = firstName;
        this.lastName = lastName;
    }
    @Override
    public String toString() {
        return "Person [firstName=" + firstName +
            ", lastName=" + lastName + "]";
    }

    @Override
    public int hashCode() {
        final int prime = 31;
        int result = 1;
        result = prime * result +
            ((firstName == null) ? 0 : firstName.hashCode());
        result = prime * result +
            ((lastName == null) ? 0 : lastName.hashCode());
        return result;
    }

    @Override
    public boolean equals(Object obj) {
        if (this == obj)
            return true;
        if (obj == null)
            return false;
        if (getClass() != obj.getClass())
            return false;
        Person other = (Person) obj;
        if (firstName == null) {
```

```
            if (other.firstName != null)
                return false;
        } else if (!firstName.equals(other.firstName))
            return false;
        if (lastName == null) {
            if (other.lastName != null)
                return false;
        } else if (!lastName.equals(other.lastName))
            return false;
        return true;
    }
}
```

> Getters and setters have been omitted for brevity, and the fields have instead been defined using the default access modifier. You can choose to use `private` fields and getters and setters in your version.

Next, you will write a short program that associates `Person` and `Address` instances:

```
package addresses;
import java.util.HashMap;
import java.util.Map;

public class MapMain {
    public static void main(String[] args) {
        Address a1 = new Address(799, "E Dragham",
            "Tucson", 85705, "USA");
        Address a2 = new Address(200, "Main Street",
            "Phoenix", 85123, "USA");
        Address a3 = new Address(100, "Main Street",
            "Seattle", 98104, "USA");

        Person p1 = new Person("Dane", "Cameron");
        Person p2 = new Person("James", "Smith");
        Person p3 = new Person("Keith", "Rogers");
        Person p4 = new Person("Owen", "Heart");

        Map people = new HashMap();
        people.put(p1, a3);
        people.put(p2, a1);
        people.put(p3, a2);
        people.put(p4, a1);

        System.out.println("Dane lives at " + people.get(p1));
        people.put(p1, a2);
        System.out.println("Now Dane lives at " + people.get(p1));
    }
}
```

This produces the following output:

```
Dane lives at 100 Main Street, Seattle, USA
Now Dane lives at 200 Main Street, Phoenix, USA
```

`Maps` enforce a number of rules:

⇒ Each key can only occur once in the `Map`, if you `put` a key that already exists, the value associated with this will be updated. This is why the `Address` for Dane changed in the example program.

⇒ `null` values can be used for both the key and the value, but there can only be a single entry with a `null` key.

`Maps` generally provide extremely good performance when accessing values based on their key. This is, however, dependent on the object being used as the key providing a `hashCode` implementation that produced well-distributed values, because, as with `Sets`, lookups are optimized through the use of the `hashCode`.

Generics

Before continuing any further it is worth taking a step back and talking about *generics*. Generics were retrofitted into the Java language with Java 5 and allow any type (for instance, `ArrayList`, `HashSet`, or types you defined yourself) to operate on other types in a type-safe manner.

The Collections you have created so far in this chapter operate on any type derived from `Object`. This means that if you wish to extract elements from a `Collection`, you need to know what type they are, and cast them appropriately. This can be a major source of run-time bugs; for instance, the following code compiles, but generates a `ClassCastException` at run-time.

```java
public static void main(String[] args) {
    List addresses = new LinkedList();
    Address a1 = new Address(799, "E Dragham",
        "Tucson", 85705, "USA");
    addresses.add(a1);
    Person p1 = new Person("Dane", "Cameron");
    addresses.add(p1);
    Address a = (Address) addresses.get(1);
}
```

The cause of the exception is obvious: a `Person` has been cast as an `Address` - an issue that only becomes apparent at run-time.

A better way to write this code is to define what types the `List` will contain, and allow the compiler to ensure all operations on the `List` conform to this type. All of the classes in the Collections API have been defined to work with generics in order to facilitate this.

You can define a `List` for `Address` objects as follows:

```java
List<Address> addresses = new LinkedList<Address>();
```

In fact, as of Java 7 this can be simplified as follows:

```java
List<Address> addresses = new LinkedList<>();
```

The key difference in this declaration is the angle brackets. The value `<Address>` is provided when the `LinkedList` is created, it therefore acts like a parameter – and represents the type that the `List` can store. Once you make this change you will notice that the following line no longer compiles:

```
addresses.add(p1);
```

The compiler has determined that you are attempting to store a `Person` in the `List`, and realizes this is invalid.

You will also notice that you are able to extract `Address` objects from the `List` without casting:

```
Address a = addresses.get(0);
```

The compiler knows this is a type safe operation; therefore it does not force you to cast the value returned from `get`.

Generics are an extremely useful feature of the Java language. They allow API designers to design a generic interface, and then allow the user of the API to specify the types that they wish to use with the API. The generic API then acts as though it had been custom written for these types. For instance, the `LinkedList` acts as though it was written specifically with our `Address` objects in mind.

In the case of `Maps` you need to specify two types: one for the key and one for the value. The example in `MapMain` can therefore be rewritten:

```
Map<Person, Address> people = new HashMap<>();
```

It is also possible to nest generic declarations. For instance, this line of code declares a `Map` where a `Person` is the key and the value is a `List` of `Address` objects:

```
Map<Person, List<Address>> people = new HashMap<>();
```

Notice that one set of angle brackets is nested inside the other.

Generics and Inheritance

It is important to understand how generics work with inheritance, because the behavior is not as intuitive as you may expect. In order to demonstrate this, you will use the `Shape` hierarchy of classes from earlier in the book.

It will probably come as no surprise that the following is valid:

```
public static void main(String[] args) {
    List<Shape> shapes = new ArrayList<>();
    shapes.add(new Square());
}
```

If a `List` is defined to store instances of `Shape`, there is no problem adding instances of `Square` to it.

Things become slightly trickier, however, when you start dealing with the `Lists` themselves rather than their contents. Consider the following invalid example:

```
public static void main(String[] args) {
    List<Square> squares = new ArrayList<>();
```

```
        squares.add(new Square());
        List<Shape> shapes = squares;
}
```

This contains the following invalid line:

```
List<Shape> shapes = squares;
```

It may not be immediately obvious why this is invalid. A `List` defined to store instances of `Square` is being assigned to a variable defined to store a `List` of `Shape` instances. The `List` of `Squares` is clearly a `List` of `Shapes`, so why would this not be valid?

Consider what may happen if this was valid: the next line of the program may perform the following operation:

```
shapes.add(new Circle());
```

From the point of view of a `List` of `Shapes`, this would be a valid line of code, because a `List` of `Shapes` can contain `Circles`: but remember that another variable has a reference to this `List`, and it thinks it is a `List` of `Squares`. If the next line of the program were the following, a `Circle` would be returned when a `Square` was expected:

```
Square s = squares.get(1);
```

This constraint can be an annoyance: consider the following invalid code:

```
public static void main(String[] args) {
    List<Square> squares = new ArrayList<>();
    List<Circle> circles = new ArrayList<>();
    squares.add(new Square());
    circles.add(new Circle());
    printFirstElement(squares);
    printFirstElement(circles);
}
private static void printFirstElement(List<Shape> shapes) {
    System.out.println(shapes.get(0));
}
```

In this example it is not possible to pass an instance of `List<Square>` or `List<Circle>` to a method that declares a parameter of type `List<Shape>`. This is a major limitation, because it prevents you from creating methods that act on a wide variety of types in an inheritance hierarchy.

Fortunately there is a solution to this problem; the method can be defined as follows:

```
private static void printFirstElement(List<? extends Shape> shapes) {
    System.out.println(shapes.get(0));
}
```

In this case you are stating that the parameter can be any `List` of a type that extends `Shape`: so both `Lists` defined in the `main` method can be passed to this method.

Obviously there is a problem here: what if `printFirstElement` adds a `Circle` to a `List` of `Squares`? Because the compiler cannot check that an object added to a `List` such as this is consistent with the underlying type, it is not possible for `printFirstElement` to add to the `List` – it must treat the `List` as read-only.

Iterators and For Loops

Probably the most common operation that is performed on a `Collection` is to iterate over its elements. Iterating simply means accessing each element one-by-one. Prior to Java 8, Java provided two primary mechanisms for this: a special type of `for` loop, and the `Iterator` class. Java 8 introduces another mechanism called a `Stream`: this will be examined in future chapters.

The most convenient way to iterate over a `Collection` is with the `for`-loop. This can be achieved as follows:

```java
public static void main(String[] args) {
    List<Address> addresses = new ArrayList<>();
    addresses.add(new Address(799, "E Dragham",
        "Tucson", 85705, "USA"));
    addresses.add(new Address(200, "Main Street",
        "Phoenix", 85123, "USA"));
    addresses.add(new Address(100, "Main Street",
        "Seattle", 98104, "USA"));
    addresses.add(new Address(8400 , "London Place",
        "Washington", 20521, "USA"));
    for (Address a : addresses) {
        System.out.println(a);
    }
}
```

Notice that the syntax is different from the `for`-loops seen earlier in the book. In this type of `for`-loop the first part of the definition - `Address a` - is a declaration of the variable the elements in the `List` should be assigned to on each iteration. The second part of the declaration is the `Collection` that will be iterated over.

This approach works for any implementation extending `Collection`. It is less common to iterate `Maps`, but this can be achieved by invoking the `values` method of `Map` to return a `Collection` of the values stored in the `Map`.

Collection-based `for`-loops are relatively new to Java. Prior to their availability `Iterators` were the conventional way to iterate over a `Collection`:

```java
public static void main(String[] args) {
    List<Address> addresses = new ArrayList<>();
    addresses.add(new Address(799, "E Dragham",
        "Tucson", 85705, "USA"));
    addresses.add(new Address(200, "Main Street",
        "Phoenix", 85123, "USA"));
    addresses.add(new Address(100, "Main Street",
        "Seattle", 98104, "USA"));
    addresses.add(new Address(8400 , "London Place",
        "Washington", 20521, "USA"));
    java.util.Iterator<Address> iter = addresses.iterator();
    while (iter.hasNext()) {
        Address a = iter.next();
        System.out.println(a);
    }
}
```

As you can see, declaring and using `Iterators` is more verbose than using `for`-loops, which is why they have fallen out of favor. The `Iterator` must first be declared, and then a `while`-loop is used to check whether there are any further elements in the `Collection` with the `hasNext` method. If there are more elements in the `Collection`, the next element is obtained inside the `while` loop using the `next` method.

> Iterators are a design pattern in their own right, and were commonly used in other languages before the advent of Java.

An important consideration with both iteration approaches is that it is typically not possible to modify the `Collection` during the iteration process. For instance, the following code throws a `ConcurrentModificationException`:

```
while (iter.hasNext()) {
    Address a = iter.next();
    System.out.println(a);
    addresses.remove(a);
}
```

> Some implementations of `List` do allow this, notably the `CopyOnWriteArrayList` implementation.

If you need to modify a `Collection` during iteration, it is possible to use the `remove` method on the `Iterator` itself, and this is one of the key reasons `Iterators` are still used:

```
Iterator<Address> iter = addresses.iterator();
while (iter.hasNext()) {
    Address a = iter.next();
    System.out.println(a);
    iter.remove();
}
```

Implementations of `List` also provide an alternative type of `Iterator` called a `ListIterator`:

```
ListIterator<Address> iter = (ListIterator<Address>) addresses.listIterator();
```

This provides all the same basic functionality of conventional `Iterators`, but allows navigation backwards as well as forwards.

18 GENERICS

In the previous chapter you learned how to use *generics* when using third party APIs. This chapter will show you how you can write your own APIs that take advantage of the power of generics.

Generics are one of the key ways you can add value to APIs you write. If you write a generic API that can be used with a variety of types you should consider incorporating generics into it. This will ensure code using your API can obtain the benefits of type safety that generics bring.

In this chapter you will explore generics by writing your own implementation of a `LinkedList`. This will not only give you an idea of how generics work, it will help consolidate your knowledge of the Collections API.

What is a Linked List?

Linked lists are common data structures in programming. A linked list always has a root node that represents the start of the list. Each node can then hold an optional reference to the next node in the list, along with a value. If a node does not have a reference to a "next" node, it is the last node in the list. A representation of a linked list is shown in figure 18-1:

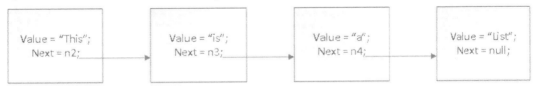

FIGURE 18-1

Implementation

You will begin your implementation by defining the class that will represent each `Node` in the list. This needs to contain two fields: the `value` of this node, and a reference to the next `Node` in the list. These fields will both use generics, because when the linked list is used, you want the user to define the type that it will store.

The following is an implementation of the `Node` class:

```
package linkedlist;
public class Node<T> {
    private Node<T> next;
    private T value;

    public Node(T value, Node<T> next) {
        this.value = value;
        this.next = next;
    }
    public Node<T> getNext() {
        return next;
    }
    public void setNext(Node<T> next) {
        this.next = next;
    }
    public T getValue() {
        return value;
    }
    public void setValue(T value) {
        this.value = value;
    }
}
```

If you look at the class declaration you will see something you have not seen before: the class is declared as `Node<T>`. Node is naturally the class name, while `<T>` represents a placeholder for the types that can be passed to this class when it is constructed.

The value `T` has no special significance. It is conventional to use single, capitalized letters as placeholders for types (e.g. `T`, `E`), but this is not enforced. If this class accepted two types (like `Map` does), it would define a comma-separated list of types, for instance, `Node<T, E>`.

Once this placeholder type has been declared you can start using it in place of concrete types. For instance, if you look at the field definition for `value` you will see it has been defined as follows:

```
private T value;
```

This essentially means that `value` will be of type `T`, where `T` will be specified when an instance of `Node` is created. The `Node` class does not care what type is provided, because it does not interact with this type in any meaningful way.

If `Node` needed the type to be restricted in some manner, it could use the following syntax:

```
public class Node<T extends Shape> {
```

This would mean any type could be provided, as long as it implemented `Shape`.

Things get slightly more complicated with the declaration of the `next` field. Remember, this field provides a reference to the next `Node` in the list. This field therefore will contain a reference to an object of type `Node`, but more specifically, it will be a `Node` operating on the same type as this `Node`. Therefore this has been declared as follows:

```
private Node<T> next;
```

Notice that the getters and setters for this field follow the same convention.

You will next turn your attention to the linked list itself. This will contain the following methods:

⇒ `addFirst` : this will add a new `Node` to the start of the list
⇒ `addLast` : this will add a new `Node` to the end of the list
⇒ `print`: this will print the list

This implementation will be kept reasonably short, because these methods alone are sufficient to gain an understanding of generics. If you want, you can extend the implementation to include more of the methods you have seen in the Collections API. You could even implement the `List` interface itself and thereby extend the Collections API.

You will call your linked list `LinkedList2` so as not to confuse it with the version provided by Java:

```
package linkedlist;
public class LinkedList2<T> {
    Node<T> head;

    public LinkedList2() {}

    public void addFirst(T value) {
        if (head == null) {
            head = new Node<T>(value, null);
        } else {
            Node<T> newHead = new Node<T>(value, head);
            head = newHead;
        }
    }
}
```

Notice that this class also accepts a type `<T>`. The fact that you have used T again is not significant, you could have used any value to denote this type: I prefer to use T because it is short for "type".

The only field that the linked list will need is a reference to the head (first node) of the list. Once it has a reference to this it can navigate the entire list using the `next` field of each `Node`.

This initial version has provided an `addFirst` method. This first checks to see if the list already has a head node. If it does not, the list is empty, and you can simply create a new `Node` to act as the head node. This will not have a value for its `next` field; therefore you simply pass `null` to the `Node` constructor.

Notice that when `Node` is instantiated you specify that it also operates on the same type as the list, as denoted by T. The list still does not know what this type will be, it just knows that `LinkedList2` and `Node` both operate on the same type.

If the list does already have a head node, you still want to construct a new `Node`, but you want to make the newly created `Node` the head of the list, and the old head of the list will be set in its `next` field.

You can also add the `addLast` method:

```
public void addLast(T value) {
    if (head == null) {
        head = new Node<T>(value, null);
    } else {
        Node<T> lastNode = head;
        while (lastNode.getNext() != null) {
            lastNode = lastNode.getNext();
        }
        Node<T> node = new Node<T>(value, null);
        lastNode.setNext(node);
    }
}
```

This method starts out the same as the `addFirst` method: if the list is empty a new `Node` is set as the `head` node.

If the list is not empty, you need to navigate the list until you find a `Node` that does not have a `next` Node – by definition this is the end of the list. When you find this `Node` you create a new `Node` to represent the new end of the list – and then tell the current last `Node` that this is its `next` Node.

Finally, you can add the `print` method to the list. This simply iterates through all the Nodes, and prints their `value`:

```
public void print() {
    Node<T> lastNode = head;
    while (lastNode != null) {
        System.out.println(lastNode.getValue());
        lastNode = lastNode.getNext();
    }
}
```

Now that you have created the API you can try it out. The following program uses the API and specifies that it contains instances of `String`:

```
package linkedlist;
public class Main {
    public static void main(String[] args) {
        LinkedList2<String> list = new LinkedList2<>();
        list.addFirst("First value");
        list.addLast("Last value");
        list.addFirst("New first value");
        list.addLast("New last value");
        list.print();
    }
```

}

If you run this program it will output the following:

```
New first value
First value
Last value
New last value
```

You can also verify for yourself that it is not possible to add anything but `Strings` to the list. For instance, the following line will produce a compilation error:

```
list.addLast(new Integer(22));
```

It is worth noting that just because your class supports generics does not mean users of the class have to provide the relevant types. It is possible to instantiate `LinkedList2` as follows:

```
LinkedList2 list = new LinkedList2();
```

In this case any type can be inserted into the list, and the `LinkedList2` class will not provide any form of type safety to the user of the API.

DANE CAMERON

19 UNIT TESTING

This chapter will take you on a slight diversion into the world of unit testing. Unit tests are automated tests used for verifying code. Java supports a popular library called JUnit that allows Unit Tests to be written in Java, and executed within the Eclipse IDE (or outside the Eclipse IDE if required). This library will be the subject of this chapter.

Unit tests are an important mechanism for maintaining code quality, and most Java programmers attempt to provide coverage for most of their code in a set of automated unit tests. The beauty of unit tests is that once they are written, it is trivial to execute a large set of tests in a short period of time, and thereby have a reasonable level of confidence that your code is correct. This is particularly useful when modifying existing code.

A typical unit test will execute a block of Java code and obtain a result. It will then make various *assertions* about that result; for instance, it may assert that the result is the number 100. If all the assertions in a test pass, the unit test is considered to have passed.

In this chapter you will develop a set of unit tests for some of the code already written in this book. The tests developed will utilize JUnit version 4. Eclipse may ask you which version of JUnit you wish to utilize; if so, choose version 4.

Basic Tests

You will begin by creating a basic test for the `Address` class in the Collections project. To begin, locate the `Address` class and right click on it. From the menu that appears choose `New -> JUnit Test Case`. This will present you with a dialog as seen in figure 19-1; simply accept the default values by clicking "Finish":

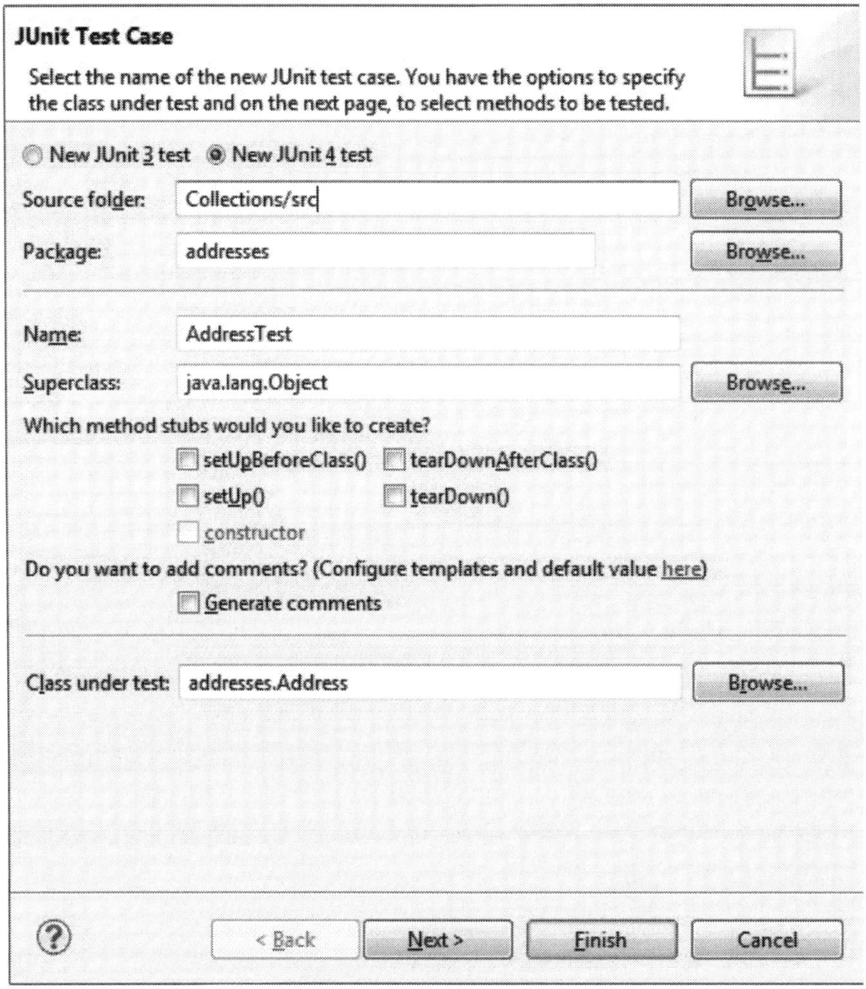

FIGURE 19-1

This will create the Unit Tests in the same folder as the source code.

It is also common to create a new source folder called `tests`: if you would prefer to use this approach right click on the project and choose `New -> Source Folder`, and call the folder `tests`. Once created, you can browse to this source folder and set it as the `Source Folder` for any tests when creating them.

Eclipse will generate the following class:

```
package addresses;
import static org.junit.Assert.*;
import org.junit.Test;
public class AddressTest {

    @Test
    public void test() {
        fail("Not yet implemented");
    }
```

}

The key feature of this class is the method marked with the annotation `@Test`. When this class is executed as a jUnit test, any methods marked with this annotation will be automatically executed, and will either pass or fail.

In order to execute this class as a unit test, simply right click on the class and select `Run As -> Unit Test`. Eclipse will open a new view for displaying the unit test results, which should appear as per figure 19-2:

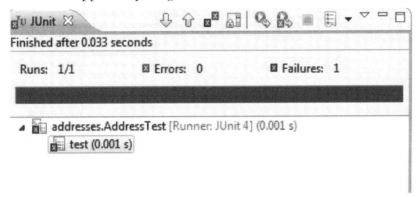

FIGURE 19-2

The red bar indicates the test has failed: this is due to the fact that the test currently calls `fail`.

You may be wondering where the `fail` method came from, because this class does not support a `fail` method, and it doesn't extend any other classes? It comes from the `static import` on the following line:

```
import static org.junit.Assert.*;
```

This statement requests that all `static` methods in the specified class be imported into the class, meaning they can be executed without prefixing them with their class name. Once a `static import` is performed, it is as though the `static` methods imported were defined in this class. Static imports are not specific to unit tests, you can use them in any of your classes.

The code is therefore effectively executing the following statement:

```
Assert.fail("Not yet implemented");
```

You will begin by adding a test for the `equals` method:

```
package addresses;
import static org.junit.Assert.*;
import org.junit.Test;

public class AddressTest {
    @Test
    public void testEquals() {
        Address a1 = new Address(1, "Main Road",
```

```
        "Vicksburg", 57332, "USA");
    Address a2 = new Address(1, "Main Road",
        "Vicksburg", 57332, "USA");
    Address a3 = new Address(2, "Main Road",
        "Vicksburg", 57332, "USA");
    assertEquals(a1, a2);
    assertFalse(a1.equals(a3));
    assertFalse(a1.equals("Hello World"));
    }
}
```

The `Assert` class contains a wide variety of `static` methods for *asserting* specific scenarios.

This test verifies three scenarios, and includes both positive and negative scenarios. If you run this as a unit test it will produce a green bar, as seen in figure 19-3:

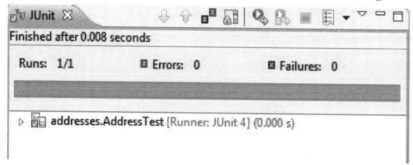

FIGURE 19-3

Next you will add a two more tests to verify the `hashCode` and `toString` methods:

```
@Test
public void testHashKey() {
    Address a1 = new Address(1, "Main Road",
        "Vicksburg", 57332, "USA");
    Address a2 = new Address(1, "Main Road",
        "Vicksburg", 57332, "USA");
    Address a3 = new Address(2, "Main Road",
        "Vicksburg", 57332, "USA");
    assertEquals(a1.hashCode(), a2.hashCode());
    assertFalse(a1.hashCode() == a3.hashCode());
}

@Test
public void testToString() {
    Address a1 = new Address(1, "Main Road",
        "Vicksburg", 57332, "USA");
    Address a2 = new Address(2, "West Road",
        "Mobile", 44332, "USA");
    assertEquals(a1.toString(), "1 Main Road, Vicksburg, USA\n");
    assertEquals(a2.toString(), "2 West Road, Mobile, USA\n");
}
```

Finally, you will add a method for verifying the `compareTo` method:

```
@Test
```

```
public void testSort() {
    Address a1 = new Address(1, "Main Road",
        "Vicksburg", 57332, "USA");
    Address a2 = new Address(1, "Main Road",
        "Mobile", 65544, "USA");
    Address a3 = new Address(2, "Main Road",
        "Los Angeles", 90787, "USA");
    List<Address> addresses = Arrays.asList(a1, a2, a3);
    Collections.sort(addresses);
    assertEquals(a1, addresses.get(2));
    assertEquals(a3, addresses.get(0));
}
```

Notice the `asList` helper method on `Arrays` can be used to construct a `List` from an array.

If you run this class as a unit test now, Eclipse should confirm all 4 tests pass, as seen in figure 19-4:

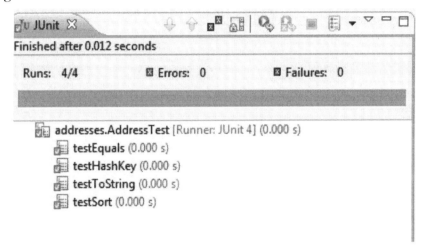

FIGURE 19-4

These examples demonstrate how simple most unit tests can be.

JUnit also supports a number of other useful annotations that you should be aware of.

Sometimes it is useful to set up the same data for all tests prior to any tests executing. This can be achieved by annotating a method with `@BeforeClass`, and performing any relevant data initialization in the body of that method:

```
@BeforeClass
public void constructList() {
}
```

jUnit also supports a `@Before` annotation that fulfills a similar role, but is executed before each test is executed. This is useful if the tests will modify the data, and where it is necessary to reset the data after each test.

Additionally, jUnit also supports `@After` and `@AfterClass` annotations that allow you to provide methods that will be executed after each test, or all the tests in the class have executed.

Eclipse will generate stubs for these methods if you select the options shown in figure 19-5 when creating a unit test:

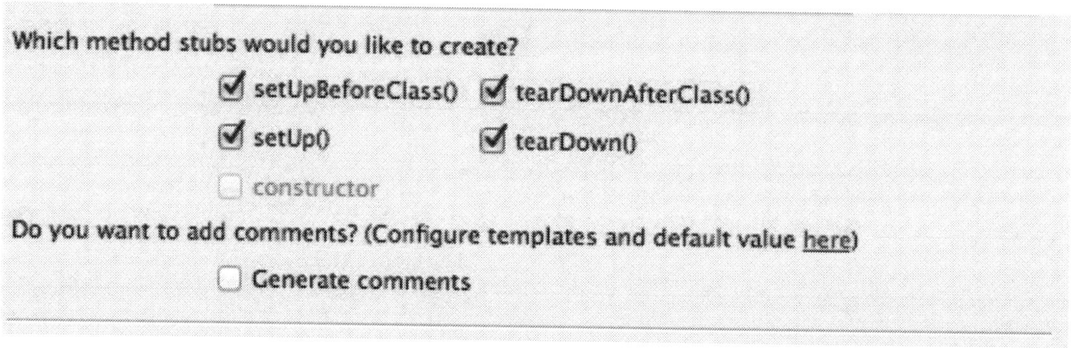

Which method stubs would you like to create?
- ☑ setUpBeforeClass() ☑ tearDownAfterClass()
- ☑ setUp() ☑ tearDown()
- ☐ constructor

Do you want to add comments? (Configure templates and default value here)
- ☐ Generate comments

FIGURE 19-5

Although unit tests are simple, they are enormously powerful. As programs grow in size it can be difficult to know what each line in the program does, and what the impact of changing a line of code will be. Unit tests are therefore designed to give you the confidence to change (or *refactor*) code: if you break existing functionality the unit tests will tell you.

In fact, many programmers actually write their unit tests before writing program logic. The unit test specifies the expected behavior of the code, and you therefore know that you have met these expectations once all the unit tests pass.

20 ENUMERATED TYPES

If you think about the `boolean` data-type, it is simply a type with a defined list of values: `true` and `false`. There are many other cases where it is convenient to define data-types with a pre-defined set of possible values. For instance, the days of the week or the months of the year both have predefined sets of values. Java provides a feature called enums (enumerated types) that allow you to define types such as this.

Working with enums

Enums are technically objects, but unlike traditional objects their types are declared as `enum` rather than a `class`:

```
package enums;
public enum DaysOfWeek {
    Monday,Tuesday,Wednesday,Thursday,Friday,Saturday,Sunday;
}
```

Notice that the list of values are not `Strings` (they do not have double quotes around them), therefore they follow the same rules as Java variables, and cannot contain spaces or other extraneous characters. Each value is separated from the next by a comma, and the list is concluded with an optional semi-colon.

Many programmers prefer to use capital letters for enumerated type values, because they are essentially constants. This remains an area where there is no strong convention in either direction, however, so you can use the convention you prefer.

Just as all classes implicitly extend `Object`, all enumerated types implicitly extend `java.lang.Enum`. This provides a set of utility methods to each `enum`.

> Enum itself extends `Object`, meaning that `enums` also support

> familiar methods such as `toString` and `equals`.

Once an `enum` has been declared, it can be used as follows:

```java
package enums;
public class UsingEnums {
    public static void main(String[] args) {
        DaysOfWeek monday = DaysOfWeek.Monday;
        DaysOfWeek sunday = DaysOfWeek.Sunday;
    }
}
```

Enumerated types can be compared against other enumerated types for equality, and they can be used as the input to a `switch` statement (something that is not possible with regular objects).

A further interesting feature of `enums` is that it is possible to associate additional data with each value. This can be achieved via a constructor on the `enum` itself that is then invoked as each value is defined. The constructor must be `private` due to the fact it can only be used by the `enum` itself:

```java
package enums;

public enum DaysOfWeek {
    Monday(true),Tuesday(true),Wednesday(true),Thursday(true),
        Friday(true),Saturday(false),Sunday(false);

    private DaysOfWeek(boolean weekday) {
        this.weekday = weekday;
    }
    private boolean weekday;
    public boolean isWeekday() {
        return weekday;
    }
}
```

In the case of an `enum`, the constructor must appear below the list of values.

Notice that enumerated types can also define a set of fields and methods for accessing this data. Each enum value stores its own independent data. Therefore, once data has been associated with each value, other objects that utilize these enumerated types can access this data:

```java
package enums;
public class UsingEnums {
    public static void main(String[] args) {
        DaysOfWeek monday = DaysOfWeek.Monday;
        DaysOfWeek sunday = DaysOfWeek.Sunday;
        System.out.println("Monday is a weekday? :" +
            monday.isWeekday());
        System.out.println("Sunday is a weekday? :" +
            sunday.isWeekday());
    }
```

}

It is important to understand that the data associated with each `enum` value should remain constant during the program execution: enumerated types represent static data, and as such, their data should not be subject to change.

Conclusion

It is not necessary to use enumerated types in your programs, in fact enumerated types did not exist in Java until relatively recently. It is perfectly feasible to use `Strings` in place of `enums`. There are, however, some real advantages to using `enums`:

- ⇒ Enumerated types clearly identify the possible values for a field. If `Strings` are used it is not always immediately obvious what value should be used. For instance, should *Tuesday* be represented as Tuesday, TUESDAY or Tues.
- ⇒ It is possible to associate extra information with each value, thereby creating more complex types.
- ⇒ It is always possible to compare `enums` with the `==` operator: as you have seen this is not always possible with `Strings`.
- ⇒ Although it may not be immediately obvious, it is possible for `enums` to implement an interface. This ensures `enum` values can be used wherever the corresponding interface is expected.

21 INNER CLASSES

Up until this point all the classes you have created have existed as independent entities, capable of being instantiated by any code with the appropriate permissions.

Java supports an additional type of class called an inner class. Inner classes provide a mechanism for nesting classes inside other classes. There are in fact four types of inner class:

⇒ Inner classes
⇒ Static inner classes
⇒ Local classes
⇒ Anonymous inner classes

This chapter will examine these four types of inner class, and take a look at where and when they can be useful.

> Don't confuse inner classes with the examples earlier in the book that defined multiple classes in the same class file. There was nothing special about these classes as a result of the way they were declared: it was simply a matter of convenience.

Before starting this chapter it is worth pointing out that Java 8 includes a new feature called lambda expressions that provide many of the benefits of inner classes, but offer other significant advantages. While the next chapter will cover lambda expressions, it is worth ensuring that you understand inner classes before moving on to an understanding of lambda expressions. Once you understand inner classes it will be far easier to understand the rationale for lambda expressions.

Inner classes

Inner classes allow a class to be nested inside another class. An instance of an inner class can only exist inside an instance of its wrapper class, and when instantiated, has special privileges when performing operations on its wrapper.

Although there is a parent and child relationship between the class and the inner class, do not fall into the trap of thinking that inner classes are related to inheritance: as you will see, inner classes and inheritance are fulfilling very different functions in the language.

In this section you will create a shopping cart program. Each shopping cart can hold a list of products; therefore start by creating a class to represent products:

```java
package innerclasses;
public class Product {
    private String name;
    private Double price;

    public Product(String name, Double price) {
        this.name = name;
        this.price = price;
    }

    public String getName() {
        return name;
    }
    public Double getPrice() {
        return price;
    }
    @Override
    public int hashCode() {
        final int prime = 31;
        int result = 1;
         result = prime * result + ((name == null) ? 0 :
            name.hashCode());
        result = prime * result + ((price == null) ? 0 :
             price.hashCode());
        return result;
    }
    @Override
    public boolean equals(Object obj) {
        if (this == obj)
            return true;
        if (obj == null)
            return false;
        if (getClass() != obj.getClass())
            return false;
        Product other = (Product) obj;
        if (name == null) {
            if (other.name != null)
                return false;
        } else if (!name.equals(other.name))
            return false;
        if (price == null) {
            if (other.price != null)
                return false;
```

```
            } else if (!price.equals(other.price))
                return false;
            return true;
        }
    }
```

This is a conventional class with two fields: name and price. It also provides implementations of equals and hashCode.

You will now create a ShoppingCart class for holding products. The Shopping cart needs to be able to hold more than one of each product and therefore you will create an inner class within ShoppingCart called Item that will encapsulate a product and a quantity. The reason for making this an inner class is that no code outside the ShoppingCart ever needs to deal with Items directly: the concept is private to ShoppingCart:

```
package innerclasses;

import java.util.ArrayList;
import java.util.List;

public class ShoppingCart {
    private List<Item> items = new ArrayList<>();
    public ShoppingCart() {}

    public void addProduct(Product p) {
        boolean found = false;
        for (Item item : items) {
            if (item.matches(p)) {
                item.increaseTotal();
                found = true;
            }
        }
        if (!found) {
            items.add(new Item(p));
        }
    }
    public void removeProduct(Product p) {
        for (Item item : items) {
            if (item.matches(p)) {
                item.decreaseTotal();
            }
        }
    }
    public void printCart() {
        double total = 0;
        for (Item item : items) {
            total += item.getTotalPrice();
            System.out.println(item.getDisplay());
        }
        System.out.printf("The total is : $%f\n\n", total);
    }
    private class Item {
        private Product product;
        private Integer qty;
```

```
        Item(Product product) {
            this.product = product;
            this.qty = 1;
        }
        void increaseTotal() {
            qty += 1;
        }
        void decreaseTotal() {
            qty = Math.max(0, qty-1);
        }
        boolean matches(Product p) {
            return this.product.equals(p);
        }
        Double getTotalPrice() {
            return qty*product.getPrice();
        }
        String getDisplay() {
            if (qty == 0) {
                return product.getName() + " has been removed";
            } else {
                return qty + " x " + product.getName() +
                    " ($" + (product.getPrice() * qty) + ")";
            }
        }
    }
}
```

The `ShoppingCart` supports three core methods:

⇒ `addProduct`: this creates an `Item` from a `Product` and adds it to the `ShoppingCart`. If the product is in the `ShoppingCart`, this method simply increases the `quantity` stored against the `Item`

⇒ `removeProduct`: this reduces the quantity purchased for the relevant `Product` by 1

⇒ `printCart`: this prints the current state of the `ShoppingCart`

As you can see, the Shopping cart contains the following inner class declaration:

```
private class Item {
```

Once the inner class has been declared, the outer class can use it just like a regular class, but because this class is `private` it is hidden from the rest of the program, and the rest of the program will be completely unaware of its existence.

In order to see this class in action run the following program:

```
package innerclasses;
public class Main {
    public static void main(String[] args) {
        Product i1 = new Product("The Sun Also Rises", 9.99);
        Product i2 = new Product("The Old Man and the Sea", 7.99);
        Product i3 = new Product("For Whom the Bell Tolls", 7.99);
        ShoppingCart cart = new ShoppingCart();
        cart.addProduct(i1);
```

```
            cart.addProduct(i2);
            cart.addProduct(i2);
            cart.addProduct(i3);
            cart.printCart();
            cart.removeProduct(i3);
            cart.printCart();
     }
}
```

This will print the following:

```
1 x The Sun Also Rises ($9.99)
2 x The Old Man and the Sea ($15.98)
1 x For Whom the Bell Tolls ($7.99)
The total is : $33.960000

1 x The Sun Also Rises ($9.99)
2 x The Old Man and the Sea ($15.98)
For Whom the Bell Tolls has been removed
The total is : $25.970000
```

In one sense inner classes are a mechanism for aiding encapsulation. Because you do not want the `Item` class exposed to any other code, declaring it inside the `ShoppingCart` class fully encapsulates its functionality in the `ShoppingCart`. Although this could have been achieved with access modifiers, nesting one class within the other makes their relationship to one another more explicit.

Inner classes also offer other advantages that would not be found in stand-alone classes:

⇒ The inner class has access to all the fields and methods of the outer class, including its `private` fields and methods.
⇒ The inner class can access the `this` reference of the outer class as follows: `ShoppingCart.this.items.clear();`
⇒ The outer class has full access to the inner class, including its `private` methods and fields.

As these points demonstrate, the outer and inner classes have a very special relationship with one another. Although they are independent in some sense, they can perform many of the same operations, and have most of the same privileges, as a method on a class.

In the previous example, the `Item` class has been made `private`. Inner classes can be declared with any access modifier required, meaning they can potentially be instantiated by classes other than their outer class.

If you were to make `Item` a `public` class, it still could not be instantiated without a `ShoppingCart` to act as its outer class. The manner in which an inner class is instantiated from outside its parent is therefore not entirely intuitive:

```
ShoppingCart cart = new ShoppingCart();
Product i1 = new Product("The Sun Also Rises", 9.99);
cart.new Item(i1);
```

Notice that the `new` keyword is invoked on an instance of `ShoppingCart`: the outer class of the newly created `Item` will therefore be the `ShoppingCart` instance represented by the variable `cart`.

Once an inner class is instantiated it is no different from any other class: its fields and methods can be accessed based on their access modifiers. The fact that the inner class may access functionality on its outer class is not apparent to an external class using the inner class.

It is also obviously possible for multiple inner classes to share the same outer class.

Static Inner Classes

Static inner classes look similar to inner classes, except they are declared with the `static` keyword. Unlike inner classes, static inner classes do not exist inside an instance of the outer class (they exist inside the class itself), and therefore do not have access to the outer class's `this` variable.

I seldom find many uses for static inner classes: essentially they provide an additional level of nesting that acts like packages. The one main advantage that they offer is that they can access `private static` fields and methods on their outer class.

The following is a simple example:

```
package innerclasses;

public class StaticInner {
    public StaticInner() {}

    public static class Helper {
        public void printHello() {
            System.out.println("Hello");
        }
    }
}
```

In this case the outer class is called `StaticInner`, and contains a static inner class called `Helper`. Notice that the static inner class can contain non-static methods and fields.

Due to the fact that `Helper` has been declared as `public`, it can be invoked directly by other classes as follows:

```
package innerclasses;
public class Main {
    public static void main(String[] args) {
        StaticInner.Helper helper = new StaticInner.Helper();
        helper.printHello();
    }
}
```

The dot notation in the declaration of `StaticInner.Helper` provides an insight into the true nature of static inner classes: the best way to think of static inner classes is as an extension to the package system. Just as a package is a container for one or more classes, a class can act as a container for one or more static inner classes.

Local Classes

Local classes are essentially the same as inner classes, but they are defined and used inside a method rather than inside a class. As a result, local classes have access to variables and parameters defined inside the method, along with the fields of the outer class itself.

Before beginning this section, it may be worth thinking about why you would want to declare a class inside a method. The most common reason is that you wish to encapsulate functionality inside a method because that functionality will not be used outside the specific method.

In order to demonstrate local inner classes you will modify the `printCart` method of `ShoppingCart` to declare and use a local inner class called `PrintAdaptor` to process and print each item.

```java
public void printCart() {
    class PrintAdaptor {
        int count = 1;
        double total = 0;
        PrintAdaptor() {}
        void processItem(Item item) {
            System.out.println("Item "+ (count++));
            System.out.println(item.getDisplay());
            System.out.println("-----------------------");
            total += item.getTotalPrice();
        }
        double getTotal() {
            return total;
        }
    }
    PrintAdaptor pa = new PrintAdaptor();
    for (Item item : items) {
        pa.processItem(item);
    }
    System.out.printf("The total is : $%f\n\n", pa.getTotal());
}
```

When declaring local inner classes you cannot use access modifiers such as `private` or `public`, because by definition the class can only be instantiated inside the method in which it is declared.

As you can see, local inner classes can still declare constructors, and can manage state.

You may be wondering whether you have really gained anything by making this code a local inner class rather than a method. It could be argued that the class has helped encapsulate the printing functionality, and the state that needs to be managed as part of this process (as seen in the `count` and `total` variables), but the argument is not particularly convincing.

I find the use of local inner classes results in code that is harder to read, so even if the `PrintAdaptor` has no value outside this method, I would still be inclined to create it as a standalone class, or potentially as an inner class.

As mentioned earlier, one benefit of local inner classes is that they can access variables or parameters from the method they are declared in. There are however limitations to this, specifically, the variables and parameters must be declared as `final`.

It is possible for a method to return an instance of a local inner class, but because the class (including its definition) is defined inside a method, the method cannot declare that it returns this type. The way around this problem is to declare that the local inner class implements an interface, and declare that the method returns this interface. Because the rest of the program knows what to expect from an interface, it will have no problem using the local inner class.

Anonymous Inner Classes

Anonymous inner classes are perhaps the most useful type of inner class. They are similar to local inner classes, but are declared and instantiated in a single step, and therefore their type is unnamed (or anonymous).

Of all the types of inner class, anonymous inner classes are the one I find the most use for in my own code. This is likely to change now that lambda expressions have been introduced, however, because anonymous inner classes were also the closest Java had to lambda expressions before Java 8 - this will all make sense after you read the next chapter.

It may not seem very useful to declare a class that does not have a name, but they turn out to be enormously useful for creating *callbacks*.

Callbacks allow a block of code to be passed from one method to another. The receiving method can then execute the code as and when required, and pass it any relevant arguments. There are three key situations where this is useful:

⇒ In situations where you need a code block to be executed when an event occurs. For instance, in a GUI application you may want a code block to be executed when a button is clicked. The code to be invoked can be encapsulated in a callback, and passed to the button. When the button is clicked it will invoke the callback, without needing to know anything about the code encapsulated in it.

⇒ You want to receive a response asynchronously, so that the invoker can continue processing other code while waiting for a response. Consider a program that invokes a service over the network: if the service was called synchronously the program would freeze while waiting for a response. By providing a callback, the program can continue with other processing while waiting for the response, knowing that the relevant code will be executed when the response is received.

⇒ You want to write a generic algorithm, and then provide an action that can be incorporated into the algorithm. It is this use of callbacks that will form the basis of the reminder of this chapter.

In this section you will create a generic algorithm for filtering `Lists` based on a condition. For instance, the condition may be to filter all the even numbers out of a `List` of numbers, or filter all the lower-case `Strings` out of a `List` of `Strings`.

Naturally this functionality could be achieved through iteration and imperative programming techniques, but another way to write this is to define a method that accepts each element in the List, and returns true or false to indicate whether the element should be retained in the List – and to define a generic algorithm for iterating the List and invoking the method on each element.

In this example, the condition returning true or false (detecting even numbers, detecting lower case Strings) will be encapsulated in a callback, and created as an anonymous inner class. The advantage of this approach is that you can reuse the generic filtering algorithm, and just replace the class that makes the filtering decision.

Callbacks in Java are typically implemented via the command design pattern. The command pattern uses an interface to represent an action that can be performed. Classes then implement this interface, allowing them to encapsulate an action (or command) that can be invoked by a generic algorithm. In this example, you can define an interface for classes that will make filtering decisions as follows:

```
package localclasses;
public interface Filter<T> {
    boolean filter(T t);
}
```

Next, you can write a static helper class that performs generic filtering. You will call this Collections2 because it is enhancing the methods Java makes available on the Collections class. This will create a new empty List, iterate through the items in the original List, and invoke the filter method on the instance of Filter passed to it with each element as an argument - those invocations that return true will have their respective element added to the new List:

```
package localclasses;
import java.util.ArrayList;
import java.util.List;

public class Collections2 {
    public static <T> List<T> filter(
            List<T> input, Filter<T> filter) {
        List<T> result = new ArrayList<T>();
        for (T t : input) {
            if (filter.filter(t)) {
                result.add(t);
            }
        }
        return result;
    }
}
```

Notice that the filter method accepts an instance of Filter: it does not care what this actually does, just as long as it returns true for any elements that should be retained in this List.

Now that you have a generic filtering API in place, you can use this functionality to filter a List. The code below will declare an anonymous class that implements Filter, and provide an implementation that returns `true` for odd numbers:

```
package localclasses;
import java.util.List;
import java.util.Arrays;
public class Main {
    public static void main(String[] args) {
        List<Integer> numbers = Arrays.asList(
                        1,5,4,2,7,9,6,4,2,6,5,8);
        List result = Collections2.filter(numbers,
            new Filter<Integer>() {
                @Override
                public boolean filter(Integer t) {
                    return t%2 == 1;
                }
            });
        System.out.println(result);
    }
}
```

Notice that the instance of `Filter` passed to the `filter` method is constructed inside the `main` method, and is never even given a name (it is anonymous):

```
new Filter<Integer>() {
    @Override
    public boolean filter(Integer t) {
        return t%2 == 1;
    }
}
```

It would have been possible to define this class as a conventional class, or an inner class, but because the implementation is irrelevant outside this context, it makes sense to create an anonymous inner class.

With the generic algorithm in place it is trivial to change its behavior to use a new condition. In this example, all States that do not begin with A are filtered out.

```
public static void main(String[] args) {
    List<String> numbers = Arrays.asList(
                    "Alabama","Arkansas","Kansas","Nebraska");
    List result = Collections2.filter(numbers,
        new Filter<String>() {
            @Override
            public boolean filter(String s) {
                return s.charAt(0) == 'A';
            }
        });
    System.out.println(result);
}
```

Although anonymous inner classes have been widely used for implementing functionality such as this in Java, they are likely to have a diminished role in the future due to a new feature added to the language in Java 8 – this feature will be the focus of the next chapter.

22 LAMBDA EXPRESSIONS

This chapter will introduce you to one of the most exciting additions to the Java language in many years: lambda expressions.

Lambda expressions had originally been slated for inclusion in Java 7, and had been requested widely for many years before that. Lambda expressions (commonly known as closures or anonymous methods) allow you to encapsulate a block of code in an anonymous method (i.e. a method without a name or enclosing class), and pass it to another method, which can invoke it. This may sound like a simple technique (and it is) but it brings tremendous benefits, especially when used in conjunction with another Java 8 feature: the Streams API.

The closest Java has had to lambda expressions in the past were anonymous and local inner classes. As you saw in the previous chapter, these were classes defined and instantiated inside a method, and often passed to other methods as callbacks.

In order to understand the limitations of anonymous inner classes, however, consider that the filter functionality implemented in the previous chapter can be implemented as follows in a language such as JavaScript:

```
[1,5,4,2,7,9,6,4,2,6,5,8]
.filter(function(v) {return v%2 == 1;})
```

The JavaScript implementation passes an anonymous function to the `filter` method natively supported by arrays.

The key to comparing these two approaches is comparing the Java implementation of an anonymous inner class:

```
Collections2.filter(numbers, new Filter<Integer>() {
    @Override
    public boolean filter(Integer t) {
        return t%2 == 1;
    }
```

})

To the JavaScript implementation of an anonymous function:

```
function(v) {return v%2 == 1;}
```

When you compare the two you can get a feeling why people have accused Java of feeling overly verbose. Admittedly, the JavaScript version does not bring the benefits of type safety, but otherwise the two examples are functionally equivalent. JavaScript is not an isolated example either; many languages now support equally concise syntaxes.

The key feature in JavaScript that allows this line of code to work is that functions can be assigned to variables and passed to other functions as arguments. To be specific: functions are first-class citizens in the language.

Up until the release of Java 8, all Java methods had to be defined inside a class – therefore methods were not first-class citizens in the language. As a result, methods could not be passed to other methods as parameters or assigned to variables.

A lambda expression is essentially an anonymous method that lives outside the scope of a class. As you will see, this is an illusion to some degree, lambda expressions are still objects, and they do have types, but the syntax for creating them removes the overhead of defining a class.

> Lambda expressions are an important component in a programming paradigm called *functional programming*. Functional programming differs from object orientated programming by emphasizing the role of functions as the core building block of a program.
>
> Java now embraces multiple programming paradigms, and is therefore referred to as a *multi-paradigm language*.

The basic format of a lambda expression is as follows:

```
(String s) -> { System.out.println(s); };
```

The first part of the expression `(String s)` denotes the parameters accepted by the lambda expression when it is invoked – in this case it will be passed a single `String` parameter. If no parameters are required by the lambda expression this can simply be defined as `()`. As you will see, this structure can be further simplified in some situations, and the types derived by the compiler based on context.

The right hand side of the expression `{ System.out.println(s); };` contains the code block that will be executed when the lambda expression is invoked – naturally this can access the parameters passed to the expression, and can use any other Java language features as required – it is just a regular code block. This block also has access to variables in scope when the lambda expression was constructed, although with certain caveats (as you will see shortly).

If the code-block consists of a single statement the { } brackets can be omitted, and the return type of the statement implicitly becomes the return type of the lambda expression. Where { } brackets are used, the lambda expression can use the `return` keyword to return a value, otherwise, as in this case, it returns `void`.

The two parts of the expression are glued together by the -> construct.

There will be plenty of examples of this construct coming up, so don't worry about understanding the details of lambda expressions too much at this point.

Functional Interfaces

As mentioned earlier, many languages supporting lambda expressions make functions first-class citizens in the language. Java does not go that far - lambda expressions are still objects. In addition, even with the addition of lambda expressions, Java remains a statically typed language; therefore it needs to know the type of every argument (including the type of any lambda expressions) passed to a method at compile time. This leads to the obvious question: what type are lambda expressions?

The answer to this lies in a new Java 8 feature called *functional interfaces*. You have already come across interfaces with no methods (for instance, `Serializable` and `Cloneable`). These are known as marker or tagging interfaces, because they are simply used to denote something about a class without requiring it to implement anything.

Java now supports a second special class of interface that contain a single method: these can be designated as functional interfaces. Many existing Java interfaces have been designated as functional interfaces including the `Comparable` interface introduced earlier in the book.

> These interfaces are also called Single Abstract Method interfaces (SAM Interfaces).

Prior to Java 8 there was nothing special about interfaces containing a single method: in Java 8 they can now act as the type for lambda expressions when tagged with the annotation `@FunctionalInterface`, for example:

```
@FunctionalInterface
public interface Example {
    void doSomething(Object obj);
}
```

One obvious use for lambda expressions is for callbacks. As discussed in the previous chapter, callbacks encapsulate a block of code that can be executed by another block of code when a specified event occurs. The event may be the user pressing a button on the GUI, or the result being received for a long running transaction.

The example below creates a functional interface to represent the printing of an object. Instances of this interface will then be passed as a callback to other methods, allowing them to print the results of an operation in the manner required by the initial invoker:

```
package printing;
@FunctionalInterface
public interface Printer {
    void print(Object obj);
}
```

Adding the `@FunctionalInterface` annotation ensures that the compiler will check that the interface meets the requirements for being a functional interface: if the interface contained anything other than one method definition the code would not compile.

Once a functional interface has been defined, you can declare a lambda expression of that type:

```
Printer printer = (Object o) -> { System.out.println(">>>" + o); };
```

This line of code will not execute the lambda expression: it is simply assigning it to a variable so that it can be executed at a later point in the code.

If you think about this line of code, it is actually very unusual from a Java point of view. The compiler is determining the type of object to construct via the type it is assigned to. This is the other way round from how Java normally works: typically an expression has a type, and the compiler determines whether that is compatible with the type it is being assigned to.

If you wanted to, you could then invoke this as follows:

```
printer.print("Hello World");
```

Generally, however you want to pass the lambda expression to another method. The following is a contrived example, but shows the basic technique:

```
package lambda;
import printing.Printer;
public class Adder {

    public static void main(String[] args) {
        int num1 = 10;
        int num2 = 20;
        Printer printer = (Object o) -> {
            System.out.printf("The result of %d and %d is %d\n"
            , num1, num2, o);
        };
        add(num1, num2, printer);
    }

    public static void add(int num1, int num2, Printer printer) {
        int result = num1 + num2;
        printer.print(result);
    }
}
```

This prints the following to standard output:

```
The result of 10 and 20 is 30
```

This is a contrived example because there is no reason for the `add` method not to return the result of the addition for the `main` method to print itself, but it provides a nice introduction to lambda expressions.

Notice that this lambda expression uses local variables from the `main` method, even though it is eventually executed in the `add` method: I will return to this subject shortly when discussing the scope that lambda expressions operate in.

As it happens, most of the time you do not need to define your own functional interfaces because Java provides a set for you. You can see this more clearly by moving to a realistic example.

A common use-case for lambda expressions is to have a method pass each element of a `Collection` to a lambda expression (just like the filter example last chapter). Java 8 provides a new method on `List` called `forEach` that accepts a lambda expression and implicitly passes each element in the `List` to it: the lambda expression it accepts must conform to the `Consumer` functional interface defined in the `java.util.function` package. This defines the following method:

```
void accept(T t)
```

The following shows a basic example:

```
package lambda;
import java.util.Arrays;
import java.util.List;
import java.util.function.Consumer;

public class Main {
    public static void main(String[] args) {
        Consumer c = (Object o) -> { System.out.println(">>>" + o); };
        List l = Arrays.asList("Hello", "World", "Print", "My", "List");
        l.forEach(c);
    }
}
```

This will produce the following output:

```
>>>Hello
>>>World
>>>Print
>>>My
>>>List
```

This approach is referred to as *implicit* rather than *explicit* iteration. Methods such as `forEach` remove the need for the programmer to describe the iteration process to the compiler – they implicitly perform it. This may sound like a minor convenience, but it will turn out to have powerful implications later in the book.

You can of course combine the declaration and use of the lambda expression into a single step:

```
l.forEach((Object o) -> { System.out.println(">>>" + o); });
```

In this case you don't even need to import the `Consumer` interface – the compiler knows to check that the lambda expression conforms to the `Consumer` interface, because that is the interface accepted by the `forEach` method.

You can even take this one step further by removing the type definition from the lambda expression's parameter, and remove the `{}` brackets from the lambda expression's code block:

```
l.forEach(str -> System.out.println(">>>" + str));
```

Because I used generics to declare that the `List` contains elements of type `String`, the compiler knows that every element in the array is a `String`. This also means that the compiler can safely assume that every element passed to the lambda expression will be a `String`.

This in turn allows you to omit the type of the `str` parameter, and simply use the following expression:

```
str -> System.out.println(">>>" + str)
```

It should now be obvious that the filtering example from the previous chapter can be implemented with lambda expressions. Java 8 refers to a filter as a *predicate* and provides a functional interface called `Predicate`. This defines the following method:

```
boolean test(T t)
```

The fundamental aspect of a predicate is that it accepts an element and returns `true` or `false`. The `List` interface also supports a new method called `removeIf`. This method passes every element in the `List` to the predicate, and removes it if the predicate evaluates to `true`:

```
package lambda;
import java.util.Arrays;
import java.util.LinkedList;
import java.util.List;

public class Main2 {
    public static void main(String[] args) {
        List<Integer> l = new LinkedList
            (Arrays.asList(4,5,88,76,55,23,7,20,45));
        l.removeIf(i -> i%2 == 0);
        System.out.println(l);
    }
}
```

The expression `i -> i%2 == 0` conforms to the `Predicate` interface because it accepts a single parameter and returns a `boolean` result – as mentioned earlier, lambda expressions implicitly return a type if they consist of a single statement without `{}` brackets.

This could alternatively have been written as a code block:

```
l.removeIf(i -> {return i%2 == 0;});
```

I far prefer the first form for readability, and this is the form that is most commonly used.

I should probably mention at this point that the `removeIf` method is a very poor example of functional programming due to the fact that it mutates (or changes) the original list. Functional programming emphasizes immutability, and therefore the preferred approach would be to create a new list of odd numbers and leave the original list untouched. As you will see in the next chapter, it is possible to achieve this relatively simply with Java 8 using the Streams API.

In case you were wondering, the fact that this method mutates the `List` meant I could not simply use:

```
Arrays.asList(4,5,88,76,55,23,7,20,45)
```

The `List` created by `asList` is a fixed-length `List` mapped to the array specified, and therefore it is not possible to remove elements.

Auto-generated Interfaces

One issue with the lambda expressions you have looked at so far is that they do not lead to very good code reuse. The examples above have all created lambda expressions on the fly and passed them as parameters to other methods. If two different classes needed lambda expressions performing the same task, they would each need to construct their own lambda expression (thereby duplicating the code).

The lambda expression API in Java 8 provides a mechanism to use any method, on any object (or static method on a class) as a lambda expression (subject to its access modifiers), as long as it conforms to the required functional interface. This feature is called auto-generated interfaces, and is facilitated by a new operator called the "double colon".

Let's take a very simple example: Suppose you want to pass each element in a `List` to the `System.out.println` method. The `println` method meets the requirements of the `Consumer` functional interface (it accepts a single parameter and returns `void`); therefore it can be used as an instance of `Consumer`:

```
List<String> l = Arrays.asList("Hello", "World",
            "Print", "My", "List");
l.forEach(System.out::println);
```

The key here is the statement `System.out::println`. Essentially this is saying that there is a method called `println` on the object represented by the variable `System.out`, and this should be used as the lambda expression accepted by the `forEach` method. Because `forEach` accepts a `Consumer`, the `println` method is implicitly converted to be an object of type `Consumer` as part of the process.

If you now go back to the example of removing even number elements from a list: suppose you already had the following utility class:

```
package lambda;
public class Detector {
    public boolean isEven(int i) {
```

```
        return i%2 == 0;
    }
    public boolean isOdd(int i) {
        return !isEven(i);
    }
}
```

This is a simple utility that detects odd and even numbers: it has nothing to do with lambda expressions, and could have pre-dated Java 8. You could rewrite the filtering example as follows:

```
package lambda;
import java.util.Arrays;
import java.util.LinkedList;
import java.util.List;

public class Main {
    public static void main(String[] args) {
        Detector d = new Detector();
        List<Integer> l = new LinkedList
            (Arrays.asList(4,5,88,76,55,23,7,20,45));
        l.removeIf(d::isEven);
        System.out.println(l);
    }
}
```

Or, if you made `isEven` a static method, you could execute the following:

```
l.removeIf(Detector::isEven);
```

This is a very useful technique, because it means existing code can be re-purposed to adapt to an interface it does not explicitly implement.

Sorting

Sorting lists is a very common operation, and is supported by the `Comparator` and `Comparable` interfaces. I have always been annoyed by the fact that the `sort` method was a static helper on the `Collections` class, rather than a method on the `List` class.

> Earlier in the book you used the `Comparable` interface: this defined a method on the class being sorted.
>
> In this section you will use the `Comparator` interface: this involves the creation of a standalone class, and is useful when the sort behavior may not always be the same for a specific class.
>
> A `Comparator` accepts two objects of a specified type and determines which sorts higher or lower by returning an `int`.

Java has rectified this situation in Java 8 via a `sort` method on `List`, which accepts an instance of `Comparator`.

To demonstrate this, create a very simple `Person` class:

```
package lambda;
public class Person {
    String firstName,lastName;
    public Person(String firstName, String lastName) {
        this.firstName = firstName;
        this.lastName = lastName;
    }
    public String getFirstName() {
        return firstName;
    }
    public String getLastName() {
        return lastName;
    }

    @Override
    public String toString() {
        return  firstName + " " + lastName;
    }
}
```

You can now create a `List` of `Person` objects, and sort it based on `firstName` as follows:

```
package lambda;

import java.util.Arrays;
import java.util.List;

public class Main5 {
    public static void main(String[] args) {
        List<Person> l = Arrays.asList(
                new Person("Albert", "Smith"),
                new Person("Jim", "James"),
                new Person("John", "Brown"),
                new Person("William", "Hughes"),
                new Person("Simon", "Fleming")
        );
        l.sort((p1, p2) ->
            p1.getFirstName().compareTo(p2.getFirstName()));
        System.out.println(l);
    }
}
```

The following statement is implicitly constructed into an object of type `Comparator` as part of this process.

```
(p1, p2) -> p1.getFirstName().compareTo(p2.getFirstName())
```

I would take a lot of convincing that the equivalent code with anonymous classes (while functionally equivalent) is as readable:

```
l.sort(new Comparator<Person>() {
    @Override
    public int compare(Person p1, Person p2) {
        return p1.getFirstName().compareTo(p2.getFirstName());
    }
});
```

Scope

As you have seen, lambda expressions can use variables that were in scope when they were created. There is a caveat however – they can use those variables as long as they do not change their values after they are declared.

As an example, consider the following functional interface:

```
package lambda;

@FunctionalInterface
public interface NumberAdder {
    int add(int x);
}
```

This has a method called `add` that accepts an `int`, and returns an `int`.

You will now create a method that returns a `NumberAdder` as follows:

```
public static NumberAdder getNumberAdder() {
    int startingNumber = 10;
    return x -> x + startingNumber;
}
```

This method declares a local variable called `startingNumber`, and then returns an instance of `NumberAdder` that will (when invoked) add `startingNumber` to the number that is passed to the lambda expression.

Under normal circumstances the `startingNumber` variable would be implicitly destroyed when the `getNumberAdder` method completes (remember, local variable references exist on the stack, and are popped off the stack when the method completes). In the case of lambda expressions, however, the variable survives when the method completes. Here is the complete example including the invoking method:

```
package lambda;

public class Main {
    public static void main(String[] args) {
        NumberAdder na = getNumberAdder();
        System.out.print(na.add(20));
    }

    public static NumberAdder getNumberAdder() {
        int startingNumber = 10;
        return x -> x + startingNumber;
    }
}
```

When this runs it will print out 30. Lambda expressions that use variables in this manner are said to be *capturing lambdas*, because they capture copies of variables that were in scope when they were constructed.

In order for this little bit of magic to work, the variable `startingNumber` must be `final` or *effectively final*. Even the following code is invalid and won't compile:

```
public static NumberAdder getNumberAdder() {
        int startingNumber = 10;
        startingNumber++;
        return x -> x + startingNumber;
}
```

The term effectively final is new. Essentially it means that the variable must behave as though it was `final`, even though it doesn't need to be marked as `final`. Basically, if the variable would not be valid with the `final` modifier added, it is not valid for use by a lambda expression.

This constraint is controversial and was added to reduce concurrency issues that could arise from mutating variables. Up until Java 8 you could never have threading issues with local variables: simply put it was impossible for two threads to be sharing the same instance of a local variable because they are created inside a method, and two threads invoking the same method would receive their own independent copies of the variables.

If lambda expressions could change a local variable, and two methods invoked the lambda expression from two separate threads at the same time, a whole new set of concurrency issues would have been introduced into the language.

It is of course possible to work around this constraint (just as it is possible to work around the constraints on `final` variables) by encapsulating the value as a field inside an object. It would then be possible to change the value of this field even after the lambda expression is created. This could be achieved by creating the following class:

```
package lambda;
public class IntegerHolder {
    public int number = 10;
}
```

And changing the main class as follows:

```
package lambda;
public class Main7 {
    public static void main(String[] args) {
        NumberAdder na = getNumberAdder();
        System.out.print(na.add(20));
    }

    public static NumberAdder getNumberAdder()
IntegerHolder ih = new IntegerHolder();
        ih.number = 10;
        NumberAdder na = x -> x + ih.number;
        ih.number = 20;
        return na;
    }
}
```

In this case, the `ih` variable is effectively final, because you do not change the object referenced after the variable is initialized. You do however change the `number` held by the object after creating the lambda expression.

In this case the result of the operation is 40, because when the lambda expression is invoked, the value of the `number` field has been changed to 20.

This approach does naturally open the code up to the concurrency issues that the specification was trying to avoid through the use of `final` variables, and therefore should not be seen as a feature.

23 STREAMS API

Java 8 also introduces a new API called the Streams API as part of the lambda expressions changes. These should not be confused with input and output streams (which will be introduced later in the book); they are a mechanism for processing a sequence of elements (such as the elements in a `Collection`). Java 8 formally defines streams as "a sequence of elements supporting sequential and parallel aggregate operations."

As you will see in later chapters, the Streams API is part of a push to simplify the way parallel algorithms (algorithms that process on multiple threads at the same time) can be implemented in Java by allowing programmers to request parallel processing rather than implement it themselves. Streams are a lot more than that, however, they provide an alternative to iteration, and provide support for a variety of operations, all of which can utilize lambda expressions.

You will begin with some very basic examples, returning to my favorite of excluding even numbers from a `List`. This can be accomplished as follows:

```
package streams;

import java.util.Arrays;
import java.util.List;

public class EvenOnly {
    public static void main(String[] args) {
        List<Integer> l = Arrays.asList(5,4,88,76,55,23,7,20,45);
        l.stream().filter(p -> p%2==1)
            .forEach(i -> System.out.print(i+" "));
    }
}
```

After creating a `List`, this program first accesses its stream using the `stream` method. This returns an object of type `java.util.stream.Stream<Integer>`. You will look at what streams are in more detail soon, but for now just think of them as a way of conveying elements from a source of data (i.e. the `List`) to a function (i.e. `filter`).

This code *internally iterates* over every element in the `List` (as seen in the previous chapter using `forEach`), and passes each element in turn to the `filter` method. This is opposed to *external iteration* with `for`-loops and iterators, because the programmer does not need to declare the fact they wish to process each element in the `List`, and they do not need to control the iteration.

External iteration may not seem like a huge inconvenience that needs to be alleviated – especially since the introduction of the Collection-based `for`-loops. Internal iteration can bring unseen benefits, however, because it may implement different strategies to iterate different collections, therefore allowing behavior to be added implicitly (such as parallel processing).

The `filter` method is referred to as an *intermediate operation*. As each element is processed, those that pass the `filter` are then passed to the `forEach` method, which is a *terminal operation*.

The type returned by the `filter` method is itself a `Stream`, and therefore it is possible to chain a whole set of intermediate operations together into a *pipeline*. Pipelines are facilitated by the fact that the output of one operation becomes the input of another operation.

> Pipelines are widely used in computing: for instance the Unix/Linux command line supports pipelines where the output of one program is passed as the input to another program via the "|" operator. For instance, the following finds any processes running for the user that contain `java` in their name:
>
> ```
> ps | grep 'java'
> ```
>
> The convention in Unix that allows this is that programs produce ASCII text to standard output, and other programs read ASCII text from standard input. The pipe operator therefore pipes the standard output of one program to the standard input of another.

As you will see throughout this chapter, pipelines provide a mechanism for describing a complex set of functionality in easy to understand chunks.

Terminal operators (as their name suggests) represent the end of a pipeline, and they are responsible for terminating the stream in some manner. `forEach` is not the most obvious example of a terminal operation, but it provides a manner of accessing all the elements after they have been processed by the pipeline, and performing some operation on them (printing them out in this case). You will notice that the `forEach` method returns `void`, therefore the pipeline cannot continue after this method has been invoked.

Unlike the `removeIf` method seen earlier, this pipeline does not alter the original `Collection` in any way: it simply provides a mechanism for processing its elements.

In the previous example, the first element in the `List` (5) is passed to the lambda expression of the `filter` method, and is evaluated to `true` (it is odd). As a result, this element is passed to the lambda expression of the `forEach` method, which causes the number to be printed.

Once the element has been all the way through the pipeline, the next number (4) is processed. Because the `filter` lambda expression will return `false` for this number it will never be passed to the `forEach` lambda expression, and so on.

Even this is not strictly speaking a true representation of the processing: intermediate operations are lazy. The intermediate operations are not executed until the terminal operation is invoked – so it is the execution of the `forEach` method with the first number (5) that causes the `filter` method to be invoked.

This approach means that the entire pipeline can be processed in a single iteration of the `List`, and can result in dramatic performance improvement for large sets of data. It also means that the stream does not need to hold all the elements in the `List` as it performs its processing.

This last point is important. An alternative implementation of `Streams` would have been to invoke the `filter` operation on all elements and capture the resulting elements in a `Collection` – once these had been captured they could be passed to the `forEach` method. I think it is fairly obvious that this implementation would not be as efficient either in terms of memory utilization or processor utilization.

In order to see lazy intermediary operations in action, re-write the `main` method as follows:

```
public static void main(String[] args) {
    List<Integer> l = Arrays.asList(5,4,88,76,55,23,7,20,45);
    Stream<Integer> s = l.stream().filter(p -> {
        System.out.println("Filter called on "+ p);
        return p%2==1;
    });
    System.out.println( "The pipeline is created - " +
        "calling terminal operation");
    s.forEach(i -> System.out.println(">>>" + i));
}
```

This produces the following result:

```
The pipeline is created - calling terminal operation
Filter called on 5
>>>5
Filter called on 4
Filter called on 88
Filter called on 76
Filter called on 55
>>>55
Filter called on 23
```

```
>>>23
Filter called on 7
>>>7
Filter called on 20
Filter called on 45
>>>45
```

Notice the first line that is output: although this was printed after the `filter` method appears to have been invoked, it is actually the first print statement to be displayed, proving this line was executed first. This shows that even with the code structured across multiple statements, the `Collection` is still processed with a single pass by the `Stream`.

There is another major benefit with the lazy invocation approach. Suppose you just wanted to find the first odd number in this `List`. This can be achieved with an alternative terminal operation called `findFirst`:

```
public static void main(String[] args) {
    List<Integer> l = Arrays.asList(5,4,88,76,55,23,7,20,45);
    Stream<Integer> s = l.stream().filter(p -> {
        System.out.println("Filter called on "+ p);
        return p%2==1;
    });
    Optional<Integer> result = s.findFirst();
    System.out.println(result.get());
}
```

This example prints the following result:

```
Filter called on 5
5
```

Because the first element in the `List` is odd, this is the only element that needs to be processed.

There is one other interesting aspect to this example. Rather than returning an `Integer`, the `findFirst` method returned an `Optional<Integer>`. You will find references to the `Optional` class throughout the Streams API: it provides a container for a value that may be `null`. This class supports a method called `isPresent` to determine whether the container holds a non-`null` value.

The `Optional` class also supports methods such as `map` and `filter` that allow the value to be modified via lambda expressions if required. There is also nothing to stop you returning `Option` instances from your own code, and it may prove a useful mechanism for extending the value of your APIs.

There are a couple more points to make about streams before continuing.

> ⇒ Once a stream has processed its elements it cannot be reused. For instance, in the previous example you could not have invoked an alternative terminal operation on the `Stream` returned by `filter` after the `forEach` operation had been executed. Technically streams can be closed, but there is no reason to explicitly close them.

⇒ Streams must be non-interfering: they cannot change the source of the stream (the `List` in the example above).

I will now turn to a slightly more complicated example, and demonstrate how a pipeline can include multiple intermediate steps. Suppose you want to do the following:

⇒ Filter the even numbers out of the list
⇒ Multiply each remaining number by itself
⇒ Sum the numbers together

In this case, the first two steps will be the intermediate operations, while the `sum` operation will be the terminal operation. This can be achieved as follows:

```
double result = l.stream()
                 .filter(p -> p%2==1)
                 .mapToInt(p -> p * p)
                 .sum()
```

The `filter` method in this example should look familiar, and because it returns a `Stream<Integer>` you can obviously execute other intermediate operations on the result.

The next intermediate operation that is executed is `mapToInt`. This is slightly different from the `filter` operation: it provides a way of transforming data. The lambda expression passed to `mapToInt` accepts any type of object as input, and returns an `int` as a result. In this case the input parameter is also an `int`, but that is not required: you could have passed a `Person` object as the argument, and returned its `salary` field (if that was a `int`).

The lambda expression passed to `mapToInt` is simply multiplying the input parameter by itself and implicitly returning the result.

The other interesting thing about `mapToInt` is that instead of returning an object of type `Stream<Integer>`, it actually returns an instance of `IntegerStream`. The difference may sound small, but `IntegerStream` provides a set of specialized terminal operations designed to work with integer values, including `min`, `max`, `average`, and the method you are using here: `sum`.

The Streams API also supports `DoubleStreams` (via `mapToDouble`) and `LongStreams` (via `mapToLong`). These classes support the same set of terminal operations seen on `IntegerStream`.

> Streams also support a general-purpose `map` operation for transforming objects of any type to any other type, but this method simply returns a `Stream<T>` where `T` is the return type of the lambda expression returned by the `map` operation.

Reducing

The `sum` method is a type of terminal operation known as a *reducing* operation: it takes a set of values and reduces them to an aggregate value. You could also have implemented the `sum` functionality via the general purpose `reduce` terminal operation:

```
l.stream()
.filter(p -> p%2==1)
.mapToInt(p -> p * p)
.reduce((a, b) -> a + b)
```

The `reduce` method starts by passing the first two elements in the stream to the lambda expression provided. The result of this operation is then passed to the lambda expression along with the third element, and so on until the elements have all been processed. The following is a print out of the values passed to the `reduce` lambda expression:

```
a = 25,   b = 3025
a = 3050, b = 529
a = 3579, b = 49
a = 3628, b = 2025
```

(There are 5 odd numbers, so the expression is invoked 4 times).

The `reduce` method returns an instance of `OptionalInt`, because the `filter` method could have potentially removed all elements from the `Stream`.

The `reduce` operation accepts a lambda expression conforming to the `BinaryOperator` functional interface. This interface has a method that accepts two parameters and returns a single parameter of the same type:

```
R apply(T t, U u)
```

Due to the power of auto-generated interfaces, you could therefore have reused one of the new `static` helper methods added to `Integer` (and the other number wrapper types) in Java 8:

```
public static int sum(int a, int b)
```

As follows:

```
l.stream()
.filter(p -> p%2==1)
.mapToInt(p -> p * p)
.reduce(Integer::sum)
```

Notice that the `sum` method is `static`, therefore you don't need an instance of `Integer` to invoke the `sum` method.

The `reduce` operation can also accept an optional first parameter representing the initial value of the aggregation:

```
l.stream()
.filter(p -> p%2==1)
.mapToInt(p -> p * p)
.reduce(100, (a, b) -> a + b)
```

This example will return 100 more than the previous example.

If omitted, this uses the default value for the data-type returned, e.g. 0 for numbers.

Collecting

Another useful terminal operation is *collecting*. Collecting provides a mechanism for accumulating or summarizing elements based on a set of criteria.

As an example, consider a `List` of objects instantiated from the `Person` class defined in the previous chapter. You may want to group all the `Person` instances together where the `firstName` is equal – this could be achieved as follows:

```
package streams;
import java.util.Arrays;
import java.util.List;
import java.util.Map;
import java.util.stream.Collectors;
public class Collecting {
    public static void main(String[] args) {
        List<Person> people = Arrays.asList(
                new Person("Albert", "Smith"),
                new Person("John", "James"),
                new Person("John", "Brown"),
                new Person("William", "Hughes"),
                new Person("William", "Fleming")
        );
        Map<String, List<Person>> groupedMap = people.stream()
            .collect(Collectors.groupingBy(Person::getFirstName));
        System.out.println(groupedMap.get("William"));
    }
}
```

The `groupingBy` operation returns a `Map` where the keys are the distinct values that were grouped by (Willian, John and Albert), and the values are `Lists` of `Person` objects matching the key.

Because you are accessing the `List` containing all `Person` instances with the `firstName` of "William" in the last line, this will print out:

```
[William Hughes, William Fleming]
```

The `collect` method accepts a `Collector`. These can be generated via a set of `static` helpers on the `Collectors` class - in this case you are using the `groupingBy` `Collector`, and specifying the method that should be used for comparison. The appropriate `Collector` instance will then be generated for you.

Once elements have been grouped it is common to run an aggregation operation on each group (for instance, count how many elements are in each group). The `groupingBy` methods therefore accept a second parameter for performing aggregate operations. As an example you will process all the time zones available in Java (you will see these again later in the book when you look at the new Date And Time API): these can be obtained as an array by executing `TimeZone.getAvailableIDs()`. These exist in the form:

```
Africa/Asmara
Europe/London
```

The convention consists of an optional first portion (Eurpoe, Africa), which represents a grouping mechanism, and the portion after the forward slash representing a specific value.

You will write a program that performs the following:

⇒ Filters out any zones that don't have a forward slash in them
⇒ Groups the zones by their group (e.g. Europe, Africa)
⇒ Counts how many zones are in each group

This can be performed in a single line as follows:

```
package streams;
import java.util.Arrays;
import java.util.Map;
import java.util.TimeZone;
import java.util.stream.Collectors;
public class Collecting5 {
    public static void main(String[] args) {
        Map<String, Long> result =
            Arrays.asList(TimeZone.getAvailableIDs())
                .stream()
                .filter(s -> s.indexOf("/") >= 0)
                .collect(Collectors.groupingBy((String s) -> s.substring(0, s.indexOf("/")),
                    Collectors.counting()));
        System.out.println(result);
    }
}
```

> This code uses two useful `String` methods:
>
> ⇒ It is possible to discover whether a specified character exists in a `String` with the `indexOf` method. If the character does not exist in the `String` this will return -1
>
> ⇒ It is possible to return a specified sub-String via the `substring` method. This accepts the starting and ending index of the sub-string to return.

Notice the use of `Collectors.counting()` as the second parameter to the `groupingBy` method. This itself is a `Collector`, and processes the result of the `groupingBy` operation. The `counting` method (unlike the `groupingBy` method) does not need any other information in order to generate a `Collector` because it operates on a data-structure in the format returned by the `groupingBy` method (a `Map` with `Lists` as its values).

This outputs the following:

```
{Europe=59, Africa=54, SystemV=13, Canada=9, Pacific=42, Etc=35, Asia=91,
America=164, Brazil=4, Mexico=3, Indian=11, Antarctica=11, Chile=2,
Australia=23, Arctic=1, Atlantic=12, US=13}
```

Partitioning is another form of `Collector` that is similar to `groupingBy`. As discussed earlier, `filter` operations return `true` or `false` for all elements in the `Stream`. Partitioning provides a mechanism to collect all the values that are `true` into one `List`, and all the values that are `false` into another `List`. In this example you will create two lists: one for the time zones that have a "/" in their name (e.g. America/Cancun), and one for the zones that don't (e.g. Greenwich)

```java
package streams;
import java.util.Arrays;
import java.util.List;
import java.util.Map;
import java.util.TimeZone;
import java.util.stream.Collectors;

public class Collecting4 {
    public static void main(String[] args) {
        List<String> zones =
            Arrays.asList(TimeZone.getAvailableIDs());
        Map<Boolean, List<String>> zonesCompare =
            zones.stream()
                .collect(Collectors.partitioningBy(s -> s.indexOf("/") > 0));
        System.out.println(zonesCompare);
    }
}
```

Another good example of collecting is adding a comma between every word in a `List`. The trick to joining is that the comma (or other delimiter) should not occur after the last element, therefore it is hard to achieve with simple iteration (because you do not know an element is the last in the `List` until you try to select the next element).

Joining can easily be achieved with `Streams` as follows:

```java
package streams;

import java.util.Arrays;
import java.util.List;
import java.util.stream.Collectors;

public class Collecting {

    public static void main(String[] args) {
        List<String> strings = Arrays.asList("This", "is", "a", "list");
        String s = strings.stream()
            .collect(Collectors.joining(", "));
        System.out.println(s);
    }
}
```

This takes advantage of the `joining` collector, which accepts the token that should be placed between each element. This prints out:

```
This, is, a, list
```

Notice that this does not add a comma after the last element.

Collectors can also be used for collecting the results of a pipeline into a new `Collection` such as a `List` or a `Set`. This can be achieved as follows:

```java
package streams;
import java.util.Arrays;
import java.util.List;
import java.util.Map;
import java.util.stream.Collectors;

public class Collecting {

    public static void main(String[] args) {
        List<Person> people = Arrays.asList(
                new Person("Albert", "Smith"),
                new Person("John", "James"),
                new Person("John", "Brown"),
                new Person("William", "Hughes"),
                new Person("William", "Fleming")
        );

        List<Person> filteredList = people.stream()
            .filter(p -> p.getFirstName().equals("William"))
            .collect(Collectors.toList());
        System.out.println(filteredList);
    }

}
```

This filters out all the `Person` instances where the first name is "William", and adds the result to a new `List`.

Other operators

The Streams API is a large API, and will take some time to learn in its entirety. The following are potentially the most useful intermediate operations provided by the Streams API that have not been introduced up until now:

⇒ `distinct`: removes any duplicate elements (based on the `equals` implementation) from the stream

⇒ `limit`: limit the elements in the stream to a specific number. This could be useful for processing search results if only a maximum of 100 results were to be shown. It can also result in performance improvements because it allows you to reduce the elements in the stream mid-way through the pipeline.

⇒ `map`: this is a generic version of the `mapToInt` method seen earlier. It takes each element in turn and returns a value (potentially of a different type) based on a transformation.

⇒ `sorted`: this provides a mechanism for sorting the elements, either based on natural order (the `Comparable` implementation) or a `Comparator`. This can be called anywhere in the pipeline prior to the terminal operation, so it is useful when a map operation may have resulted in an unordered stream.

The following are the most useful terminal operators available on `Stream` not discussed so far:

⇒ `allMatch`: this accepts a `Predicate` and returns true if all elements return `true` from the `Predicate`
⇒ `anyMatch`: this accepts a `Predicate` and returns `true` if any elements return `true` from the `Predicate`
⇒ `noneMatch`: this accepts a `Predicate` and returns `true` if none of the elements return `true` from the `Predicate`
⇒ `count`: counts the number of elements in the `Stream`

Creating Streams

So far you have focused on how `Streams` can be created from `Collections`. There are in fact several ways to create `Streams`.

The Streams API contains a concept called a *range*. A range allows a Stream to be constructed as a sequence of numbers, for instance:

```
IntStream.range(0, 10).forEach(n -> System.out.println(n));
```

This generates an `IntStream` with the numbers 0 through 9. The alternative `rangeClosed` method can be used if you want the range to be inclusive of the final number (e.g. 0 to 10).

Once the `Stream` has been created it can be processed just like any other `Stream`, therefore ranges provide a streams based alternative to `for`-loops.

An alternative mechanism for creating streams is via *builders*. The following is an example of a builder that adds three `Strings` to a `Stream`, and then invokes the `forEach` terminal operation:

```
Stream.builder().add("Hello").add("World").add("!").build()
   .forEach(s -> System.out.print(s));
```

The builder is obtained via a `static` method on `Stream`. Once all elements have been added, the `build` method is invoked to return a `Stream` of the elements.

> Builders are also a design pattern. Instead of providing a variety of constructors to instantiate an object in different ways, they expose methods that allow the object to be built bit by bit.
>
> In the case of streams, the builder simply provides an `add` method

> to include an object in the stream, and then a `build` method to generate the stream.
>
> You can choose to use builders to create your own objects, and they are especially useful when objects can accept a large number of optional arguments when they are created.

Naturally `IntStream`, `LongStream` and `DoubleStream` support corresponding builders for generating `Streams` of `ints`, `longs` and `doubles` respectively.

Another way to construct streams is to concatenate two `Streams` together:

```
Stream s1 = Stream.builder().add( "Hello").add("World").add("!").build();
Stream s2 = Stream.builder().add( "Another").add("Stream").build();
Stream.concat(s1, s2).forEach(s -> System.out.print(s));
```

The `Stream` created in the final line above will process 5 elements.

`Streams` can also be generated via `static` helpers on the `Random` class. `Random.ints()`, `Random.longs()` and `Random.doubles()` provide mechanisms for returning an unlimited stream of random `ints`, `longs` and `doubles` respectively (although the quantity of values can be bound by an optional parameter). It is also possible to define a range for the numbers; for instance you could request a `Stream` of 100 random `ints` between 0 and 100,000 as follows:

```
Random.ints(100, 0, 100000)
```

Naturally these return `Streams` appropriate for the type of number, so the previous example returns an `IntStream`.

> Random numbers in Java are technically *pseudo*-random numbers – they appear to be random but in fact are not. Random numbers are generated based on a 48-bit seed – if you know what this seed is, or can determine it, you can calculate the next random number that will be created.
>
> This usually does not matter, but Java also supports a class called `SecureRandom` – this should be used if you need more secure random numbers.

Possibly the most useful source of `Streams`, outside of `Collections`, however, is `Streams` created from files. Although you will look at more conventional mechanisms for interacting with files later in the book, this functionality provides a useful introduction to the way textual files can be processed.

Java 7 introduced a `Files` class with a set of `static` helpers. This has been enhanced in Java 8 to include methods that return `Streams`. In order to see this in action, start by creating a text file on your file system, and add a few lines to it.

The following example shows how that file can be read as a `Stream`, and processed with the operations you have seen earlier:

```
package streams;
import java.io.IOException;
import java.nio.file.*;
import java.util.logging.*;

public class FileReading {
    public static void main(String[] args) {
        Path path = Paths.get("/tmp/test.txt");
        try {
            Files.lines(path).distinct()
              .forEach(s -> System.out.println(s));
        } catch (IOException ex) {
            Logger.getLogger(FileReading.class.getName())
              .log(Level.SEVERE, "IO Error", ex);
        }
    }
}
```

This program looks for a file called `/tmp/test.txt` and converts it into a `Stream` via the `Files.lines()`. Be sure to change this to a location such as `C:/tmp/test.txt` on Windows. The intermediary operation (`distinct`) is then used to remove duplicate lines, and the results are printed out with the terminal `forEach` operator.

Notice that this never needs to read the whole file into memory: it can simply `Stream` one line at a time through the pipeline, and then move on to the next line.

Finally, it is possible to generate a `Stream` from an array using a static helper on `Arrays`. The following is a very simple example that prints out the sum of the numbers in an array. Due to the fact that the array is of type `int`, the `Stream` returned is an `IntegerStream`, and therefore the `sum` aggregate operation can be used:

```
package streams;

import java.util.Arrays;

public class ArraysStream {
    public static void main(String[] args) {
        int[] intArray = {4,2,5,7,66,4,3};
        int result = Arrays.stream(intArray).sum();
        System.out.print(result);
    }
}
```

You will return to the subject of streams later in the book when you investigate how streams can be processed in parallel, allowing you to simply take advantage of multi-processor hardware.

24 DATES AND CALENDARS

Dates are one of those subjects you think are very simple until you start writing code that uses them. We all use dates and calendars on a regular basis outside of coding, and no one seems to have much of a problem with them.

There are several aspects to dates that make them complex for computer programs to handle. One of these is the concept of a time zone. Typically the same computer program must be capable of running in different time zones, and may even have users simultaneously using it in multiple time zones. Presenting a date such as `20/May/2014 11:10am` is therefore ambiguous if a user on the West Coast sends it to a user on the East Coast.

Another thing that makes dates complex is that computer programs need to be very precise about dates, whereas we typically use dates in a more generic sense. Every `Date` in Java must be defined to millisecond granularity, whereas in real life we easily refer to dates such as "tomorrow", "next week" or "before the end of the year". As you will see in the next chapter, this problem has finally been resolved in Java through the introduction of a new API.

Dates are not even consistent throughout the year. Most regions have daylight savings time for a portion of the year, and therefore the time effectively changes. If a date was saved as `10 July 2013 11:14 am` during daylight saving time, how should it be displayed if you print this date when the clocks have gone back to standard time?

Additionally, not all years are the same. Some years have 366 days, while most only have 365. Additionally, not even all days are the same; some days contain a mysterious "leap seconds", meaning that there are 86401 or 86399 seconds in the day rather than 86400.

Finally, the ways in which dates are presented vary from country to country. For instance, the following date will be interpreted as the 10th of December in some countries, and the 12th October in other countries.

10/12/2014

Java supports two APIs for dealing with dates and times. This chapter will introduce the Date and Calendar API, which has existed in Java in some form since the very first release of the language. The next chapter will introduce you to a new API introduced in Java 8 called the Date and Time API. The Date and Time API brings significant advantages, but it is likely that the Date and Calendar API will remain in common use for the foreseeable future. My advice is to get to know both APIs, and decide on a case-by-case basis which one best fits your requirements.

With the Dates and Calendar API dates are represented by an number (a `long` as it happens) containing the number of milliseconds that have elapsed since 1st January 1970 UTC (Coordinated Universal Time – essentially the same thing as Greenwich Mean Time). This date is known as the *epoch*.

Working with dates

Java encapsulates the number of milliseconds since the epoch inside a `Date` object, and provides a set of methods for interacting with this date. The following is a simple program that constructs a `Date` and prints out the time in milliseconds it represents, along with a human readable translation of this date:

```
package dates;
import java.util.Date;
public class CurrentDate {
    public static void main(String[] args) {
        Date date = new Date();
        System.out.println("The time in milliseconds is "+
            date.getTime());
        System.out.println("The date is "+date.toString());
    }
}
```

Notice that you have imported `Date` from the `java.util` package. There is also a `Date` class in the `java.sql` package, but this is not relevant for this chapter.

By default a `Date` is initialized with the current date and time, as taken from the system clock of the computer running the program.

For me, this printed the following:

```
The time in milliseconds is 1393119625394
The date is Sun Feb 23 14:40:25 NZDT 2014
```

Notice for me Java has converted the date into my current time zone (New Zealand Daylight Savings time) when it printed the date. It has picked up this information from the computer I am working on.

If you had run this program at exactly the same point of time, but on the other side of the world, the time in milliseconds would have been the same, but the representation of the date would have been different.

If I wanted to run the program as though I was in a different time zone, I can do this by providing a system parameter. Right click on the class and choose `Run as -> Run Configurations...`

Inside the dialog, choose the arguments tab and add a VM argument:

`-Duser.timezone=UTC`

This is shown in figure 24-1:

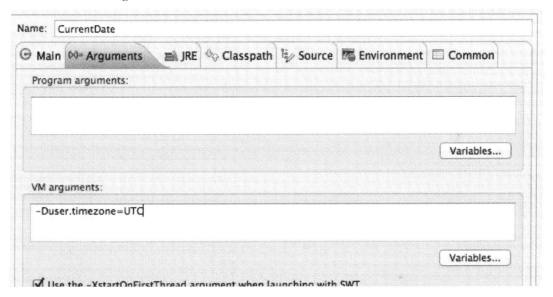

FIGURE 24-1

When you select the "Run" option at the bottom of the dialog, the program will now run as though you are in UTC time:

```
The time in milliseconds is 1393119625394
The date is Sun Feb 23 01:40:25 UTC 2014
```

Notice that the time in milliseconds are the same (or almost the same), but the displayed time differs by 13 hours.

Due to the fact `Dates` are simply numbers, it is possible to manipulate dates with standard arithmetic operations. For instance, if I want to add 1 day to a date, it is possible using simple arithmetic:

```
package dates;
import java.util.Date;
public class CurrentDate {

    public static void main(String[] args) {
        Long timeMs = System.currentTimeMillis();
        timeMs += 24*60*60*1000;
```

```
        Date date = new Date(timeMs);
        System.out.println("The date tomorrow is "+date.toString());
    }
}
```

This program uses a helper on the `System` class to obtain the current time in milliseconds. It then adds one day to this by adding 24 hours * 60 minutes * 60 seconds * 1000 milliseconds. Of course, if I knew there were 86,400,000 milliseconds in a day I could have bypassed the arithmetic and simply written:

```
timeMs += 86400000;
```

Although it is possible to manipulate `Dates` in this manner, it is discouraged. The next section introduces `Calendars`, which are a far superior way of manipulating dates. For instance, it is not easy to add one month to a date (or even one year) using this mechanism, because each month can have a different number of milliseconds.

Calendars

Up until this point I have been assuming you want `Dates` to be populated with the current date. What if you want to create a date representing 20th January 2015?

You may have noticed that the `Date` class does support a constructor for creating specific dates, and technically this could be used for the purpose:

```
Date date = new Date(115, 0, 1);
```

There are a few things to note about this constructor however:

⇒ The year is specified as 115. This is because the constructor assumes a base year of 1900 – I have no idea why.
⇒ The month is 0, because Java uses the months 0-11 rather than 1-12.
⇒ The day of month still starts at 1 rather than 0 – again, I have no idea why.

This is all a bit of a mess – and is why you will notice the line through the constructor when you attempt to use it, as seen in figure 24-2:

```
public static void main(String[] args) {
    Date date = new Date(114, 1, 1);
    System.out.println(date.toString());
}
```

FIGURE 24-2

This line means that the constructor is *deprecated*. Deprecated code is code that the author does not want anyone to use anymore. Rather than removing it from the codebase, which would immediately break any code that used it, they mark it as deprecated to indicate you should look for alternatives.

> You can mark code you have written as deprecated by using the following annotation:
> ```
> @Deprecated
> public void deprecatedMethod() {
> }
> ```
> Deprecated code still works the same as non-deprecated code; it is just a way of suggesting to people not to use it.

In this particular case, the constructor has been deprecated (along with a lot of other methods in `Date`) because the correct way to construct historic or future dates in Java is via `Calendars`.

Calendars provide a way of thinking about dates within a *calendar system*. Most of us are familiar with a calendar of 12 months, each with 28, 29, 30 or 31 days: but this calendar system (called the Gregorian calendar) is just one of many calendar systems used around the world. Other countries use different Calendars, such as the Japanese Imperial Calendar or the Thai Buddhist Calendar. Because Java needs to support users in every country, it also provides support for these calendars.

In this chapter you will only focus on the Gregorian calendar, because it is unlikely most readers will ever encounter another calendar system.

In order to obtain a `Calendar` instance representing the current date you can use the following code:

```
Calendar c = Calendar.getInstance();
```

Once the Calendar is created you can access its properties, as seen in the next example. If you run the following example you will notice that the month printed is still 0 based, so February is 1. (The `Calendar` class does support a constant for each month, however, for instance `Calendar.JANUARY`). Java also uses numbers for the day of the week when an enumerated type would make more sense (although, again, constants are provided, for instance `Calendar.FRIDAY`).

```
System.out.println("The year is "+ c.get(Calendar.YEAR));
System.out.println("The month is "+ c.get(Calendar.MONTH));
System.out.println("The day is "+ c.get(Calendar.DATE));
System.out.println("The hour is "+ c.get(Calendar.HOUR));
System.out.println("The day of the week is "+
   c.get(Calendar.DAY_OF_WEEK));
```

If you inspect the concrete type of the `Calendar` in the debugger, you will see that its type is `GregorianCalendar`. Java has determined from the locale of your computer that this is the most appropriate calendar for you. Typically it is not necessary to cast the `Calendar` to `GregorianCalendar`, because `Calendar` contains all the methods typically needed for accessing and manipulating dates.

> GregorianCalendar is actually an amalgamation of two calendar systems: the Gregorian and Julian Calendars – in case you are interested, all dates before October 15th, 1582 use the Julian calendar system (in the real world the cutover from one calendar system to the other was far messier) – the only real difference between the two systems is the way they handle leap years.

You can also use the `GregorianCalendar` constructor to construct arbitrary dates; for instance, the following constructs a `Calendar` object mapped to the date 15th March 2015:

```
Calendar c = new GregorianCalendar(2014, 2, 15);
```

This constructor is overloaded, so you can just set the date elements (in which case the time is set to midnight), or you can set the date and time.

> Although not supported by a constructor, it is possible to map a `Calendar` to a specific `Date` using the `setTime` method, which accepts a `Date` as a parameter.

Once a Calendar has been constructed you can also change any of its elements (such as the year) individually using the `set` method, for instance:

```
c.set(Calendar.MONTH, 5);
```

Alternatively, you can use the `add` method to increment or decrement an element of the date. For instance, the following will add 2 months to the date backing the calendar.

```
c.add(Calendar.MONTH, 2);
```

A `Calendar` can also be converted back into a `Date` by using the badly named `getTime` method.

Formatting Dates

The previous sections have given you an appreciation for the way dates can be created and manipulated. This section will address the manner in which dates can be converted into `Strings` for display.

Java uses the concept of *formatters* for converting objects or primitives into `Strings` for display. These same formatters are also capable of acting in reverse: accepting a `String` and parsing it to produce an object or primitive of the appropriate type.

With dates, the base interface responsible for formatting is `DateFormat`, and its principle implementation is `SimpleDateFormat`.

In order to operate on Dates, the DateFormat needs to know the pattern the textual String should adhere to. The following are all valid representations of the same date (although to varying degrees of accuracy):

- ⇒ 26 January 2015 15:34:00
- ⇒ 2015-1-26 3:34pm
- ⇒ Jan 26, 2015
- ⇒ 2015
- ⇒ January 15

Java provides an *expression language* that can be used to define date formats.

The following is an example of a program that uses a Calendar to construct a Date, and then uses an instance of SimpleDateFormat to print the date in the formats listed:

```
package dates;
import java.text.DateFormat;
import java.text.SimpleDateFormat;
import java.util.Calendar;
import java.util.Date;
import java.util.GregorianCalendar;

public class Formatting {
    public static void main(String[] args) {
        Calendar c = new GregorianCalendar(2014, 0, 26, 15, 34, 0);
        Date date = c.getTime();
        DateFormat df1 = new SimpleDateFormat("dd MMMM yyyy HH:mm:ss");
        System.out.println(df1.format(date));

        df1 = new SimpleDateFormat("yyyy-M-dd h:mm aa");
        System.out.println(df1.format(date));

        df1 = new SimpleDateFormat("MMM dd, yyyy");
        System.out.println(df1.format(date));

        df1 = new SimpleDateFormat("yyyy");
        System.out.println(df1.format(date));

        df1 = new SimpleDateFormat("MMMM yy");
        System.out.println(df1.format(date));
    }
}
```

I will not provide a full description of the formatting rules, because these can easily be looked up when needed. There are, however, a few key rules to remember:

- ⇒ Each component of a date (e.g. hours, days, year) is represented by a letter, but these are case sensitive: "M" represents month, "m" represents minutes, "s" represents seconds. This is a common source of bugs, at least for myself.
- ⇒ The number of times the letter is repeated may impact the presentation. For instance MMMM produces January, MMM produces Jan, MM produces 01, M produces 1.

⇒ It is possible to interweave date components with other formatting symbols such as "-" and ":".

Java also supports a set of "default" formats based on the user's *locale* (the concept of locales will be discussed in future chapters). For instance, the following can be used to print the day, month and year in a format appropriate to the user running the program:

```
DateFormat df2 = DateFormat.getDateInstance(DateFormat.SHORT);
System.out.println(df2.format(date));
```

The constants `MEDIUM`, `LONG` and `FULL` can also be used, and each provides different output.

As mentioned, you can also use `SimpleDateFormat` to convert `Strings` into `Dates`. The following program demonstrates this:

```java
public static void main(String[] args) throws ParseException {
    Calendar c = new GregorianCalendar(2015, 0, 26, 15, 34, 0);
    Date date = c.getTime();
    DateFormat df1 = new SimpleDateFormat("dd MMMM yyyy HH:mm:ss");
    System.out.println(df1.parse("26 January 2015 15:34:00"));

    df1 = new SimpleDateFormat("yyyy-M-dd h:mm aa");
    System.out.println(df1.parse("2015-1-26 3:34 PM"));

    df1 = new SimpleDateFormat("MMM dd, yyyy");
    System.out.println(df1.parse("Jan 26, 2015"));

    df1 = new SimpleDateFormat("yyyy");
    System.out.println(df1.parse("2015"));

    df1 = new SimpleDateFormat("MMMM yy");
    System.out.println(df1.parse("January 15"));
}
```

This is an interesting example, because in many of these cases the format does not provide a value for all elements of the date. For instance, in the second last case the only date element you are providing is the year. If a value is not provided for a date component, Java simply defaults in the first value; if no month is provided it is set to January. The example above prints out:

```
Sun Jan 26 15:34:00 NZDT 2015
Sun Jan 26 15:34:00 NZDT 2015
Sun Jan 26 00:00:00 NZDT 2015
Wed Jan 01 00:00:00 NZDT 2015
Wed Jan 01 00:00:00 NZDT 2015
```

25 DATE AND TIME API

As of Java 8, an entirely new Date and Time API has been provided alongside the Date and Calendar API discussed in the previous chapter.

Many Java programmers have complained about the Date and Calendar API over the years, and a popular open source library called Joda-time has commonly been used in its place.

Not all programmers disliked the Date and Calendar API, and not all programmers liked the Joda API, but the Java language committee has ultimately decided to incorporate a "Joda-like" API to give Java programmers the choice without needing to resort to external libraries.

This chapter will introduce the Date and Time API. If this chapter were to provide an overview of the entire API it would become very boring, very quickly, and contain an enormous amount of duplication. This chapter will therefore attempt to set out the core principles of the API: once these are understood it is straightforward to extend this knowledge to other tasks with the API.

The Date and Time API is designed to take into account two distinct ways of representing date and time:

⇒ In human terms: this uses the familiar concepts of months, days, hours and durations.
⇒ In machine terms: this measures the amount of time that has passed (in nano-seconds) from an epoch.

> A nano-second is one-billionth of a second. Put another way, there are a million nano-seconds in a millisecond.

When dealing with the Date and Time API you can decide the date and time implementation that best suits your needs from the following options:

- `LocalDate`: this represents the year, month and day portion of a date independent of any time zone. This is useful for representing dates such as holidays, because 25 December is a holiday regardless of whether you are in the US, Australia or the United Kingdom.
- `LocalTime`: this is essentially the same as `LocalDate`, but it only represents a time, e.g. 12:55:21 (times are always captured to nano-second precision).
- `LocalDateTime`: this is the same as `LocalDate`, but contains time information as well as date information.
- `ZonedDateTime`: this is the same as `LocalDateTime`, except it contains a time zone offset from UTC time (e.g. -05:00) and a zone ID (e.g. America/Detroit).
- `OffsetDateTime`: this is identical to `ZoneDateTime` but does not contain a zone id, it only contains an offset.
- `OffsetTime`: this is similar to `OffsetDateTime`, but only contains the time portion of the date, e.g. 13:00:21+12:00
- `Year`: this simply contains the year portion of a date
- `Month`: this is an enumerated type representing the 12 months of the year
- `MonthDay`: this represents a day and month, and can therefore be used to represent a day of the year in a year-agnostic manner.
- `YearMonth`: as expected, this contains a year and a month.
- `DayOfWeek`: this is an enumerated type representing the 7 days of the week
- `Instant`: an instant represents the number of nanoseconds that have occurred between 1/1/1970 and an instance in time. Due to the fact this is a number larger than can be accommodated by a long, the seconds since 1/1/1970 are stored in a long, and the nanoseconds offset are stored in an int.
- `Duration`: a duration is an amount of time that has elapsed between two `Instants`. Like `Instant`, the duration is recorded in terms of seconds and nano-seconds.
- `Period`: a period is a date based amount of time. This records a duration in terms of years, months and days.

Now that the basic types have been introduced it is worth jumping in and looking at some examples. Although the classes are quite different in the way they represent date and time, they tend to support a standard set of methods; these methods will be introduced in the examples following. The first example will deal with the `LocalDateTime` class and examine some of the ways it can be constructed and manipulated:

```
package datetime;
```

```java
import java.time.LocalDateTime;
import java.time.ZoneOffset;
public class DateTime {

    public static void main(String[] args) {
        LocalDateTime dt = LocalDateTime.now();
        System.out.println(dt);
        System.out.println(dt.getMonth());
        System.out.println(dt.getDayOfWeek());
        dt = dt.plusDays(2);
        System.out.println(dt.getDayOfWeek());
        dt = dt.plusHours(5).plusMinutes(10);
        System.out.println(dt);
        System.out.println(dt.atOffset(ZoneOffset.ofHours(-11)));
        dt = dt.minusWeeks(20);
        System.out.println(dt);
        dt = dt.withDayOfMonth(4) .withYear(2009);
        System.out.println(dt);
    }
}
```

This produced the following result:

```
2014-03-06T19:38:34.933
MARCH
THURSDAY
SATURDAY
2014-03-09T00:48:34.933
2014-03-09T00:48:34.933-11:00
2013-10-20T00:48:34.933
2009-10-04T00:48:34.933
```

This short example demonstrates a number of useful methods. For a start, there is a `now` method for creating a `LocalDateTime` representing the current date and time:

```
LocalDateTime dt = LocalDateTime.now();
```

There are also a variety of methods for accessing a specific portion of the date or time (such as the year or month). You may recall that these methods were deprecated on `Date`, but are available in a similar form on `Calendar`:

```
dt.getMonth()
dt.getDayOfWeek()
```

Next, there are a wide array of methods for adding or subtracting units of time (e.g. weeks, years, hours) from a `LocalDateTime`. Because `LocalDateTime` is immutable, these always return a new instance of `LocalDateTime`. These are somewhat similar to the methods on `Calendar`, but cover a wider array of options, and, unlike `Calendar`, do not mutate (or change) the object:

```
dt.plusDays(2)
dt.plusHours(5).plusMinutes(10)
```

An alternative way of manipulating a `LocalDateTime` is with the methods prefixed "with", for instamce, `withMonth`, `withYear`. These methods also return a new `LocalDateTime`, manipulated to have the appropriate unit set to the value specified in the request:

```
dt.withDayOfMonth(4).withYear(2009)
```

Finally, there are ways to convert this type of date object into other types of date. This example shows `atOffset`, but `atZone` is also supported:

```
dt.atOffset(ZoneOffset.ofHours(-11))
```

In addition to creating a `LocalDateTime` with the static `now` method, the static `of` method can be used. For example:

```
LocalDateTime dt = LocalDateTime.of(2014, Month.MARCH, 3, 12, 24, 33);
```

This method is overloaded, so you can choose how precise you want the value to be by optionally providing seconds and nanoseconds.

`LocalDateTime` instances can also be parsed from a textual string (this will be examined in more detail later):

```
LocalDateTime.parse("2014-03-20T20:12:33", DateTimeFormatter.ISO_DATE_TIME);
```

Finally, they can be generated from a different type of date/time object:

```
LocalDateTime.from(Instant.now());
```

Now that you have a general understanding of the methods supported by the API, it is worth focusing on a couple of principles used by the API:

Chaining methods

Most of the classes in the `time` package support pipelining (or chaining). This is a technique whereby the output of one method call becomes the input for another method call. You have already seen examples of this earlier in the book with the intermediate operations on the Streams API. Chaining works on the principle that the return type of a method is the type the original method was invoked on (either `this` or a new instance of the type the method was invoked on).

The following are examples of chaining:

```
dt.withDayOfMonth(4).withYear(2009)
dt.plusHours(5).plusMinutes(10)
```

Immutable objects

The classes defined in the Date and Time API are immutable. This means that once their value is set it can never be changed. Even when their value appears to change Java is actually creating a new instance of the object.

There has been a move towards immutable classes in Java because they tend to be easier to use in multi-threaded environments, and also lead to better practices in general, since the state of a variable will not be modified without the knowledge of one of its references. For instance, consider the following code from the Calendar API:

```
Calendar c = new GregorianCalendar();
Calendar c2 = c;
c.add(Calendar.DATE, 1);
```

The value in the `Calendar` referenced by c2 is changed without its knowledge. This situation can never occur with the Date and Time API.

Year and MonthDay

You can now look at a different set of examples with the `Year` and `MonthDay` classes (remember, these only deal with a subset of the fields needed to fully represent a date):

```
package datetime;

import java.time.Month;
import java.time.MonthDay;
import java.time.Year;

public class YearMonth {
    public static void main(String[] args) {
        Year y = Year.now();
        System.out.println(y.isLeap());
        System.out.println(y.isBefore(Year.of(2013)));
        System.out.println(y.isAfter(Year.parse("2013")));

        MonthDay md = MonthDay.of(Month.FEBRUARY, 29);
        System.out.println(md.atYear(2011));
        System.out.println(md.isValidYear(2012));
        System.out.println(md.isValidYear(2013));
    }
}
```

This produces the following result:

```
false
false
true
2011-02-28
true
false
```

As you can see, different classes in the Date and Time API sometimes support additional methods. The `Year` class supports an `isLeap` method that indicates if the year specified is a leap year, while the `MonthDay` class supports an `isValidYear` method to indicate if the day and month represent a valid date in a particular year.

All date/time classes also support `isBefore` and `isAfter` methods for comparing two instances of the same type.

Instant

As mentioned earlier, an `Instant` represents a point in time, and is stored as a `long` and `int` pair, representing the number of nanoseconds that have passed since 1 January 1970 (midnight UTC).

As it happens, timekeeping in nanoseconds is surprisingly complex. Seconds are defined via atomic clocks: such seconds are referred to as *SI seconds*. There are very close to 86400 SI seconds in a day (24 x 60 x 60).

Unfortunately the devil is in the detail – very close is not the same as exactly. To make matters worse, not all days are exactly the same length, and the length of a day is not predictable. Although the variants are tiny, they do add up after time, therefore – as mentioned earlier - UTC incorporates a concept called *leap-seconds*.

Due to these complexities of the UTC time-scale, the designers of the Date and Time API decided to create their own time-scale called the Java Time-scale. This time-scale always has 86400 seconds in a day – but each second may not be the same length as an SI second. This allows Java to reflect the tiny changes in the length of each day without moving away from the simplicity of 86400 seconds in a day.

How this works is largely up to the Java implementation. According to the documentation: "Implementations of the Java time-scale using the JSR-310 API are not required to provide any clock that is sub-second accurate, or that progresses monotonically or smoothly. "

If you are using Java in environments where extreme precision is required you probably want to investigate the implications of this statement in relation to your chosen JVM.

Now that the details have been addressed, the following is a code example using `Instants`:

```
package datetime;
import java.time.Instant;
import java.time.temporal.ChronoUnit;

public class InstantExample {
    public static void main(String[] args) {
        Instant now = Instant.now();
        System.out.println("Epoch seconds = "+ now.getEpochSecond());
        System.out.println("Offset nanoseconds = "+ now.getNano());
        System.out.println(now.toString());

        now = now.minusSeconds(86400 );
        System.out.println(now.toString());

        System.out.println(now.until(Instant.now(), ChronoUnit.HOURS));
    }
}
```

This uses the familiar `now` method to construct an `Instant`, and then prints its seconds and nanoseconds.

As the example shows, it is possible to add or subtract seconds from an `Instant` to create a new `Instant` reflecting that offset.

It is also possible to use the `until` method to determine how far apart two `Instants` are in the required unit – hours in this example.

Duration and Period

The final classes you will examine are `Duration` and `Period`, which are both mechanisms for recording the passing of time. As mentioned earlier, durations are used to track a period of time in seconds and nanoseconds, while a period is used to track a period of time in years, months and days.

The following is an example program that constructs a `Duration` as the difference between two `Instants` roughly 1050 milliseconds apart:

```
package datetime;
import java.time.Duration;
import java.time.Instant;

public class Durations {
    public static void main(String[] args) {
        Instant i1 = Instant.now();
        try {
            Thread.sleep(1050L);
        } catch (InterruptedException ex) {
        }
        Instant i2 = Instant.now();
        Duration d = Duration.between(i1, i2);
        System.out.printf("%d seconds and %d nanoseconds elapsed\n",
                d.getSeconds(), d.getNano());
    }
}
```

Once a `Duration` has been created, it can be used conveniently with other types of Date or Time:

```
LocalDateTime ldt = LocalDateTime.now();
ldt = ldt.plus(d);
```

This code adds the duration to an instance of `LocalDateTime`.

`Periods` are used to find the number of years, months and days between two dates. The following code constructs a `Period` representing the difference between two `LocalDate` instances:

```
package datetime;

import java.time.LocalDate;
import java.time.Month;
import java.time.Period;

public class Periods {
    public static void main(String[] args) {
        LocalDate ldt1 = LocalDate.of(2008, Month.JANUARY, 22);
        LocalDate ldt2 = LocalDate.of(2014, Month.MARCH, 12);
        Period p = Period.between(ldt1, ldt2);
        System.out.printf("%d years, %d months, %d days\n",
                p.getYears(), p.getMonths(), p.getDays());
    }
}
```

This prints:

```
6 years, 1 months, 18 days
```

It is also possible to construct `Periods` from their static constructor methods:

```
Period p2 = Period.ofDays(2000);
```

If you were to print the years and months of this `Period` it would print 0 – in fact the `printf` statement above would produce the following:

```
0 years, 0 months, 2000 days
```

This is because you have not specified the period in relation to any fixed date, therefore it is not possible to know how many months and years it is. For instance, 366 days could be 1 year and 1 day or 1 year and 0 days depending on the context, for instance, does the period include the date 29 February?

Formatting and Parsing

The Date and Time API provides its own parsing and formatting API. You have already briefly seen an example of parsing dates using the following code:

```
LocalDateTime.parse("2014-03-20T20:12:33", DateTimeFormatter.ISO_DATE_TIME);
```

In this case, the expression `DateTimeFormatter.ISO_DATE_TIME` is an instance of the `DateTimeFormatter` class. This defines a date and time format as follows:

```
'2011-12-03T10:15:30+01:00[Europe/Paris]'
```

Because I am constructing a `LocalDateTime`, the time zone and offset are irrelevant. I have therefore omitted them.

`DateTimeFormatter` provides a whole set of predefined date and time formats, such as:

- ISO_DATE
- ISO_TIME

If the existing patterns do not meet your needs, you can of course define your own patterns. The pattern language for `DateTimeFormatter` is the same as for `SimpleDateFormat`:

```
DateTimeFormatter formatter = DateTimeFormatter.ofPattern("MMM dd yyyy");
LocalDate ldt = LocalDate.parse("Jan 22 2014", formatter);
```

This particular pattern can be used for parsing a textual date into an object that only contains date information; for instance, the following code is perfectly legal and constructs a `Year` with the value 2014:

```
DateTimeFormatter formatter = DateTimeFormatter.ofPattern("MMM dd yyyy");
Year year = Year.parse("Jan 22 2014", formatter);
```

This code is not valid however:

```
DateTimeFormatter formatter = DateTimeFormatter.ofPattern("MMM dd yyyy");
LocalDateTime ldt = LocalDateTime.parse("Jan 22 2014", formatter);
```

This produces a `DateTimeParseException`, because the format does not contain time information, and therefore is insufficient for populating all the fields on a `LocalDateTime` instance.

Formatting is the reserves of parsing. The main constraint of formatting is that the pattern can only contain elements that are relevant for the given object. Therefore, the following code is valid:

```
LocalDate ld = LocalDate.now();
ld.format(DateTimeFormatter.ofPattern("yyyy MM"));
```

While the following code will result in an `UnsupportedTemporalTypeException`:

```
LocalDate ld = LocalDate.now();
ld.format(DateTimeFormatter.ofPattern("yyyy MM dd hh"));
```

In this particular case I am attempting to format the hour of a `LocalDate` – which is not possible.

It is also possible to format dates based on the defaults of the user's locale. For instance, the following will print the date in a locale specific manner:

```
LocalDate ld = LocalDate.now();
ld.format(DateTimeFormatter.ofLocalizedDate(FormatStyle.SHORT));
```

DANE CAMERON

26 INPUT AND OUTPUT

Input and output are key aspects of nearly all computer programs. For instance, a typical command line program will accept input, perform an operation on that input, and produce a result as output.

You have already seen many examples of output in this book through the methods on `System.out`. I have not really stopped to look at what `System.out` is, however, or how it relates to Java's broader approach to input and output.

Java has historically used two key approaches for dealing with input and output:

⇒ **Streams**: streams are byte orientated, meaning they work with arrays of bytes. Do not confuse this use of "Stream" with the Steams API – they are not related.
⇒ **Readers/writers**: readers and writers are character orientated, meaning they deal with arrays of characters or strings.

The first key to working with input or output in Java is deciding which approach is relevant for the task at hand.

> This chapter will use the Java I/O library. Java supports an alternative library called Java NIO (Java non-blocking I/O) – you may choose to investigate this on your own, although typically Java I/O will meet your needs.
>
> Java NIO uses a different set of constructs to represent interaction with the underlying file-system, and may be more efficient for intensive I/O operations.

> In addition, several other helper classes have been added to Java over the years to ease interaction with the file system – these will be covered in passing – but are not the main focus of this chapter.
>
> Despite these alternatives to Java I/O – and although these alternatives are better in many respects – it is important to gain an understanding of the Java I/O, because it is still very widely used, and you are likely to encounter code that uses it.

As it happens, `System.in` and `System.out` are both streams. This may seem odd because you have been passing them `Strings` in most instances. If you look at the overloaded `print` methods, however, you will see that they can also accept primitive types.

Streams are more generic than readers/writers, because any type of data can be represented as an array of bytes if required, but not all data can be (conveniently) represented as an array of characters. This is the reason that `System.out` is a stream.

The next key to working with input and output is determining the source or destination of the data, for instance:

⇒ The source may be a network socket
⇒ The source may be a file on the local file system
⇒ The destination may be the standard output
⇒ The destination may be a file on a remote file system

Finally, it is necessary to determine the approach that should be taken when reading or writing data:

⇒ Should ever byte/character be written one at a time?
⇒ Should a whole set of bytes/characters be buffered and written at once?
⇒ Should a checksum be verified when reading the data to ensure it has not been corrupted?
⇒ Should the data be decrypted as it is read or encrypted as it is written?

The approach is actually more complex because it may be necessary to use more than one approach. For instance, it may be necessary to buffer the data as it is read, decrypt it, and then verify a checksum.

Due to this complexity, Java comes with a wide array of classes descending from `Reader`, `Writer`, `InputStream` or `OutputStream`. It is then possible to nest instances of these classes inside each other to add additional functionality. If this sounds confusing it will be explained in detail below.

Files

In the first section of this chapter you will work with files, because they remain a very popular source and destination for data. You have already seen that the Streams API provides an elegant mechanism for reading the contents of a file line by line, but this section will look at more fundamental mechanisms that can be used for reading and writing files.

InputStreams and OutputStreams

You will begin by working with streams. Begin by creating a new project in Eclipse: I have called mine `InputOutput`. Create a file inside the `src` folder called `bytes.txt`. Simply right-click on the `src` folder and select New -> File.

Add some random characters to this file, for instance:

```
1js7j4gsj0dm
```

Now, create a program for reading this data and printing it to Standard Output:

```
package streams;
import java.io.File;
import java.io.FileInputStream;
import java.io.IOException;

public class ReadFile {
    public static void main(String[] args) {
        File f = new File("src/bytes.txt");
        FileInputStream fis = null;
        try {
            fis = new FileInputStream(f);
            int content;
            while ((content = fis.read()) != -1) {
                System.out.println(content);
            }
        } catch (IOException e) {
            e.printStackTrace(System.out);
        } finally {
            try {
                fis.close();
            } catch (IOException e) {
                e.printStackTrace(System.out);
            }
        }
    }
}
```

There is quite a lot going on here, so I will go through it line by line.

The program starts by defining the `File` that will be read:

```
File f = new File("src/bytes.txt");
```

The location of the `File` is relative to the root directory of the project. This is called a relative file location, because the location is relative to the location of the project. It is also possible to define absolute file paths:

```
File f = new File("c:/projects/inputoutput/src/bytes.txt");
```

Or

```
File f = new File("/projects/inputoutput/src/bytes.txt");
```

The forward slash is always used to separate elements in the path, even on Windows systems. Because Java uses the underlying system libraries, the file name will be case sensitive if the machine enforces case sensitive file names.

> Although the `File` class is supported in all versions of Java, newer versions of Java support a class called `Path` that adds additional functionality – and is now generally favored. You can convert a `File` to a `Path` by invoking `toPath` on it – this will then give you access to the functionality defined by `Path` – should you need it.
>
> A class called `Files` contains a large number of static utility methods that utilize `Path`s. This should be your first port of call for methods allowing you to copy, move or delete files.

`FileInputStream` can accept a `String` representing the file path, but it is best practice to encapsulate the file path in a `File` object because this gives you access to a set of utility methods, for instance:

```
f.exists();
f.canRead();
f.canWrite();
f.length();
```

Constructing a `File` object in this manner does not ensure a corresponding file exists on the file-system; it is merely the representation of a possible location on the file-system, where a file may or may not reside.

I then create a `FileInputStream` and pass it the `File` as a parameter. You will see that this is occurring inside a `try/catch` block: If the `File` does not exist a `FileNotFoundException` will be thrown at this point. This exception extends `IOException`, therefore the code will simply catch `IOException`.

The next portion of code loops through all the content in the file one byte at a time, and assigns the content of each location to the variable `content`. If the value of this is `-1` then the end of file has been reached, and the loop ends.

The `catch` block prints out any exception that occurs by passing a stream (`System.out`) to the `printStackTrace` method of `Exception`. You will notice that `printStackTrace` accepts an `OutputStream`, therefore I could have passed it any kind of `OutputStream`, including a `FileOutputStream`. This highlights the flexibility of programming to a common interface.

After the `catch` block you will notice a `finally` block that closes the `FileInputStream`. You want to attempt to close the `FileInputStream` regardless of whether the method completed successfully, because an error may have occurred during the `read` operation. You will notice you also need to wrap the call to `close` in a further `try/catch` block, because this will generate an exception if the `File` did not exist originally.

It is important to always close files after using them; otherwise the file descriptor will continue to utilize Operating System resources.

Java 7 introduces an alternative mechanism for ensuring resources are always closed – the *try-with-resources* statement. This allows the previous example to be written as follows:

```
package streams;
import java.io.File;
import java.io.FileInputStream;
import java.io.IOException;

public class ReadFile2 {
    public static void main(String[] args) {
        File f = new File("src/bytes.txt");
        try (FileInputStream fis = new FileInputStream(f)) {
            int content;
            while ((content = fis.read()) != -1) {
                System.out.println(content);
            }
        } catch (IOException e) {
            e.printStackTrace(System.out);
        }
    }
}
```

Notice in this case that the `FileInputStream` is declared within brackets in the `try`-statement. Any object that implements `java.io.Closeable` can be declared in a statement such as this, and the Java platform will ensure the resource is automatically closed at the end of the `try`-block whether an exception occurs or not.

If you run this you may be surprised at the result, in my case it was:

```
49
106
115
55
106
52
103
115
106
48
100
109
```

The call to read returns an `int`. Because a byte consists of 8 bits, it is capable of holding

2 to the power of 8 values (256): the numbers 0 through 255 represents these values (with -1 representing the special end-of-file value). The read method does not return a `byte`, because Java needs an extra value to represent -1– and therefore all possible values could not fit into a `byte`. Technically it could return a `short`, but `int` values are typically easier to use.

> An alternative way of implementing this is to invoke `Files.readAllBytes`, and pass a `Path` argument representint the file. This method returns a `byte[]`.

The file that was read is an ASCII text file. Each character in the file therefore occupies one byte of space, and the call to `read` always returns the byte value representing this character. The number represents the position of the character in the ASCII table: 49 represents "1", 106 represents "j" etc.

It is trivial to turn this numeric representation back into the ASCII representation by changing this line:

```
System.out.println(content);
```

To this:

```
System.out.println((char)content);
```

The cast here tells Java that you want the `int` to be interpreted as a `char`, which implicitly converts the byte sequence into a character sequence.

It is important to remember that although one byte equals one character in ASCII character encoding, characters can take up more than one byte in Unicode encoded files; therefore it is not generally a good idea to read textual data in this manner.

In order to write data using streams you need to use an `OutputStream`. As you have already seen, `System.out` is an `OutputStream`, but naturally you can create your own `FileOutputStreams`. When writing data to a file it is inefficient to write bytes one at a time. It is better to gather together a chunk of bytes, and write them all in one go: this is called buffering and flushing.

The downside of buffering is that if the program crashes before it completes, any data still in the buffer (referred to as un-flushed data) will be lost – therefore it is not appropriate for all situations.

In the example below I will demonstrate how to add buffering to a `FileOutputStream` by wrapping one `OutputStream` in another. This wrapping can continue almost indefinitely by wrapping this output stream in another stream adding even more functionality.

When data is written to the output stream, each stream gets a change to process the data from the outside in. They perform any processing that is necessary, and then pass the data to the next stream in the hierarchy.

> This is referred to as the decorator design pattern. This pattern is used to extend (or decorate) the functionality in a specific class with functionality from another class, without requiring one of the classes to extend the other.
>
> This pattern works well in cases where many different classes can be responsible for adding functionality, because there may not be clear cases of one class extending the other – they are all simply adding additional functionality to the same base, and can be mixed and matched accordingly.
>
> As an example, `BufferedOutputStream` cannot extend `FileOutputStream`, because you may also want to use it with different types of `OutputStream`, such as those that write to a network connection.

In the next example you will create a `File` object representing a file you want to write to, even though this does not exist yet. The process of writing to the `File` will implicitly create it:

```java
package streams;
import java.io.BufferedOutputStream;
import java.io.File;
import java.io.FileOutputStream;
import java.io.IOException;

public class WriteFile {
    public static void main(String[] args) {
        File f = new File("src/bytes_output.txt");
        FileOutputStream fos = null;
        BufferedOutputStream bos = null;
        try {
            fos = new FileOutputStream(f);
            bos = new BufferedOutputStream(fos);
            for (int i = 0; i < 100; i++) {
                bos.write(("Hello world "+i+"\n").getBytes());
                if (i%10 == 0) {
                    bos.flush();
                }
            }
        } catch (IOException e) {
            e.printStackTrace(System.out);
        } finally {
            try {
                bos.flush();
                fos.close();
            } catch (IOException e) {
                e.printStackTrace(System.out);
```

```
                }
            }
        }
    }
}
```

Notice that the `FileOutputStream` is nested inside a `BufferedOutputStream`. In addition, you need to call `flush` on the `BufferedOutputStream` whenever you want it to write data to the file. If you do not call this before closing the file then any data still in the buffer will be lost.

Readers and Writers

Readers and writers are similar to streams. Not only can they be nested inside one another to add additional functionality, the names of the various readers and writers provided by Java tend to match the names of their stream counterparts relatively closely.

You will first write a program for reading file data one line at a time and storing the line in a `String`. This is a very common operation with textual data, and as you have already seen, can also be achieved with the Streams API introduced in Java 8.

This example will be slightly more complicated because it will read all the files in the `src` directory one by one. In order to do this you create a `File` and pass it the path of the `src` directory. Files and directories are both represented by the `File` object in Java, but they can be distinguished by the `isDirectory` and `isFile` methods.

Once you have a reference to a `File` representing the directory, you can use it to list all the files in the directory and store the list in an array of `Files`. This array will contain both files and child directories of the `src` directory, therefore when you loop through the `Files` you only read the contents if the `isFile` method evaluates to `true`.

```
package streams;
import java.io.BufferedReader;
import java.io.File;
import java.io.FileReader;
import java.io.IOException;

public class ReaderExample {
    public static void main(String[] args) {
        File srcDirectory = new File("src");
        System.out.println(srcDirectory.isDirectory());
        File[] files = srcDirectory.listFiles();
        for (int i = 0; i < files.length; i++) {
            File f = files[i];
            if (f.isFile()) {
                System.out.printf("Processing file %s\n\n", f.getName());
                BufferedReader br = null;
                FileReader fr = null;
                try {
                    fr = new FileReader(f);
                    br = new BufferedReader(fr);
                    String line;
                    while ((line = br.readLine()) != null) {
                        System.out.println(line);
```

```
                    }
                    System.out.println("\n");
                } catch (IOException e) {
                    e.printStackTrace(System.out);
                } finally {
                    try {
                        br.close();
                    } catch (IOException e) {
                        e.printStackTrace(System.out);
                    }
                }
            }
        }
    }
}
```

Notice also that you have wrapped a `FileReader` in a `BufferedReader`: it is the `BufferedReader` class that provides the `readLine` method.

Although there is nothing inherently wrong with this code, and is the way this functionality has traditionally been written, this is another example where recent improvements to the Java language can result in more stream lined code. The following program achieves the exact same result.

```
package streams;
import java.io.IOException;
import java.nio.file.FileVisitResult;
import java.nio.file.Files;
import java.nio.file.Path;
import java.nio.file.Paths;
import java.nio.file.SimpleFileVisitor;
import java.nio.file.attribute.BasicFileAttributes;

public class ReaderExample {
    public static void main(String[] args) throws IOException {
        Path path = Paths.get("src");
        MyFileVisitor fileVisitor = new MyFileVisitor();
        Files.walkFileTree(path, fileVisitor);
    }

    private static class MyFileVisitor extends SimpleFileVisitor<Path> {
        @Override
        public FileVisitResult visitFile(Path path, BasicFileAttributes attributes) throws IOException {
            for (String line : Files.readAllLines(path)) {
                System.out.println(line);
            }
            System.out.println("\n");
            return FileVisitResult.CONTINUE;
        }

        @Override
        public FileVisitResult preVisitDirectory(Path directory, BasicFileAttributes attributes) throws IOException {
            return FileVisitResult.CONTINUE;
        }
```

        }
    }

Notice in this example that a `Path` is initially constructed (rather than a `File`), and then you instruct the API to walk the file tree using this `Path` as the root (recursively process every file and directory). Whenever a file or directory is encountered it invokes a method on an instance of `SimpleFileVisitor` – this can process the files or directories via the overloaded `visitFile` and `preVisitDirectory` methods respectively – and then instruct the `SimpleFileVisitor` to continue processing the next file.

Also notice in this example that the lines in a file are read as a `List<String>` using `Files.readAllLines`.

Writing files with `FileWriters` is also a straightforward process. In this example you will slightly complicate the process by creating a directory for the file being written. The file will be nested inside two new directories: you will utilize the `mkdirs` method to create these the first time the program is executed – on subsequent executions this method will realize the directories already exist.

When you create the file for the output you will specify the directory as one parameter, and the file name as the other parameter.

```
public static void main(String[] args) {
    File dir = new File("src/newdir/childdir");
    dir.mkdirs();
    File output = new File(dir, "output.txt");
    try (BufferedWriter br =  new BufferedWriter(new FileWriter(output))) {
        for (int i = 0; i <= 100; i++) {
            br.append("Line number "+i+"\n");
        }
    } catch (IOException e) {
        e.printStackTrace(System.out);
    }
}
```

> The `BufferedWriter` is automatically flushed when declared inside a try-with-resource expression.

This example uses `append` rather than `write`. This ensures that subsequent executions of the program do not overwrite the file that already exists.

Notice in this case how the `BufferedWriter` is created in a single statement, allowing it to be declared in a try-with-resources statement.

Sockets

Although the examples up until this point have used files as their input and output destinations, the basic approaches used here work equally well for transmitting data across a network.

In this section you will look at Java sockets. Sockets provide a lightweight mechanism for transmitting an array of bytes over a network.

Socket connections require one party to act as the server (called a `SocketServer`). This party will open a port that clients can connect to. When clients send data to a `SocketServer` they will block and wait for a response.

The examples in this chapter will involve the client and server running on the same machine, and therefore they will use `localhost` as the hostname. If you like, you can run these examples over a network, and specify the appropriate IP address; you will however need to ensure the firewall on the server machine allows traffic to be received on the appropriate port (`9090` in these examples).

In this example you will transmit Java objects over a network. In order to transmit them over the network you need to serialize them on the client, and then deserialize them when they reach the server. You have already seen the process of serialization in the chapter that demonstrated object cloning.

This example will send an instance of `Address` over the network, where the server will populate the `postcode` field and return the `Address` to the client.

Because the client and server will typically run on different machines, each of them will need access to the `Address` class. This may present a problem however, because the client and server may have different versions of the `Address` class, for instance, extra fields may be added to the client version but not the server version.

In order to protect against this, Java supports the concept of the `serialVersionUID` field that ensures you are informed when incompatible versions of a class are used. This can be set to any `long` value, and you should change the value any time you make a material change to a class. Eclipse will also offer to generate one for you whenever a class is declared as implementing `Serializable`. Additionally, if you do not declare a `serialVersionUID`, Java will generate a default (unseen) one. If the client and server have classes with different values for `serialVersionUID` an `InvalidClassException` will be generated during deserialization.

> Although Java creates a `serialVersionUID`, it is recommended that you generate your own, because the default version will change with any minor change to a class definition, even if this does not affect serialization.

The `Address` class in the next example also introduces a new concept of a `transient` field. If a field is marked `transient`, it is not serialized as part of the serialization process. This is useful for sensitive data that should not be sent over the network, or for fields that simply are not needed. Although omitted, be sure to add getters and setters for all fields.

```java
package server;
import java.io.Serializable;
import java.util.Date;

public class Address implements Serializable {
    private static final long serialVersionUID = -7256403555699920549L;
    private String street;
    private Integer streetNumber;
    private String city;
    private Integer postcode;
    private transient Date createDate;

    public Address() {
        createDate = new Date();
    }

    public Address(String street, Integer streetNumber, String city) {
        this();
        this.street = street;
        this.city = city;
        this.streetNumber = streetNumber;
    }
/* Getter and setter fields have been omitted for brevity, but are required by the program */
}
```

I will begin by outlining the server program:

```java
package server;
import java.io.IOException;
import java.io.ObjectInputStream;
import java.io.ObjectOutputStream;
import java.net.ServerSocket;
import java.net.Socket;

public class SocketServer {

    public static void main(String[] args) {
        try {
            ServerSocket serverSocket = new ServerSocket(9090);
            System.out.println("The server is running");
            while (true) {
                Socket client = serverSocket.accept();
                System.out.println("Client accepted");
                ObjectInputStream ois = new
                   ObjectInputStream(client.getInputStream());
                Address address = (Address)ois.readObject();
                ObjectOutputStream oos = new
                   ObjectOutputStream(client.getOutputStream());
                address.setPostcode((int)System.currentTimeMillis() %100000);
                oos.writeObject(address);
                oos.flush();
            }
```

```
        } catch (IOException e) {
            e.printStackTrace(System.out);
        } catch (ClassNotFoundException e) {
            e.printStackTrace(System.out);
        }
    }
}
```

The server will accept connections from clients continually. In order to facilitate this, you first create an instance of `ServerSocket`, and then place a call to `accept` inside a `while(true)` loop. This loop will loop forever, therefore the server will continue running even after accepting the first connection. The `ServerSocket` is configured to listen on port 9090 – but you can change this if required.

Although this is an infinite loop, it is not going to consume CPU like typical infinite loops, because the `accept` method waits until it is notified that a connection has been received. While it is in the waiting state it is not consuming resources.

Once a connection is received, the call to `accept` will return an instance of `Socket` representing the communication between the server and this single client. The server can access the clients `InputStream`: this gives the server access to the bytes the client has sent over the socket.

For the purposes of this example, you will assume that the `InputStream` will always contain the bytes representing a serialized `Address` object, therefore you wrap the `InputStream` inside an `ObjectInputStream`, and call `readObject` on it.

Notice from the point of view of the program, however, this `InputStream` is no different from a file based input stream: Java has abstracted the underlying data source as an `InputStream`.

Once you have updated the `Address` object you need to return it to the client. In order to do this you access the `OutputStream` from the `Socket`, wrap this in an `ObjectOutputStream`, call `writeObject` on it, and `flush` the stream.

You should be able to run this program and have it print that it is waiting for a connection.

You now come to the client program. This program will have its own `main` method, because it will run completely independently of the server. This program will first construct an `Address` object, and then connect to the server. The behavior of this program is the inverse of the server: it first writes to the `OutputStream`, and then reads from the `InputStream` and prints the result:

```
package server;
import java.io.IOException;
import java.io.ObjectInputStream;
import java.io.ObjectOutputStream;
import java.net.Socket;

public class SocketClient {
```

```java
    public static void main(String[] args) {
        try {
            Socket s = new Socket("localhost", 9090);
            ObjectOutputStream oos = new
               ObjectOutputStream(s.getOutputStream());
            Address a = new Address("Main Road", 99, "Montgomory");
            oos.writeObject(a);
            oos.flush();
            ObjectInputStream ois = new
                ObjectInputStream(s.getInputStream());
            a = (Address)ois.readObject();
            System.out.println("The postcode is "+a.getPostcode());
        } catch (IOException e) {
            e.printStackTrace(System.out);
        } catch (ClassNotFoundException e) {
            e.printStackTrace(System.out);
        }
    }
}
```

Although the `InputStream` can be obtained by simply invoking `s.getInputStream`, the code will automatically block until a response is received from the server socket.

If you run this program (while ensuring that the server is running), it should print out a postcode to the console.

Because there are two programs running, each will have its own console. You can switch between consoles by clicking on the console icon at the bottom of the screen, as shown in figure 26-1 (it is the button on the far right hand side):

FIGURE 26-1

If you switch to the server program's console you will see that it has printed that it has accepted a client.

You can run the client program as many times as you like, each time it will print a different postcode.

27 PROPERTIES FILES

You saw earlier in the book that it is possible to pass arguments to a program when it is invoked. This enabled the same program to behave differently depending on the value of the runtime arguments provided.

While program arguments are an important technique for passing information to a program at runtime, they can become unwieldy when there are a large number of arguments involved. In many cases it is generally better to use an approach called *properties files*.

A properties file is a plain-text file with a set of name/value pairs, where an equals sign separates the name and value. Each property is listed on a new line in the file, and the overall file is given a `.properties` extension.

Getting started

You will begin by creating a properties file for a set of messages that will appear in a program that performs basic arithmetic. Start by creating an Eclipse project, and add a file called `messages.properties` to the `src` folder by right clicking on the "src" folder and choosing `New -> File`. Add the following content to the file:

```
introduction.message=Welcome to the adder program
input.message=The input values are {0} and {1}
result.message=The result is {0}
```

This file contains three properties. On the key side of each property you should use dots rather than spaces, and I prefer to only use lower case characters.

You can see that two of these property values contain special character sequences, for instance, {1}. These are placeholders for values that will be provided at runtime.

Now, add a class with a `main` method called `Adder`:

```java
package adder;
import java.io.IOException;
import java.text.MessageFormat;
import java.util.Properties;
public class Adder {
    private Properties properties = new Properties();
    public Adder() {
        try {
            properties.load(getClass().getResourceAsStream(
                "/messages.properties"));
            System.out.println(properties.getProperty(
                "introduction.message"));
        } catch (IOException e) {
            e.printStackTrace(System.out);
        }
    }

    public void add(int a, int b) {
        String inputMessage = properties.getProperty(
            "input.message");
        String resultMessage = properties.getProperty(
            "result.message");
        System.out.println(MessageFormat.format(
            inputMessage, a, b));
        System.out.println(MessageFormat.format(
            resultMessage, a + b));
    }

    public static void main(String[] args) {
        Adder adder = new Adder();
        adder.add(20, 30);
        adder.add(23, 12);
    }
}
```

When the `Adder` class is constructed it populates a `Properties` object from the values in `messages.properties`. The `Properties` object is essentially a `Map`: it is possible to `get` and `put` properties based on their key.

The `load` method simply accepts an `InputStream`. Although it would be possible to use a `FileInputStream`, and alternative approach has been used: Because the properties file is in the `src` directory, it is copied to the `bin` directory when the program is compiled (along with the class file). It is therefore possible to use the following line of code to create an `InputStream` backed by the properties file:

`getClass().getResourceAsStream("/messages.properties")`

The `getClass` method returns a representation of the object's class as a `Class` object. You can use a helper method on this (and every `Class`) called `getResourceAsStream`. This method can be used to read any resource on the *classpath* – and because `messages.properties` is in the root directory of the classpath, you add a leading forward slash.

> You may remember from earlier in the book that the classpath is the collection of resources (primarily classes) available to a program when it executes.

If you had used a `FileInputStream` you would need to know the location of the file at runtime.

Once the properties file is loaded you can begin to use it as follows:

```
properties.getProperty("introduction.message")
```

The value is always returned as an instance of `String`.

The use of the properties in the `add` method is slightly more complex because you need to provide values for the placeholders provided in the message. In order to achieve this, you use the `MessageFormat` helper class. This accepts a `String` with placeholders as its first parameter, and the values required for the placeholders in the remaining parameters:

```
MessageFormat.format(inputMessage, a, b)
```

Resource Bundles

Although properties files can be used for storing any runtime information needed by a program, the example in the previous section is technically called a *resource bundle*. A resource bundle typically contains the text that the program will output, allowing this text to be changed without changing and recompiling source code. They are actually a lot more interesting than that however.

Before jumping in to look at resource bundles I need to address the concept of a *locale*. Whenever a program runs it runs in a locale – this captures the language of the user, and the region where the user is based. This information is derived from the user's operating system settings, and is encapsulated in an instance of `Locale`.

If you want to see what locale you are in, run the following program:

```
package adder;
import java.util.Locale;
public class MyLocale {
    public static void main(String[] args) {
        Locale l = Locale.getDefault();
        System.out.println(l.getLanguage());
        System.out.println(l.getDisplayCountry());
    }
}
```

Before looking at how useful locale information can be, you will first rewrite the example above to treat `messages.properties` as a `ResourceBundle`.

```java
package adder;
import java.text.MessageFormat;
import java.util.Locale;
import java.util.ResourceBundle;
public class Adder {
    private ResourceBundle resourceBundle;
    public Adder() {
        resourceBundle = ResourceBundle.getBundle("messages");
        System.out.println(resourceBundle.getString(
            "introduction.message"));
    }
    public void add(int a, int b) {
        String inputMessage = resourceBundle.getString(
            "input.message");
        String resultMessage = resourceBundle.getString(
            "result.message");
        System.out.println(MessageFormat.format(
            inputMessage, a, b));
        System.out.println(MessageFormat.format(
            resultMessage, a + b));
    }

    public static void main(String[] args) {
        Adder adder = new Adder();
        adder.add(20, 30);
        adder.add(23, 12);
    }
}
```

As you can see, the process for reading a resource bundle is slightly simpler: You can simply use the syntax:

```
resourceBundle = ResourceBundle.getBundle("messages");
```

Java assumes that the file is on the classpath, and assumes that the file has a `.properties` extension.

Imagine now, however, that you want to provide a French version of the program. In order to support this, you can create a new properties file called `messages_fr.properties`, and add the following content:

```
introduction.message=Bienvenue dans le programme adder
input.message=Les valeurs d'entrée sont {0} et {1}
result.message=Le résultat est {0}
```

The `_fr` suffix is not arbitrary; this is the official ISO code for the French language:

You can now change the code that reads the resource bundle as follows:

```java
public Adder() {
    Locale french = new Locale.Builder()
        .setLanguage("fr")
        .setRegion("FR").build();
    resourceBundle = ResourceBundle.getBundle("messages", french);
```

On the first line you are explicitly constructing a `Locale` for the program to use. In this you are setting both the region and the language – although in this case only the language is important.

If you run the program now it should produce the following output:

```
Bienvenue dans le programme adder
Les valeurs dentrée sont {0} et {1}
Le résultat est 50
Les valeurs dentrée sont {0} et {1}
Le résultat est 35
```

On a side note, you could have used the following `static` field to obtain a French locale:
`Locale french = Locale.FRENCH;`

> Users who had set French as their operating system language should have automatically picked up the French resource bundle without constructing a `Locale` object.
>
> I tend not to rely on the default locale set on user's computers however. It is common that this does not accurately reflect the wishes of the user. I tend to ask the user to choose the locale they wish to use.

The region can also be used to choose the appropriate resource bundle. For instance, you may want different resource bundles for American English and British English.

In this case, you could make a default version of the resource bundle for American English, and then an alternative version called `messages_en_GB.properties` for British English. In fact, you can add as many English language resource bundles as you need for all the different variants of the language.

Internationalization and Localization

The approach outlined in the previous section is referred to as Internationalization and Localization. Because these are very long words they are sometimes abbreviated to I18n and L10n. Internationalization is the process of ensuring a program can be adapted for a specific language or region (for instance, by using resource bundles rather than literal `Strings`), while Localization is the process of adapting the Internationalized program to a specific region or language.

Resource bundles are an important component in I18N and L12N, but they are not the full story. Another very important component is the use of formatters.

For instance, the number 999,999.00 is commonly output as 999.999,00 in many European countries. As a result, it is always sensible to use locales when formatting or parsing numbers.

The following program shows how a number can be formatted as a simple number, a currency and a percentage using the Italian `Locale`:

```java
package adder;
import java.text.NumberFormat;
import java.util.Locale;
public class Numbers {
    public static void main(String[] args) {
        NumberFormat nf = NumberFormat.getInstance(Locale.ITALY);
        System.out.println(nf.format(999999.99));
        nf = NumberFormat.getCurrencyInstance(Locale.ITALY);
        System.out.println(nf.format(999999.99));
        nf = NumberFormat.getPercentInstance(Locale.ITALY);
        System.out.println(nf.format(999999.99));
    }
}
```

This produces the following result:

```
999.999,99
€ 999.999,99
99.999.999%
```

28 DEFAULT METHODS

The chapter will offer something of a diversion into a new feature added to Java 8.

Java 8 has made significant changes to the way interfaces are defined. You have already seen the changes that have been added to support *functional interfaces*, but another important change has been included called *default methods*: these allow implementation details to be included in interfaces.

> Default methods are also commonly referred to as *defender methods* or *virtual extension methods*.

It may sound a strange decision to allow interfaces to contain implementation details, because it largely goes against the whole ethos of interfaces: they are designed to provide contracts that classes can choose to implement.

Default methods have mainly been added to Java to support some of the other changes in Java 8. If you consider the Collections API, many fundamental types (such as `List` and `Set`) are interfaces. Java 8 wanted to add new methods to these interfaces to support Streams, but adding new methods would suddenly break existing code for anyone who had implemented these interfaces themselves.

Interfaces have historically been very difficult to modify if third parties have implemented them, because the changes will never be backwards compatible with their code. As soon as new methods are added, they are obliged to implement them.

Java 8 now allows methods to be added to interfaces along with default implementations. This means that new methods can be added to interfaces, along with default implementations. Any existing implementations of the interface will automatically pick up the default implementation, while new classes implementing the interface can either choose to provide their own implementation or use the default implementation.

Because Java classes can implement multiple interfaces, this change essentially brings a form of multiple inheritance to the Java language. Before jumping in to look at the changes, it is therefore perhaps worth taking a step back and looking at one of the primary reasons Java did not historically support multiple inheritance: *the diamond problem.*

Start by defining a very simple interface:

```
package diamond;
public interface A {
    void doSomething();
}
```

Next, implement this interface in two separate classes:

```
package diamond;
public class B implements A {
    @Override
    public void doSomething() {
        System.out.println("Doing something the B way");
    }
}
```

and

```
package diamond;
public class C implements A {
    @Override
    public void doSomething() {
        System.out.println("Doing something the C way");
    }
}
```

Now, consider what would happen if you were to write a class that extended both B and C (let's call it D), which implementation of doSomething should it use? This is called the diamond problem because a class diagram of this structure looks like a diamond, as seen in figure 28-1:

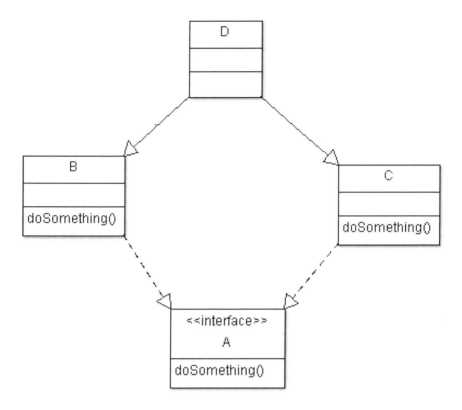

FIGURE 28-1

Before looking at how the diamond problem is resolved in Java 8, you can begin by writing an interface with a default method:

```
package defaultmethods;
public interface A {
    public default void doSomething() {
        System.out.println("I am A");
    }
}
```

Notice the use of the `default` keyword. Previously this keyword has only had meaning inside `switch` statements and annotation declarations; it now takes on meaning inside interfaces.

Although this interface contains an implementation for its only method, it still is not possible to directly instantiate an instance of this interface: a class still must implement it in order for it to be used.

You can now implement this interface as follows:

```
package defaultmethods;
public class B implements A {
}
```

Notice that you do not have to implement the `doSomething` method if you don't want to.

You can now instantiate B, and invoke the `doSomething` method:

```
package defaultmethods;
public class DefaultMethods {
    public static void main(String[] args) {
        B b = new B();
        b.doSomething();
    }
}
```

This will print I am A.

You can now create a second interface with the same `doSomething` method signature:

```
package defaultmethods;
public interface A2 {
    public default void doSomething() {
        System.out.println("I am A2");
    }
}
```

And change class B to implement both interfaces:

```
package defaultmethods;
public class B implements A, A2 {
}
```

This will result in a compilation error, because the compiler cannot know which version of the `doSomething` this class wants to use.

You now have three choices:

⇒ Change B to only implement either A or A2
⇒ Provide an implementation of `doSomething` on B
⇒ Explicitly tell the compiler to use the implementation in A or A2

The first two options are fairly self-explanatory; the third option can be achieved as follows:

```
package defaultmethods;
public class B implements A, A2 {
    @Override
    public void doSomething() {
        A2.super.doSomething();
    }
}
```

This tells the compiler to utilize the implementation on A2.

One important point to note with default methods is that they cannot provide implementations for any of the methods defined on `Object`. For instance, they cannot provide implementations of `toString` or `equals`. The primary reason for this is that all objects already have default implementations for these methods; therefore a decision was made to disallow interfaces from providing an alternative default implementation.

Although default methods provide a form of multiple inheritance, they do have limitations. The default methods do not have access to the state of the object (as captured by fields) that has implemented them, and they cannot store state of their own. If you need to access the state of the object you can only do this via methods defined on the interface, and implemented on the class.

Interfaces may also now provide `static` methods – previously they could only define `static` fields. A `static` method on an interface looks identical to a `static` method on a class:

```
package defaultmethods;
public interface A {
    public default void doSomething() {
        System.out.println("I am A");
    }

    public static void staticMethod() {
        System.out.println("I am a static method");
    }
}
```

Adding `static` methods to interfaces is less controversial than default methods, because there is no concept of inheritance with static methods. In fact they work particularly well in cases where an interface only contains `static` methods, because it is clear that it should not be instantiated.

29 THREADING

Up until this point in the book, the programs developed have consisted of a single thread of execution. The thread of execution is initiated when the `main` method begins executing, and continues until the `main` method ends, or an unhandled exception occurs. In a single threaded program, the program is performing one task at a time; and not moving on to the next task until that is completed.

> Although not shown in any examples up until this point, it is also possible to instruct the program to end by invoking `System.exit`, and passing an `int` argument representing an exit code.

There are many reasons why a single thread of execution is not optimal for many programs. Most computing devices now provide multiple cores or processors, and therefore it is feasible to execute multiple instructions simultaneously; therefore increasing the overall level of computation that is performed in any period of time.

> A Java program executes as a single process: all threads execute within the context of this process.
>
> A thread is essentially a *lightweight process*. Like a process, each thread has its own execution environment (for instance, its own stack), but threads share many resources from their parent process, such as file descriptors and memory on the heap. This means it is generally more efficient for an operating system to switch between threads than processes.

Java has provided native support for multi-threading since its initial release. At the time native threading was a major point of difference from other languages, but as time has gone on, and computers have increased in the number of processors and cores they offer, most mainstream languages have adopted multi-threading APIs either natively or through libraries.

If you consider a computer with 8 cores, a single threaded program can use, at most, 12.5% of the overall CPU at any point in time. If, on the other hand, there is a way of using multiple threads to distribute processing across all 8 cores, it is conceivable that the task could be completed 8 times faster.

In this chapter you will begin by examining the core building blocks and concepts of the threading APIs in Java. Once these core building blocks are understood you will take a look at the built in libraries Java provides for simplifying the process of writing multi-threaded programs – most notably parallel processing of Streams.

Programming with Threads

The first aspect of writing a multi-threaded program is identifying aspects of the program that can be executed in a separate thread from the main program thread. Ideally this aspect of the program should be relatively self-contained, and therefore keep inter-thread communication to a minimum.

The program you will write in the first section of this chapter will accept a set of numbers, and determine whether each number is a prime number using a very simple algorithm. The key to this program is that a new thread will be spawned for determining whether each number is a prime number: if 10 numbers are passed to the program, 10 threads will be created.

To begin, create a new project called `Threads`. Inside this, create a new class called `NumberProcessor` in a package called `primes`.

```
package primes;
public class NumberProcessor {
    public boolean isNumberPrime(long number) {
        long end = number / 2;
        for (long i = 2; i <= end; i++) {
            if (number % i == 0) {
                return false;
            }
        }
        return true;
    }
}
```

The `isNumberPrime` method simply loops through all possible factors of the number passed to it, from 2 to half the value of the dividend. For instance, if the number passed in is 30, it will divide the number by every number from 2 to 15. It will then perform a modulus operation on this number using the % operator: if the result of this is 0 then the dividend is divisible by that denominator and not prime. If you have not found any factors for the number when the loop finishes the number must be prime, so it returns `true`.

Obviously this is a very inefficient mechanism for finding prime numbers.

The next step is to inform Java that this class can be run in a separate thread. In order to do this you must declare that the class implements the `Runnable` interface. In addition, just as programs begin execution in a `main` method, you must provide a method for each thread to begin execution in: the equivalent to the `main` method for threads is the `run` method (which is defined on the `Runnable` interface).

In the next example you will notice that the `run` method does not accept any parameters (unlike the `main` method). In order to pass a number to this class, therefore, you will define a constructor that accepts that number, and then pass that number to `isNumberPrime` inside the `run` method:

```java
package primes;
public class NumberProcessor implements Runnable {
    private long numToProcess;

    public NumberProcessor(long numToProcess) {
        this.numToProcess = numToProcess;
    }
    public boolean isNumberPrime(long number) {
        long end = number / 2;
        for (long i = 2; i <= end; i++) {
            if (number % i == 0) {
                return false;
            }
        }
        return true;
    }
    @Override
    public void run() {
        boolean result = isNumberPrime(numToProcess);
        if (result == true) {
            System.out.println(numToProcess + " is a prime number");
        } else {
            System.out.println(numToProcess +
                " is not a prime number");
        }
    }
}
```

You now have an independent unit of code that is capable of processing a number and printing out whether it is a prime number. With this in place you can create the `Main` class that will accept an array of arguments (as `String`s), convert them to numbers, and pass each in turn to an instance of `NumberProcessor`.

```java
package primes;
public class Main {
    public static void main(String[] args) {
        for (int i = 0; i < args.length; i++) {
            long number = Long.valueOf(args[i]);
            NumberProcessor numberProcesssor = new
                NumberProcessor(number);
```

```
            Thread t = new Thread(numberProcesssor);
            t.start();
        }
    }
}
```

This class has a `main` method, because it is the starting point for the program. When the `main` method begins it loops through all the arguments passed in, and converts each parameter to a `long` value.

Once each number has been extracted, a new instance of `NumberProcessor` is created and passed the appropriate number. You might be thinking you can now simply call `run` on the instance of `NumberProcessor`. In fact calling `run` on `NumberProcessor` would be valid, but the invocation would not execute on a separate thread: the call would block the `main` thread until it completed.

In order to run the execution on a separate thread you create an instance of the `Thread` class, and pass it an object implementing `Runnable` (in our case, an instance of `NumberProcessor`). Once the thread has been created you call `start` on it.

Try running the program with the following arguments:

`85126773864 2860486313 1500450271 1200450280`

(this took approximately 20 seconds to execute on my computer)

The output this produced for me was as follows:

```
85126773864 is not a prime number
1200450280 is not a prime number
1500450271 is a prime number
2860486313 is a prime number
```

As you can see, even though `1200450280` was the last number to begin processing, it was the second to complete: this is because the algorithm very quickly detected this was not prime: all four numbers are processed in parallel, and their results printed as soon as they finish processing (meaning the order in which the results are printed is indeterminate – and could vary from one execution, or one machine, to the next).

Additionally, if you monitor your CPU utilization while running this example, you should see that two processors are running at 100% (the other two numbers return almost immediately).

Sleeping

The list of numbers passed to the `main` method dictates the number of threads generated by this program. It does not matter, however, if the number of threads exceeds the physical number of cores on the computer. For instance, it is possible to create 10 threads on a computer that only has 2 cores, and therefore only supports 2 concurrent threads of execution.

Where the number of threads exceeds the cores on the hardware, the operating system will allocate processing time to the various threads. This ensures that all threads receive some processing time, and no single thread can dominate the processor.

> Even though it is possible, generally you do not want to create 100s of threads for a single program. If too many threads are created, more and more time will be spent context switching (switching between threads), and more memory will be used to capture the stack of each executing thread.
>
> There is typically no benefit creating more threads than there are processors on the hardware. You can determine this with the following code:
>
> `Runtime.getRuntime().availableProcessors();`

Even though the operating system ensures all threads receive their fair share of processor time, there are times where it makes sense for a thread to voluntarily yield to other threads. For instance:

⇒ A thread may be waiting on data that it knows will not be available for a period of time.
⇒ A thread may determine that other threads have a higher priority, and therefore it will yield processor time for a period of time.

As an example, imagine in the previous example that you want to prioritize the smallest numbers, because they can potentially be processed quickest, and you can begin producing results for the user.

In order to achieve this, you will use the `Thread.sleep` method built into Java. When you execute this (and pass it the amount of milliseconds you wish the thread to sleep for), the currently executing thread will yield control of the processor, and will not be allocated anymore processor time until the specified length of time has passed.

Change the run method in `NumberProcessor` as follows:

```
@Override
public void run() {
    try {
        Thread.sleep((long) Math.log(numToProcess));
    } catch (InterruptedException e) {}
    System.out.println("Beginning to process " + numToProcess);
    boolean result = isNumberPrime(numToProcess);
    if (result == true) {
        System.out.println(numToProcess + " is a prime number");
    } else {
        System.out.println(numToProcess + " is not a prime number");
    }
}
```

This code is using the following call to obtain a number related to the number passed in, but an order of magnitude lower (so it does not sleep for ever):

```
(long) Math.log(numToProcess)
```

Before beginning processing, the `NumberProcessor` then sleeps for this period of time.

As can be seen, the call to sleep must be surrounded in a `try/catch` block: the `catch` block will be invoked when the time has elapsed. This is one situation where it is typical to go against best practice, and not place any code in the `catch` block.

When I ran this code I received the following output:

```
Beginning to process 1200450280
1200450280 is not a prime number
Beginning to process 1500450271
Beginning to process 2860486313
Beginning to process 85126773864
85126773864 is not a prime number
1500450271 is a prime number
2860486313 is a prime number
```

As can be seen, a result is produced for the smallest number even before the other numbers begin processing.

If you pass the following arguments:

```
85126773864 2860486313 1500450271 1200450280 90 6
```

The effect is even more pronounced:

```
Beginning to process 6
6 is not a prime number
Beginning to process 90
90 is not a prime number
Beginning to process 1500450271
Beginning to process 1200450280
1200450280 is not a prime number
Beginning to process 2860486313
Beginning to process 85126773864
85126773864 is not a prime number
1500450271 is a prime number
2860486313 is a prime number
```

It should be pointed out that the `sleep` method is a `static` method on the `Thread` class: it automatically causes the currently executing thread (i.e. the thread that invoked the code) to sleep. It is not possible to call `sleep` on another `Thread`.

The other thing to note about the `sleep` method regards the number of milliseconds passed to it. Although the thread will sleep for at least this long, there is no guarantee it will be interrupted from its sleep immediately at the end of this period: that will depend on the number of other threads executing, and the overall operating system resources available to the program.

Synchronized

Moving from a single-threaded to a multi-threaded programming model presents additional challenges that may not be immediately obvious. For instance, the same block of code may be invoked simultaneously from two separate threads. This can present a problem if the code block updates fields on an object.

In order to see this in action, you will write a new class that will be responsible for keeping track of how many threads are currently running; and print when they start and stop running:

```java
package primes;
public class ThreadTracker {
    private int threadsRunning = 0;
    public void setThreadRunning() {
        threadsRunning++;
        System.out.println(threadsRunning + " threads running");
    }
    public void setThreadFinished() {
        threadsRunning--;
        System.out.println(threadsRunning + " threads running");
    }
}
```

You will then pass the same instance of this class to each `NumberProcessor`, which will be responsible for recording when processing starts and finishes:

```java
package primes;
public class NumberProcessor implements Runnable {
    private long numToProcess;
    private ThreadTracker tracker;
    public NumberProcessor(long numToProcess,
            ThreadTracker tracker) {
        this.numToProcess = numToProcess;
        this.tracker = tracker;
    }
    public boolean isNumberPrime(long number) {
        long end = number / 2;
        for (long i = 2; i <= end; i++) {
            if (number % i == 0) {
                return false;
            }
        }
        return true;
    }
    @Override
    public void run() {
        try {
            Thread.sleep((long) Math.log(numToProcess));
        } catch (InterruptedException e) {}
        tracker.setThreadRunning();
        boolean result = isNumberPrime(numToProcess);
        if (result == true) {
            System.out.println(numToProcess + " is a prime number");
        } else {
            System.out.println(numToProcess
```

```
            + " is not a prime number");
        }
        tracker.setThreadFinished();
    }
}
```

The `Main` class then needs to be changed as follows:

```
package primes;
public class Main {
    public static void main(String[] args) {
        ThreadTracker tracker = new ThreadTracker();
        for (int i = 0; i < args.length; i++) {
            long number = Long.valueOf(args[i]);
            NumberProcessor numberProcesssor = new
                NumberProcessor(number, tracker);
            Thread t = new Thread(numberProcesssor);
            t.start();
        }
    }
}
```

There is a bug lurking in this code that could easily be missed. Consider two threads calling the `setThreadRunning` method at exactly the same time.

⇒ Thread 1 executes the first line and changes `threadsRunning` from 0 to 1
⇒ Thread 2 executes the first line and changes `threadsRunning` from 1 to 2
⇒ Thread 1 calls the second line and prints `2 threads running`
⇒ Thread 2 calls the second line and prints `2 threads running`

Clearly this is not producing the correct results: both threads have printed that 2 threads are running, while none have printed that 1 thread is running. Although this would not be a major problem in this case, there are many scenarios where bugs such as this can be both hard to detect, and have a major impact on processing.

> I have mentioned several times throughout this book that various APIs are not thread-safe. Essentially this means that they are prone to these types of bug if used in multi-threaded programs.

This issue can occur even on devices with a single processor: the operating system will periodically interrupt threads and allow other threads to run, and this may occur in the middle of a method such as this.

In order to circumvent this issue, you need a way of ensuring only a single thread can execute a block of code at a time. Java provides an in-built mechanism for achieving this: the `synchronized` keyword. The `setThreadRunning` method can therefore be changes as follows:

```
public synchronized void setThreadRunning() {
```

Java implements synchronization via a locking mechanism. Every object has a single lock that it can make available. Any code wishing to invoke a `synchronized` method must obtain this lock before entering the method (although this happens automatically). The lock will then we automatically released once the method completes. This guarantees that the bug outlined in the previous example cannot occur.

There are potential implications to adding `synchronized` to many methods on a class. Because each object only has a single lock, it is not possible for two different threads to invoke two different `synchronized` methods on the object at the same time, even if those methods are unrelated. Therefore if there are a large number of `synchronized` methods, or a large number of threads, the `synchronized` methods may become a bottleneck for performance.

> Because each object only has a single lock, it is less likely that you will run into deadlocks. Consider a case where two methods (a and b) both had their own locks, rather than having a single lock for the entire object.
>
> Two threads may simultaneously acquire locks for each of these methods. Imagine a case where method a invokes method b, and vice versa. One thread will have a lock on a, and wait till it can acquire a lock on b – the other will have a lock on b and wait till it can acquire a lock on a.
>
> This is called a deadlock, because both threads are waiting on something that will never occur.
>
> Deadlocks are still possible in multi-threaded Java programs, but only where multiple objects are involved.

It is important to consider the cases where you should use the `synchronized` keyword, and equally, the situations where there is no need to use this keyword. As a general rule, methods that only use local variables or method parameters will not need to use the `synchronized` keyword, because each invocation of the method will have their own copies of these variables.

> As mentioned earlier in the book – due to the introduction of lambda expressions this is now not *entirely* true. It is still a good rule of thumb however.

The key case where it is important to use the `synchronized` keyword is where a method updates shared state (such as fields), and then relies on this state not being modified while it performs additional processing.

In addition to each object having a single lock, each class also has a lock. This ensures that `static` methods can also use the `synchronized` keyword. This lock works in an identical manner: any code wishing to invoke a `synchronized static` method must obtain the class lock before entering the method, and will then release it when the method completes.

There is an alternative way to use the `synchronized` keyword. Consider a case where `ThreadTracker` was provided by a third party library, and did not declare the `synchronized` keyword on its methods. In this case the `ThreadTracker` is not *thread safe*, so you can make it thread safe in your code as follows:

```
synchronized (tracker) {
   tracker.setThreadRunning();
}
```

The code `synchronized (tracker)` is responsible for obtaining the lock on the `tracker` object. The code inside the block following is then only executed while holding this lock. Once the block completes, the lock is automatically released. As long as all code using the unsafe method uses this approach, the class becomes thread-safe.

This technique can also be used to make a subset of a method thread-safe. Due to the potential bottlenecks that can occur with `synchronized` code, it makes sense to limit the synchronized code to a minimum. Rather than making a whole method `synchronized`, therefore, a method could place a subset of its code in a block such as this:

```
public void methodA() {
    // non-synchronized code goes here
    synchronized (this) {
        // this code is synchonized
    }
    // non-synchronized code goes here
}
```

Whenever the method needs to execute code in a `synchronized` block, it does so by obtaining a lock on itself (`this`). It then holds this until the block concludes; meaning only a few lines of a long method may be placed in the `synchronized` block.

Wait/notify

The final fundamental building block for multi-threading relates to three methods found on `Object` itself:

⇒ `wait`
⇒ `notify`
⇒ `notifyAll`

These methods can be used to wait for a specific scenario to occur without utilizing CPU.

Consider the following scenario:

⇒ A pool of 10 threads is responsible for each obtaining results from a remote server, and therefore will take an indeterminate amount of time to complete.
⇒ You program can only continue once it has received a minimum of five results.

Clearly our program needs to wait for a specific scenario to occur. It needs to also be notified when this scenario has occurred, so it knows to continue.

The `wait/notify` methods allow you to implement this scenario. A thread can indicate that it wishes to wait for a specified condition to be `true` by invoking the `wait` method on itself. When this is invoked, the thread is put to sleep, and does not consume any CPU.

When other threads perform a task that they think may be relevant for waiting threads they can call `notify` on that same object (to invoke a single random waiter) or `notifyAll` (to invoke all waiters). Any threads that have issued a call to `wait` on the object will then be awakened, and can determine whether the specified event has occurred. If it has, the waiter will perform its processing, if not, it will invoke `wait` on itself again.

The following program demonstrates this scenario:

```
package threads;
public class WaitExample implements Runnable {
    private int resultsObtained = 0;

    public static void main(String[] args) {
        WaitExample we = new WaitExample();
        for (int i = 0; i < 10; i++) {
            Thread t = new Thread(we);
            t.start();
        }
        we.printResults();
    }

    public synchronized void printResults() {
        while(resultsObtained < 5) {
            try {
                System.out.println("Waiting for enough results");
                wait();
            } catch (InterruptedException e) {}
        }
        System.out.println("We have received enough results");
    }

    public synchronized void addResult() {
        resultsObtained++;
        System.out.println("A result has been added");
        notifyAll();
    }
    @Override
    public void run() {
        try {
            Thread.sleep((long) (Math.random()*10000));
        } catch (InterruptedException e) {}
```

```
        addResult();
    }
}
```

This method starts by creating 10 instances of `Thread`, and starting them. When this occurs, the `run` method will be invoked, and the new thread will sleep for a random interval of up to 10 seconds (which simulates a call to a remote server). Once this time passes, it invokes `addResult` to record the fact that it has obtained a result from the server.

Once all the threads are started, the `main` method invokes `printResults`. This method checks to see whether 5 results have been obtained inside a loop. If not, it invokes `wait` on itself, otherwise it prints the result.

The key to understanding this functionality is the call to `notifyAll` inside the `addResult` method. When this is invoked, any waiting threads will be woken, and given the opportunity to see whether the event they are waiting for has occurred.

When I run this, it prints the following results:

```
Waiting for enough results
A result has been added
Waiting for enough results
A result has been added
Waiting for enough results
A result has been added
Waiting for enough results
A result has been added
Waiting for enough results
A result has been added
We have received enough results
A result has been added
A result has been added
A result has been added
A result has been added
A result has been added
```

Notice that after each result is added, the waiting thread has an opportunity to assess whether the condition has been met. Once five results are received it determines that the condition has been met and prints:
`We have received enough results`

Calls to `wait`, `notify` and `notifyAll` must occur inside `synchronized` blocks of code. This is important, because otherwise your code may check that a condition has not occurred on one line, and invoke `wait` on the next. In between these, however, a separate thread may have performed an operation notifying you the relevant event has occurred – it would therefore be conceivable your thread would be left waiting forever for an event that has already happened.

30 PARALLEL PROGRAMMING

The previous chapter introduced all the basic building blocks required to create multi-threaded programs capable of performing complex parallel processing.

The main problem with the threading concepts introduced in the previous chapter is that they can be difficult to work with, and it is easy to make mistakes. What makes matters even worse is that mistakes in multi-threaded code can be particularly difficult to diagnose and resolve.

The ability for algorithms to perform parallel processing is becoming increasingly important however. Due to the fact that all modern computers (and even smart phones) contain multiple cores, any program that is not performing parallel processing is by definition not exploiting the full potential of the hardware for CPU bound operations.

At the same time, the quantities of data that programs are required to process is growing exponentially, and will continue to grow. Before looking at Java APIs that can be used to simplify multi-threaded code, therefore, it is perhaps worth examining a common real-world algorithm for processing large quantities of data in parallel called MapReduce. The popularity of this algorithm has had a big impact on the direction Java is heading with its own APIs.

MapReduce

The MapReduce algorithm was popularized by Google researchers in a paper written in 2004, (http://research.google.com/archive/mapreduce.html) but the operations of map and reduce have been around far longer. Google's insight was to realize how these operations could be used to process massive quantities of data on thousands of computers simultaneously (called a cluster).

MapReduce consists of two primary operations:

⇒ During the map step (which can be run in parallel across many machines) each element in the dataset is filtered, transformed or sorted as required. This obviously relates to the intermediate operations you have already seen in the Stream API such as `map` and `filter`.

⇒ Once the map step is complete the results are passed to the reduce step (which may or may not be run in parallel). The reduce step is responsible for aggregating the data in some manner. This step is obviously related to the terminal operations you have seen on the Stream API.

Many MapReduce implementations have sprung up since Google published their paper, including Hadoop, which is an open source Java implementation. Typically these implementations designate one computer to be the controller: this farms out work to other nodes, which operate independently of one another, and collects the results. For instance, a 20GB file may be split into 10MB chunks, and each chunk sent to a different computer to be processed.

The benefits of implementations like Hadoop is that the programmer does not need to focus on the implementation of the multi-threaded code: they simply need to provide a set of operations and the framework takes care of the farming out the algorithm to potentially thousands of cores.

Fork/Join API

As the previous section demonstrated, the key to processing large data sets in a parallel manner is derived from splitting the data up (a process also known as forking), and processing sub-sets of the data in parallel. Once this data has been processed, it is joined back together (a process known as joining) and aggregated in some manner. Fork and join are therefore akin to the terms map and reduce.

It has been possible to write code in this manner since the very first release of Java using the APIs introduced in the previous chapter, and other threading concepts such as the `synchronized` keyword. Writing multi-threaded code is difficult for many programmers, however, and error prone even for experienced programmers. Concurrency issues and race conditions meant many programmers would rather avoid multi-threaded code if possible.

In order to alleviate some of the inherent problems with multi-threaded code, Java introduced a Fork/Join framework in Java 7. The key to this framework is the `ForkJoinPool` class. Using the fork/join framework was a major advance: it essentially provided a pool of worker threads who all competed to accept jobs – the programmer could then simply create jobs and have them processed in an efficient manner. It also provided a set of management methods to monitor the behavior of the pool.

Even with the Fork/Join framework, however, the programmer was still in control of the threading process to some degree, and had to write code in the manner dictated by the API. This is where the Streams API re-enters the story.

Parallelism with Streams

The Streams API heads in a different direction from the Fork/Join API (and all the other concurrency APIs that have been added to Java since Java 5). The Streams API takes the position that parallelism should be explicit – but non-intrusive. You have to ask for parallelism but you do not actually have to do anything in terms of implementing it.

Requiring the programmer to ask for parallelism is important, because the same program may behave differently when processed in parallel – particularly when ordering is important. Once it has been asked for, however, the Java platform takes care of optimizing the algorithm across the available hardware.

In order to see how simple it can be to change a Stream from serial to parallel processing, the following line:

`l.stream().filter(p -> p%2==1).mapToInt(p -> p * p).sum()`

could be written:

`l.parallelStream().filter(p -> p%2==1).mapToInt(p -> p * p).sum()`

Naturally, on a small List you are unlikely to see any benefits from parallel processing, so let's try it out on a more intensive example. The following program sets up a Stream of all the positive integers, and then finds the average of the even numbers. The first version uses a parallel implementation (the Stream returned from the range method is turned into a parallel stream by invoking the parallel method). The second version is serial.

```
package streams;
import java.util.OptionalDouble;
import java.util.stream.IntStream;
public class LargeRange {
    public static void main(String[] args) {
        long start = System.currentTimeMillis();
        OptionalDouble result = IntStream.range(0, Integer.MAX_VALUE)
            .parallel()
            .filter(i -> i % 2 == 0)
            .average();
        System.out.printf("Parallel version took %d\n",
            System.currentTimeMillis()-start);
        start = System.currentTimeMillis();
        OptionalDouble result2 = IntStream.range(0,
            Integer.MAX_VALUE)
            .filter(i -> i % 2 == 0)
            .average();
        System.out.printf("Serial version took %d\n",
            System.currentTimeMillis()-start);
    }
}
```

When I ran this on a reasonably old MacBook Air I obtained the following results:

```
Parallel version took 4800
Serial version took 9629
```

Unsurprisingly, when I looked at CPU usage, the parallel version was using twice as much CPU. Naturally, results may vary from machine to machine, so try this out yourself.

The great thing about this example is that I have doubled performance by invoking a single method.

Although parallel processing is simply an option, it can highlight issues that are not apparent in the same code when processed serially. A prime candidate of this is where any of the lambda expressions passed to operations in the pipeline have side effects: i.e. they change (or mutate) state that is used by other lambda expressions.

As discussed earlier, mutating the state of an object in lambda expressions is discouraged – but allowed. For instance, there is nothing to stop code in the pipeline adding elements to a common `Collection` – this is likely to cause problems when parallel processing is used, however, because most `Collection` implementations are not thread-safe.

Before considering parallelization, therefore, it is worth asking the following questions:

Will parallel processing improve performance?

Parallel processing will not necessarily improve performance. Some operations, such as sorting and collecting, are not always quicker in parallel. It is therefore always wise to benchmark algorithms in serial and parallel mode to confirm that parallelism is actually providing benefits.

If you consider the `groupingBy` examples from earlier in the book, these added all related elements to a common `List`. Java `Lists` are not thread-safe, therefore the `groupingBy` method will need to `synchronize` access to the `List`, and this could easily negate the benefits of parallel processing.

Likewise with sorting, it is possible to perform parallel sorts: each thread can use an algorithm such as quicksort to process a subset of the elements, and then these sets of sorted elements can be sorted using merge sort: depending on the quantity of data, this will not necessarily be quicker that performing a serial sort.

Finally, the `distinct` operation is another example of an operation that is hard to perform with parallel processing – particularly on an unsorted set of data. Each thread can easily determine the distinct elements amongst the data it has been asked to process – but naturally these distinct sets from each thread would need to be joined back together to get a definitive list of distinct elements.

Can the algorithm be parallelized?

Not all algorithms can be parallelized without resulting in bugs. This is particularly common for `reduce` operations - specifically, reduce operations need to be *associative* in order to be parallelizable.

As an example, summing a `List` of numbers is always associative. This is because it does not matter which order you process the numbers in. If you take the numbers 8, 6 and

3: you can sum these as (8 + 6) + 3 or 8 + (6 + 3). No matter how you add these three numbers the result will be 17.

Other `reduce` operations are not associative. Subtraction, for instance, depends on the order of the elements (8 − 6) − 3 = -1 whereas (3 − 8) − 6 = -11.

To see this in action, consider the following program:

```
package streams;
import java.util.OptionalInt;
import java.util.stream.IntStream;
public class Associative {
    public static void main(String[] args) {
        OptionalInt result =  IntStream.range(1, 1000)
            .parallel()
            .reduce((a, b) -> a-b);
        System.out.println(result.getAsInt());
        result =  IntStream.range(1, 1000)
            .reduce((a, b) -> a-b);
        System.out.println(result.getAsInt());
    }
}
```

In both cases the `Stream` contains identical elements, and the reduce operation contains an identical implementation, but the first reduce occurs in the context of parallel processing. If I run this I get the following output.

```
-124
-499498
```

The first result is clearly incorrect.

If, however, I change this `reduce` operation to perform a sum:

```
IntStream.range(1, 1000).reduce((a, b) -> a+b);
```

Both examples produce identical results:

```
499500
499500
```

This is dangerous: the compiler is not able to detect that you are performing a non-associative operation; therefore you have introduced a bug that is not easy to spot.

The point to learn from this is that you should not introduce parallelism for the sake of it: you should decide what you are trying to achieve with parallelism, and you should check that your algorithm functions correctly as a parallel operation.

Another important consideration for parallel streams is sorting. The two lines below may look like they would print out the same results:

```
package streams;

import java.util.stream.IntStream;

public class Associative2 {
```

```
public static void main(String[] args) {
    System.out.println("Running in parallel");
    IntStream.range(1, 1000)
       .parallel()
       .filter(a -> a %2 == 1)
       .limit(10)
       .sorted()
       .forEach(a -> System.out.println(a));
    System.out.println("Running in serial");
    IntStream.range(1, 1000)
       .filter(a -> a %2 == 1)
       .limit(10)
       .forEach(a -> System.out.println(a));
}
}
```

In fact, they do print out the same numbers, but the order the numbers are printed is not sequential in the first case. Even though the numbers are sorted before being passed to forEach, they are not printed in the sorted order. There is a way around this – if the parallel version is changed to use forEachOrdered it will print the numbers in sorted order:

```
IntStream.range(1, 1000).parallel()
.filter(a -> a %2 == 1)
.limit(10)
.forEachOrdered(a -> System.out.println(a));
```

The reason why this works is because the forEachOrdered operation is actually being run in serial mode: which brings me back to the first point – check that parallelism is actually bringing benefits.

One final consideration to bear in mind with parallelism has to do with the way parallelism is implemented. Under the hood, all parallel streams use a common instance of ForkJoinPool containing as many threads as you have processors:

```
Runtime.getRuntime().availableProcessors()
```

This means that if you perform a long running operation with this pool you may starve other code in the application trying to run other parallel algorithms.

It is useful to complete this discussion by comparing parallel streams to MapReduce frameworks such as Hadoop. Essentially parallel streams provide similar capabilities as Hadoop – but on a far smaller scale. Where Hadoop farms out and coordinates processing with many computers, parallel streams farm out and coordinates processing with many processors on the same machine.

31 JAVA DOC

Up until this point you have not really looked at code comments to any great extent. Hopefully you are aware of the importance of adding comments to code, both to help other people understand your code, and to ensure you remember how your code works yourself in the future.

Commenting code is always something of a fine line. You do not want to go over-board and state the obvious; otherwise no one will bother reading the comments. You want to keep your comments concise and focus on the aspects of the code that could most easily be misunderstood.

As mentioned earlier in the book, there are two ways comments can be added to Java code. Where the comment is a single line it is customary to use the // approach:

```
// this is a comment
```

If, on the other hand, the comment spans multiple lines, this form generally leads to greater readability:

```
/*
* This is a comment that spans
* multiple lines, so it uses
* a different syntax
*/
```

In this example, the asterisks on lines 2-4 are entirely optional, but they tend to add to the readability of the comment. This could have just as easily been written as follows:

```
/* This is a comment that spans
multiple lines, so it uses
a different syntax*/
```

There is actually far more to Java comments than meets the eye. Java itself supports a documentation language called JavaDoc that allows comments to be annotated in specific ways so that more readable API documentation (for instance, HTML documentation) can be generated directly from of the comments.

As an example of JavaDoc in action, navigate to the following site in your favorite browser: https://docs.oracle.com/javase/8/docs/api

This will display the website seen in figure 31-1:

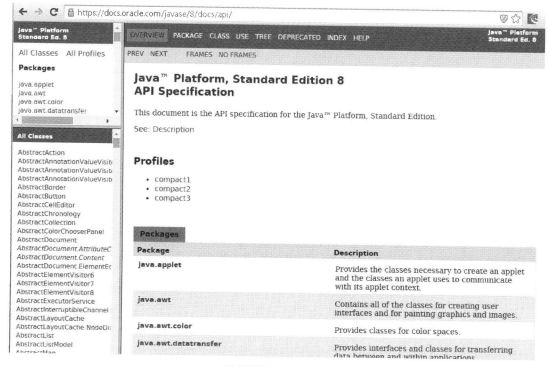

FIGURE 31-1

This is the JavaDoc for the core libraries provided by Java. If you navigate through this site using the two windows on the left hand side you will see each package is documented and each class within the package is documented. When you click on a class, its JavaDoc is displayed in the right hand window.

The purpose of this documentation is to allow you to understand the API of the libraries provided by Java, but it has actually been generated directly from the JavaDoc in the source code itself.

JavaDoc in Action

In order to understand JavaDoc you will write documentation for the `LinkedList2` class written earlier in the book. If you remember, it looked like this:

```
package linkedlist;
public class LinkedList2<T> {
    Node<T> head;
```

```java
    public LinkedList2() {}
    public void addFirst(T value) {
        if (head == null) {
            head = new Node<T>(value, null);
        } else {
            Node<T> newHead = new Node<T>(value, head);
            head = newHead;
        }
    }

    public void addLast(T value) {
        if (head == null) {
            head = new Node<T>(value, null);
        } else {
            Node<T> lastNode = head;
            while (lastNode.getNext() != null) {
                lastNode = lastNode.getNext();
            }
            Node<T> node = new Node<T>(value, null);
            lastNode.setNext(node);
        }
    }

    public void print() {
        Node<T> lastNode = head;
        while (lastNode != null) {
            System.out.println(lastNode.getValue());
            lastNode = lastNode.getNext();
        }
    }
}
```

To begin, you will start by writing JavaDoc for the class itself. This will explain the purpose of the class, and will also expose a set of attributes providing metadata about the class. Add the following immediately before the class declaration:

```
/**
 * This class provides a container for a set of elements,
 * where each element contains a link to the next element
 * in the list.
 * The container allows elements to be added to either the start
 * or the end of the list, and the entire list can be printed.
 * <p/>
 * This class uses generics to provide type safety to the
 * consumer of the list.
 *
 * @version 1.0
 * @author  Dane Cameron
 * @see     Node
 * @since   26 April 2014
 */
```

There are a number of points to note about this sample. Firstly, the comment starts with /** rather than /*. This means that the comment should appear in documentation generated from the class. A lot of your documentation should not be exposed to the wider world, because it is documenting a feature about the internal implementation that is not relevant to users of the API.

Secondly, the comments can include HTML. Because JavaDoc is usually output as HTML it can be useful to add HTML to the comments to make them more readable. In this example, paragraph tags have been added <p/>, but it is possible to add a wide array of HTML tags.

Finally, the comments contain a number of special markers starting with the @ symbol. These are special tags that add specific meaning to the class. These should be fairly self-explanatory.

If you now select Window->Show view->Javadoc, and click on the class in the editor, you should see an Eclipse view with the content shown in figure 31-2:

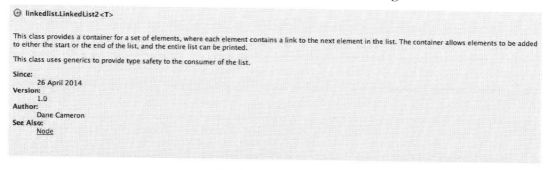

FIGURE 31-2

Notice that Eclipse has been able to format the documentation based on the HTML and tags. Also note that Node is a link, and clicking on this will take you to the Javadoc for Node (which is currently empty).

Probably in a real example you would not have provided the link to Node, because anyone using LinksedList2 does not need to know that elements are stored internally using the Node class, but it does highlight an approach that can be useful in other cases.

You can now start providing JavaDoc for the methods in the class. With methods the most important thing to document are:

⇒ The purpose of the method
⇒ The parameters defined by the method
⇒ The value returned by the method
⇒ Any exceptions generated by the method, and the reasons they will be generated

In order to get started, simply type /** and then enter above the addFirst method. When you do this Eclipse will automatically generate the following stub for you to get started:

```
/**
 *
 * @param value
 */
```

You can now fill in the relevant details yourself:

```
/**
 * Adds a new element at the start of the list.
 * <p/>
 * This must adhere to the type specified when constructing the List
 *
 * @param value The value that will be added to the list
 */
```

You will notice that if you click on the method in the Editor, the JavaDoc will display, as seen in figure 31-3:

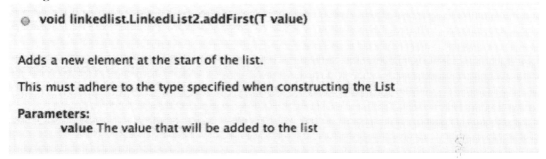

FIGURE 31-3

Because this method did not declare exceptions or a return type it does not contain any tags for those features. If you imagine a hypothetical method that accepted two parameters, returned a String, and throws an exception called SomeExceptrion, the tags may look like this:

```
 * @param value This is the first parameter
 * @param value2 This is the second parameter
 * @return String This is the return value
 * @throws SomeException this is thrown if...
```

Just as it is possible to add JavaDoc for methods, it is also possible to add JavaDoc for methods. This tends not to be necessary however – JavaDoc should generally be used for documenting the public API of the class, and fields are typically not part of this API.

You have only scratched the surface of JavaDoc in these examples. The tags and approaches outlined in this chapter are the fundamental features that should be added to all classes you write, however, especially classes that you expect other programmers to use.

32 ANNOTATIONS AND REFLECTION

This chapter will introduce two entirely new subjects; reflection and annotations. This chapter will also provide an opportunity to create a more advanced program than many other examples in the book.

Before describing annotations and reflection, consider a program that allows objects to be created from values in a CSV file. This program has the following requirements:

⇒ It can be passed a CSV file and a class name as arguments – it does not need any prior knowledge of either the file or the class
⇒ The program should create one instance of the class to encapsulate the data in each row of the file (except the header row)
⇒ The header row will contain column names for identifying the contents of the column, but these do not need to conform to the field names of the class.
⇒ The class may contain fields of type `String`, `Integer`, `Double` or `Date`, and it is up to the processor to populate these based on the data in the file.
⇒ If the file contains dates it is up to the class to specify the date format: there is not a single format that all files must use.

If you think about these requirements I think you will agree that, based on what you know about Java so far, it would not be possible to write a generic file processor that fulfilled these requirements.

In this chapter you will learn how you can use annotations and reflection to create more generic code that is capable of interacting with classes, even if it has no prior knowledge of the structure of those classes. This will mean it is possible to write code that meets these requirements.

Annotations

You will start by looking at annotations. You have already seen annotations in action when you looked at both inheritance and functional interfaces. For instance, you saw how an annotation could be placed before a method declaration to indicate it was overriding a method from a super-class or interface:

```
@Override
public void overriddenMethod() {
}
```

This annotation ensured that if the underlying method definition changed, you would receive a compilation error. This is useful, because it prompts you to also change your method definition.

One way of thinking about annotations is that they are extending the functionality of the compiler. If the underlying method definition was changed, your code would still be valid: it just wouldn't be doing what you thought it was doing (overriding a method).

The annotations you have looked at so far are all built-in annotations, and are processed at compile time. In this chapter you will look at how you can write your own custom annotations, and access these at run-time.

The requirements for the program outlined at the start of this chapter stated that the name of the columns in the CSV file do not need to match the field names in the class. You will therefore create an annotation that can be used to specify the CSV column name that a setter method on a class relates to.

Start by creating a new project in Eclipse, I have called mine `GenericProcessor`. Next, right click on the project and choose `New -> Annotation`. Name the annotation `Column`, and place it in a package called `processor.annotations`.

You will notice that Eclipse generates code that looks like an interface, but contains an @ symbol:

```
public @interface Column {
}
```

The annotations you have looked at earlier in the book have been *tagging* annotations: they contained no information beyond the presence of the annotation. It is also possible to pass arguments to an annotation: in order to allow this you need to add a method signature to the annotation – the return type of this method will be the type accepted by the annotation. You will first add the ability for a column name from the CSV file to be specified:

```
public @interface Column {
    String comumnName();
}
```

You will also add another parameter that can be used for specifying a date format if the column contains date information. In this case you will also provide a default value for the parameter:

```
public @interface Column {
    String comumnName();
    String format() default "yyyy-MM-dd";
}
```

Next, you need to specify how the annotation should be used. In this case the annotation will be used at runtime (you will access the annotation as the program executes), and that it should be applied to methods (rather than classes):

```
package processor.annotations;
import java.lang.annotation.ElementType;
import java.lang.annotation.Retention;
import java.lang.annotation.RetentionPolicy;
import java.lang.annotation.Target;

@Retention(RetentionPolicy.RUNTIME)
@Target({ElementType.METHOD})
public @interface Column {
    String comumnName();
    String format() default "yyyy-MM-dd";
}
```

Now that you have created your annotations, you can define a CSV file that you may want to process. The file you will use contains stock trading information for Oracle Corporation from 2014 to1996. This file is available on the book's website, and is called `ORCL.csv`. This file should be placed in the base directory of your project. The first few lines of the file look like this:

```
Date,Open,High,Low,Close,Volume,Adj Close
2014-05-23,17.26,18.90,16.96,17.30,168500,17.30
2014-05-22,16.97,17.25,16.85,17.21,135500,17.21
2014-05-21,16.80,17.23,16.69,17.00,180200,17.00
2014-05-20,16.86,17.01,16.61,16.73,161700,16.73
2014-05-19,16.79,17.16,16.67,16.88,129100,16.88
2014-05-16,16.79,17.25,16.50,16.91,148200,16.91
2014-05-15,16.53,16.87,16.53,16.86,235500,16.86
2014-05-14,16.01,16.90,16.01,16.67,254100,16.67
2014-05-13,15.96,16.09,15.79,15.81,78000,15.81
```

As you can see, the file contains 7 columns. The first column is the date the row relates to, and the remaining columns contain a variety of price and volume information.

You will now write a class containing 7 fields, and map the setters for these fields to the columns in the file using the `Column` annotation. This ensures that the field names on the class can differ from the field names in the CSV file:

```
package processor;
import java.util.Date;
import processor.annotations.Column;

public class StockData {
    private Date date;
    private Double openingPrice;
    private Double highestPrice;
    private Double lowestPrice;
    private Double closingPrice;
```

```java
    private Integer volume;
    private Double adjustedClosingPrice;

    public StockData() {}

    public Date getDate() {
        return date;
    }
    @Column(comumnName = "Date", format = "yyyy-mm-dd")
    public void setDate(Date date) {
        this.date = date;
    }
    public Double getOpeningPrice() {
        return openingPrice;
    }
    @Column(comumnName = "Open")
    public void setOpeningPrice(Double openingPrice) {
        this.openingPrice = openingPrice;
    }
    public Double getHighestPrice() {
        return highestPrice;
    }
    @Column(comumnName = "High")
    public void setHighestPrice(Double highestPrice) {
        this.highestPrice = highestPrice;
    }
    public Double getLowestPrice() {
        return lowestPrice;
    }
    @Column(comumnName = "Low")
    public void setLowestPrice(Double lowestPrice) {
        this.lowestPrice = lowestPrice;
    }
    public Double getClosingPrice() {
        return closingPrice;
    }
    @Column(comumnName = "Close")
    public void setClosingPrice(Double closingPrice) {
        this.closingPrice = closingPrice;
    }
    public Integer getVolume() {
        return volume;
    }
    @Column(comumnName = "Volume")
    public void setVolume(Integer volume) {
        this.volume = volume;
    }
    public Double getAdjustedClosingPrice() {
        return adjustedClosingPrice;
    }
    @Column(comumnName = "Adj Close")
    public void setAdjustedClosingPrice(Double adjustedClosingPrice) {
        this.adjustedClosingPrice = adjustedClosingPrice;
    }
}
```

You have now explicitly linked column names in a CSV file with field names in a class.

The annotations still do not do anything, but they have annotated your code in such a way that you can now start writing code to take advantage of them.

You will now write a processor that can accept a class name and a file name, and construct a `List` of objects of the specified type from the file.

Before writing the code, you will put the basic structure in place, and look at how the processor will be invoked. The processor will have the following basic structure:

```
package processor;
import java.util.ArrayList;
import java.util.List;
public class FileProcessor<T> {
    List<T> processFile(Class className, String filename) {
        List<T> result = new ArrayList<>();

        return result;
    }
}
```

And will be invoked as follows:

```
package processor;
public class Main {
    public static void main(String[] args) {
        FileProcessor<StockData> fileProcessor =
            new FileProcessor<>();
        fileProcessor.processFile(StockData.class, "ORCL.csv");
    }
}
```

To get started you need to write a method that looks at the class passed in, scans all the methods on the class, and determines which ones have `Column` annotations.

In order to achieve this you are going to use a feature called *reflection*. Reflection allows you to examine a class at runtime and determine which fields and methods it contains, and even to invoke instances of those methods on specific instances of the class.

Reflection is very useful for writing generic algorithms, because it allows code to make decisions at runtime based on the structure of the classes it has been given to work with. For instance, the `FileProcessor` in this example will not need any compile time knowledge of the `StockData` class: everything it needs to know about it will be discovered via reflection.

The following is the next version of `FileProcessor`. It constructs a map where the keys are the column names in the file (as discovered from the annotations), and the values are the related setter methods on `StockData`:

```
package processor;
import java.lang.annotation.Annotation;
import java.lang.reflect.Method;
import java.util.ArrayList;
import java.util.HashMap;
import java.util.List;
import java.util.Map;
```

```
import processor.annotations.Column;
public class FileProcessor<T> {
    List<T> processFile(Class className, String filename) {
        List<T> result = new ArrayList<>();
        Map<String, Method> headerMap = new HashMap<>();
        mapFieldNames(className, headerMap);
        return result;
    }

    private void mapFieldNames(Class c,
            Map<String, Method> headerMap) {
        for (Method method : c.getMethods()) {
            Column column = method.getAnnotation(Column.class);
            if (column != null) {
                headerMap.put(column.comumnName(), method);
            }
        }
    }
}
```

In order to access all the methods on a given class, the code simply calls `c.getMethods()`. Each method is then represented as an instance of the `Method` class.

Notice also that once a `Column` annotation is identified on a method using `getAnnotation`, it is possible to extract its value for `columnName` as follows:

`column.comumnName()`

You will now write code to process the header line in the file, and determine which position each column name has. This will ensure that it is possible to change the order of the column names after the program is written, and still have the program function correctly. The method looks as follows:

```
private void mapColumnPositions(
        Map<Integer, String> headerPositionMap, String firstLine) {
    StringTokenizer st = new StringTokenizer(firstLine, ",");
    int i = 0;
    while (st.hasMoreTokens()) {
        headerPositionMap.put(i++, st.nextToken());
    }
}
```

You will look at how this is called shortly, but it will accept a `Map` and the header line from the file, and populate the `Map` with the position of each column.

Now, you will create a method that accepts each line of the file and processes it, returning an instance of the required class at the end.

```
private T processLine(Class className, String line,
        Map<Integer, String> headerPositionMap,
        Map<String, Method> headerMap) throws Exception {
    T t = (T)className.newInstance();
    int i = 0;
    StringTokenizer st = new StringTokenizer(line, ",");
    while (st.hasMoreTokens()) {
        String columnName = headerPositionMap.get(i);
        Method setter = headerMap.get(columnName);
```

```java
            Parameter parameter = setter.getParameters()[0];
            if (parameter.getType().equals(Date.class)) {
                Column column = setter.getAnnotation(Column.class);
                DateFormat df = new SimpleDateFormat(column.format());
                setter.invoke(t, df.parse(st.nextToken()));
            } else if (parameter.getType().equals(Double.class)) {
                setter.invoke(t, Double.valueOf(st.nextToken()));
            } else if (parameter.getType().equals(Integer.class)) {
                setter.invoke(t, Integer.valueOf(st.nextToken()));
            } else {
                // assume it accepts a String
                setter.invoke(t, st.nextToken());
            }
            i++;
        }
        return t;
    }
}
```

This method is reasonably complex at first glance, but if you work through it line-by-line it is reasonably straightforward.

You start by constructing an instance of the class that will hold the data in the line (an instance of `StockData` in this case). You instantiate it using a mechanism you have not seen so far: using the `newInstance` method on the `Class` itself.

```java
T t = (T)className.newInstance();
```

Next, you split the line based on commas, and process one token at a time. You use the index of the token to determine which column name you are processing, and access the appropriate setter for that column on the newly created object:

```java
String columnName = headerPositionMap.get(i);
Method setter = headerMap.get(columnName);
```

Once you obtain a reference to the setter you need to determine what type of parameter it accepts. You know that a setter always accepts one argument; therefore you can access this via reflection also:

```java
Parameter parameter = setter.getParameters()[0];
```

The next section of the method contains a set of if-else blocks that invoke the setter based on its type. For instance, if it accepts an `Integer` you invoke it as follows:

```java
setter.invoke(t, Integer.valueOf(st.nextToken()));
```

The first block, which handles `Date` parameters, is the most complex, because in this case you also need to find the format of the date from the annotation using the following code:

```java
Column column = setter.getAnnotation(Column.class);
DateFormat df = new SimpleDateFormat(column.format());
```

You can now put it altogether:

```java
package processor;
import java.io.FileNotFoundException;
import java.io.FileReader;
```

```java
import java.io.IOException;
import java.lang.annotation.Annotation;
import java.lang.reflect.InvocationTargetException;
import java.lang.reflect.Method;
import java.lang.reflect.Parameter;
import java.nio.file.Files;
import java.nio.file.Path;
import java.nio.file.Paths;
import java.text.DateFormat;
import java.text.ParseException;
import java.text.SimpleDateFormat;
import java.util.ArrayList;
import java.util.Date;
import java.util.HashMap;
import java.util.List;
import java.util.Map;
import java.util.StringTokenizer;
import java.util.logging.Level;
import java.util.logging.Logger;
import processor.annotations.Column;
public class FileProcessor<T> {

    List<T> processFile(Class className, String filename) {
        List<T> result = new ArrayList<>();
        Map<String, Method> headerMap = new HashMap<>();
        Map<Integer, String> headerPositionMap = new HashMap<>();
        mapFieldNames(className, headerMap);
        Path path = Paths.get(filename);
        try {
            Files.lines(path).limit(1).forEach(
                s -> mapColumnPositions(headerPositionMap, s));
            Files.lines(path).skip(1).forEach(s -> {
                try {
                    result.add(processLine(className,
                        s, headerPositionMap, headerMap));
                } catch (Exception e) {
                    Logger.getLogger(FileProcessor.class.getName()).
                        log(Level.SEVERE, "Error occurred", e);
                }
            });
        } catch (IOException ex) {}
        return result;
    }

    private void mapFieldNames(Class c, Map<String, Method> headerMap) {
        for (Method method : c.getMethods()) {
            Column column = method.getAnnotation(Column.class);
            if (column != null) {
                headerMap.put(column.comumnName(), method);
            }
        }
    }

    private T processLine(Class className, String line, Map<Integer, String> headerPositionMap, Map<String, Method> headerMap) throws Exception {
        T t = (T)className.newInstance();
        int i = 0;
```

```
        StringTokenizer st = new StringTokenizer(line, ",");
        while (st.hasMoreTokens()) {
            String columnName = headerPositionMap.get(i);
            Method setter = headerMap.get(columnName);
            Parameter parameter = setter.getParameters()[0];
            if (parameter.getType().equals(Date.class)) {
                Column column = setter.getAnnotation(Column.class);
                DateFormat df =
                    new SimpleDateFormat(column.format());
                setter.invoke(t, df.parse(st.nextToken()));
            } else if (parameter.getType().equals(Double.class)) {
                setter.invoke(t, Double.valueOf(st.nextToken()));
            } else if (parameter.getType().equals(Integer.class)) {
                setter.invoke(t, Integer.valueOf(st.nextToken()));
            } else {
                // assume it accepts a String
                setter.invoke(t, st.nextToken());
            }
            i++;
        }
        return t;
    }

    private void mapColumnPositions(Map<Integer, String> headerPositionMap,
String firstLine) {
        StringTokenizer st = new StringTokenizer(firstLine, ",");
        int i = 0;
        while (st.hasMoreTokens()) {
            headerPositionMap.put(i++, st.nextToken());
        }
    }
}
```

Notice that you are using the `limit` function on `Streams` to process the first line from the file:

```
Files.lines(path).limit(1).forEach(s -> mapColumnPositions(headerPositionMap, s));
```

And then using the `skip` function the second time you process the file to skip over the header.

```
Files.lines(path).skip(1).forEach(s -> {
    try {
        result.add(processLine(className, s,
            headerPositionMap, headerMap));
    } catch (Exception e) {
      Logger.getLogger(FileProcessor.class.getName()).
        log(Level.SEVERE, "Error occurred", e);
    }
});
```

Now that we have code to construct `StockData` instances, you can write a `main` method that uses the `List` returned to find:

⇒ The highest volume for any date

- ⇒ The date with the greatest difference between the opening and closing price
- ⇒ The highest and lowest prices in the file

```
package processor;

import java.util.List;
import java.util.OptionalDouble;
import java.util.OptionalInt;

public class Main {
    public static void main(String[] args) {
        FileProcessor<StockData> fileProcessor =
            new FileProcessor<>();
        List<StockData> data = fileProcessor.processFile(
            StockData.class, "ORCL.csv");
        // find the maximum volume
        OptionalInt resultVolume = data.stream().
            mapToInt(sd -> sd.getVolume()).max();
        // find the maximum difference between the opening price
        // and the closing price
        OptionalDouble resultPrice = data.stream().mapToDouble(
            sd -> sd.getClosingPrice()-sd.getOpeningPrice()).max();
        // find the minimum opening price
        OptionalDouble lowestPrice = data.stream().mapToDouble(
            sd -> sd.getOpeningPrice()).min();
        // find the maximum opening price
        OptionalDouble highestPrice = data.stream().mapToDouble(
            sd -> sd.getOpeningPrice()).max();
        System.out.println("Highest volume: "+
            resultVolume.getAsInt());
        System.out.println("Highest price change : "+
            resultPrice.getAsDouble());
        System.out.println("Lowest price : "+
            lowestPrice.getAsDouble());
        System.out.println("Highest price : "+
            highestPrice.getAsDouble());
    }
}
```

Before ending this chapter, take a step back and look at the `FileProcessor` you have written. This knows nothing about the file it is going to be passed, or the class you are going to ask it to instantiate for each line in the file, yet it manages to perform the task through the combined power of annotations and reflection.

Code such as this is very valuable, because it can work with files and classes that have not even been written yet.

33 BUILDING AND DEPLOYING

So far you have focused on developing standalone Java programs. Obviously if you want other people to use your programs you don't want them to install Eclipse, compile the source code, and run the program: you want to distribute a pre-compiled version to them.

Put simply, you need a way of packaging together all the class files and resources that a program needs, and providing the user with a convenient mechanism to execute the appropriate `main` method to start the program running.

JARs

The basic technology for collecting a set of class files and resources together is the JAR file (short for Java ARchive). A JAR file is similar to a zip file – with a `.jar` extension. In fact if you change the extension of a JAR file from `.jar` to `.zip`, your favorite compression utility will happily un-zip it.

JAR files are actually more direct related a Unix style TAR files (Tape ARchive) – TAR files are a format for grouping together a set of files, it is not a format for compressing these files.

The Java JDK contains a command line utility called `jar` that can be used to create JAR files. If you are familiar with the Unix `tar` program, the Java `jar` program will be relatively easy to use, because it follows the same conventions.

Instead of using `jar` from the command line, you will instead utilize the utilities provided by Eclipse itself.

Before beginning, it is worth pointing out that there are two reasons to create a JAR file:

⇒ You want to group together a set of classes for use by a third party – or another of your programs. In this scenario you are creating a library, and your classes do not need to incorporate a `main` method

⇒ You want to group together a set of classes that can be run by an end user: in such cases a `main` method is obviously required.

You will examine both of these scenarios in order.

Creating a library

Cast your mind back to the `LinkedList2` class you wrote earlier in the book – imagine that you want to make this available as a library.

This class has a dependency on another class called `Node`, therefore you can create a JAR file with the `LinkedList2` and `Node` classes in it, and distribute this file.

To begin, right click on the project that contains these two classes and choose `Export...`.

On the first screen, as seen in figure 33-1, choose "JAR file" and choose "Next":

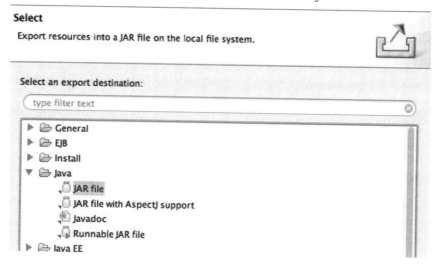

FIGURE 33-1

On the next screen, as shown in figure 33-2, you will get to choose which resources to include in the JAR file.

Click on the `linkedlist` package in the `src` directory and choose not to export the `Main` class (as seen in figure 33-2). Also choose a name and location for the JAR file to be exported to – I have called mine `list2.jar`, but use whatever name you want:

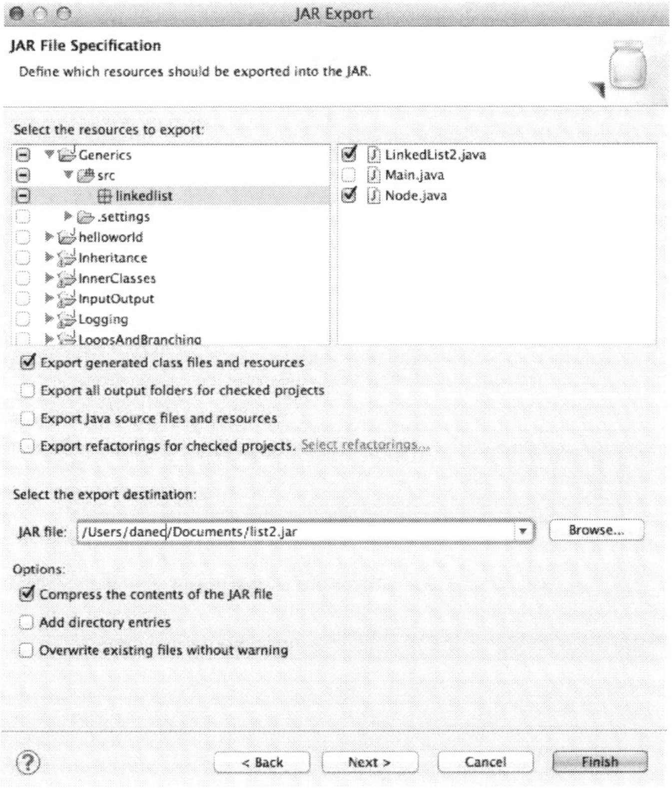

FIGURE 33-2

When you press "Finish" the JAR file will be created.

You will now use this JAR file in a separate project. By default Eclipse does not allow you to use the classes from one project in another project – each project is considered a self-contained entity.

Start by creating a new project, and add the following class:

```
package usejar;
import linkedlist.LinkedList2;
public class Main {
    public static void main(String[] args) {
        LinkedList2 list = new LinkedList2();
    }
}
```

You will notice that this does not compile due to the fact that `LinkedList2` cannot be found. Now, right click on the project in the Package Explorer and choose `Build Path -> Configure Build Path`. Next, select the libraries tab and choose `Add External Jars`. From the file chooser select the JAR file you created in the previous section, and select "Finish".

This has added the JAR with `LinkedList2` to the classpath of the program, and therefore the code will now compile, and you can begin using the `LinkedList2` class.

There are a number of sources for open source Java libraries on the Internet, and these libraries will always be provided in the form of JAR files. This means it is possible to download these libraries and add them to your Eclipse project just as you have done here.

Possibly the best source of open source Java libraries is Apache Commons, which can be found here http://commons.apache.org. This contains a long list of libraries that can be incorporated into your Java programs.

Executable Jar Files

You will now create an executable JAR file. This will allow an end user to execute one of your programs by double clicking on it, or executing it from the command line. It is important to note, however, that the user will still need to have a JVM installed on their computer, although they will most likely have the Java Runtime Environment (JRE) installed rather than a Java Development Kit (JDK).

> This chapter is ignoring one other Java technology that can be used for deploying Java programs (particularly rich GUI applications) to end users called Java Web Start. Java Web Start allows users to download and install a Java program from the Internet, and create desktop icons.
>
> If you ever need to deploy a Java program to a large group of people, and need to manage updates to the Java program, you may want to look into Java Web Start.

In this section I will create an executable JAR file for the file processor created in the Reflections and Annotation chapter.

Start by finding that project, right clicking on it, and selecting `Export...` This time in the dialog you will choose to create a Runnable JAR file, as seen in figure 33-3:

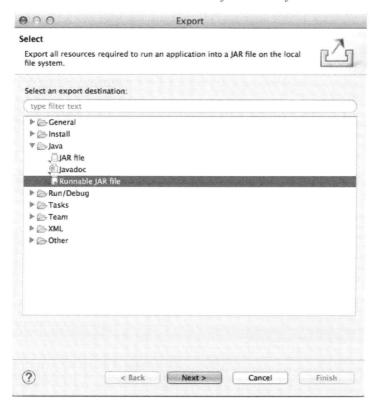

FIGURE 33-3

After clicking "Next", you will be presented with the options seen in figure 33-4. In this dialog you need to choose a "Launch configuration" – this is the configuration you used when running the program in Eclipse, and is automatically generated:

You can now select "Finish" to save the JAR file.

If you were to extract the contents of this JAR file, you would notice one main difference. A file called META-INF/MANIFEST.MF has been created for you, and contains the following:

```
Manifest-Version: 1.0
Class-Path: .
Main-Class: processor.Main
```

This instructs the `jar` tool which class contains the `main` method.

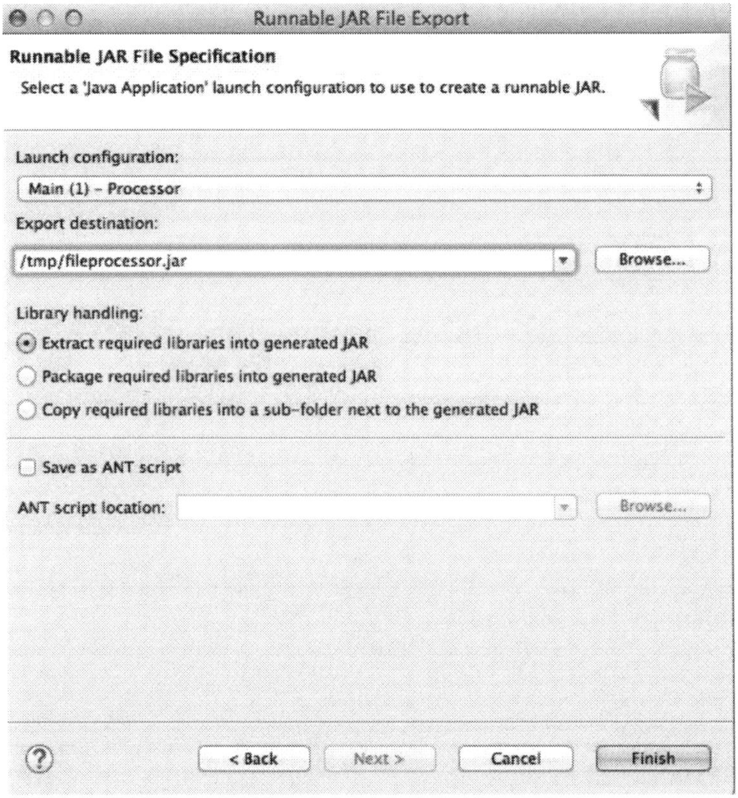

FIGURE 33-4

You can now execute JAR this from the command line. Make sure to copy ORCL.csv to the same directory as the JAR file, and then execute it in your operating system console as seen in figure 33-5:

```
Danes-iMac:tmp danemoodie$ java -jar fileprocessor.jar
Highest volume: 2073400
Highest price change : 2.25
Lowest price : 1.19
Highest price : 28.88
```

FIGURE 33-5

Notice that this still needs to be run inside a console, because the standard output needs to be written somewhere. If this was a graphical program, or wrote to a file, the user could simply double click on the JAR file.

34 LOGGING

Most real world applications will log information as they execute. Logging is a useful mechanism for outputting the state and behavior of a program as it executes so that it is possible to "manually debug" the program if an issue is encountered.

I use the words "manually debug" here, because typically you will not be able to debug programs if they are being executed by a third party, or in a production environment, but you still need some way of finding out what the program is doing if an issue occurs.

Logging can be used for outputting error information such as stack traces, or any other general information that may be useful when attempting to determine the behavior of a program.

Java includes a logging API that is suitable for most needs. There are also several other open source logging libraries available for more advanced needs. This chapter will limit itself to the logging API provided natively by Java.

Getting started

The heart of the logging API is a class called `Logger`. This is the class that is responsible for outputting log information. The following shows a simple example of a class declaring a `Logger` and outputting a message:

```
package logging;
import java.util.logging.Logger;

public class SimpleLogging {
    public static void main(String[] args) {
        Logger log = Logger.getLogger(SimpleLogging.class.getName());
        log.info("This is an information message");
    }
}
```

If I run this program in Eclipse it produces the following output:

```
Apr 25, 2014 2:39:02 PM logging.SimpleLogging main
INFO: This is an information message
```

In many ways this is similar to using `System.out.println`, but you can already see some advantages.

⇒ The output includes the current date and time that the message was logged
⇒ The output includes information about the class that produced the output

You will look at these features in more detail shortly, but for now, turn your attention to the line that creates the logger:

```
Logger log = Logger.getLogger(SimpleLogging.class.getName());
```

The `getLogger` static helper returns an object that can be used for logging messages. Because there will be many `Loggers` in a complex program it is important to associated a `String` with each `Logger` so that it is possible to differentiate the output of one `Logger` from another.

The most common `String` to associate with a `Logger` is the name of the class the `Logger` is declared in – and this is the reason that the previous example output the class name – in reality it was outputting the `Logger` name.

Notice that the method I have used in this example is `info`. When you log messages you assign an importance to them via a *level* – `info` indicates that the output is for informational purposes only. The level can also be assigned explicitly:

```java
package logging;
import java.util.logging.Level;
import java.util.logging.Logger;

public class SimpleLogging {
    public static void main(String[] args) {
        Logger log = Logger.getLogger(SimpleLogging.class.getName());
        log.log(Level.FINEST, "This is a finest message");
        log.log(Level.FINER, "This is a finer message");
        log.log(Level.FINE, "This is a fine message");
        log.log(Level.INFO, "This is a info message");
        log.log(Level.WARNING, "This is a warning message");
        log.log(Level.SEVERE, "This is a severe message");
    }
}
```

This example shows the six most common levels, from the least important to the most important.

If you run this example you may be surprised by the results. I received the following output:

```
Apr 25, 2014 3:24:01 PM logging.SimpleLogging main
INFO: This is a info message
Apr 25, 2014 3:24:01 PM logging.SimpleLogging main
```

```
WARNING: This is a warning message
Apr 25, 2014 3:24:01 PM logging.SimpleLogging main
SEVERE: This is a severe message
```

The first three messages have not been printed. The reason for this is that each `Logger` has a default level set against it, and unless the logged message is at least as important as this level, the message will not be printed.

The reason for this becomes obvious when you reflect back on the reason you are logging information. Information is being logged typically to help understand what is happening with the program. In some situations, however, you may only want to know about severe messages (when the program is being run by end users), while other times you may want much more information (when the program is being run in development or by testers).

If you want the `Logger` to print all messages (or messages above a specified importance), you begin by specifying this on the `Logger` before logging any information:

```
log.setLevel(Level.ALL);
```

You may think this would be sufficient to print the extra messages. The beauty of levels, however, is that you may wish to log `fine` messages to the console, while you want to log `severe` messages to a file – therefore each output destination also has a default logging level.

In order to see this, create an executable JAR from this project using the techniques described in the previous chapter (I called mine `simplelogging.jar`). Place this somewhere on your file system, create a file called `logging.properties` in the same directory, and add the following to it:

```
handlers=java.util.logging.ConsoleHandler
java.util.logging.ConsoleHandler.level=FINE
```

This configuration file states that you want to perform logging to the console, and that you want to log all messages that are `FINE` or higher.

If you now execute this as follows:

```
java -Djava.util.logging.config.file=logging.properties -jar simplelogging.jar
```

(make sure you are in the directory with the JAR file and the `logging.properties` file).

It should print the following:

```
Apr 25, 2014 4:30:59 PM logging.SimpleLogging main
FINE: This is a fine message
Apr 25, 2014 4:30:59 PM logging.SimpleLogging main
INFO: This is a info message
Apr 25, 2014 4:30:59 PM logging.SimpleLogging main
WARNING: This is a warning message
Apr 25, 2014 4:30:59 PM logging.SimpleLogging main
SEVERE: This is a severe message
```

If you play around with the level you will see more or fewer lines logged.

The console is an example of a handler, but you can add others. Change the `logging.properties` file as follows:

```
handlers=java.util.logging.FileHandler, java.util.logging.ConsoleHandler
java.util.logging.ConsoleHandler.level=FINE
java.util.logging.FileHandler.level=INFO
java.util.logging.FileHandler.pattern=simple.log
java.util.logging.FileHandler.limit=10000
java.util.logging.FileHandler.formatter=java.util.logging.SimpleFormatter
```

This now states that the program should log messages to both a file and the console. The file logger will only log messages that are `INFO` or higher, and these will be logged to a file called `simple.log`. This can grow in size to a maximum of 10000 bytes, at which time it will be recycled.

The last line associates a formatter with the `FileHandler`. By default the `FileHandler` creates XML output, whereas I just want the simple output that is logged to the console.

If you run this now you should see a file called `simple.log` created with the following contents:

```
Apr 25, 2014 4:38:44 PM logging.SimpleLogging main
INFO: This is a info message
Apr 25, 2014 4:38:44 PM logging.SimpleLogging main
WARNING: This is a warning message
Apr 25, 2014 4:38:44 PM logging.SimpleLogging main
SEVERE: This is a severe message
```

Handlers do not need to be limited to consoles and files. There are many other potential destinations for log messages, such as emails, databases and phone alerts. The handler mechanism abstracts the manner in which messages are logged from the process of logging messages. This is a very flexible design, because it means any program with logging code can be extended to support different approaches to logging without changing the program itself.

So far I have focused on logging messages, but another important consideration is logging stack traces. The following program demonstrates the logging of an error. In this program the `c` method will generate an exception when it is invoked by `main` because it is being passed a `null String`:

```java
package logging;
import java.util.logging.Level;
import java.util.logging.Logger;

public class SimpleLogging {
    public static void main(String[] args) {
        Logger log = Logger.getLogger(SimpleLogging.class.getName());
        log.setLevel(Level.ALL);
        try {
            a(null);
        } catch (Exception e) {
```

```
            log.log(Level.SEVERE, "An error occured in main", e);
        }
    }
    public static void a(String s) {
        b(s);
    }
    public static void b(String s) {
        c(s);
    }
    public static void c(String s) {
        s.substring(0, 10);
    }
}
```

When you run this it should produce the following output:

```
Apr 26, 2014 2:13:57 PM logging.SimpleLogging main
SEVERE: An error occured in main
java.lang.NullPointerException
    at logging.SimpleLogging.c(SimpleLogging.java:27)
    at logging.SimpleLogging.b(SimpleLogging.java:23)
    at logging.SimpleLogging.a(SimpleLogging.java:19)
    at logging.SimpleLogging.main(SimpleLogging.java:12)
```

Notice how simply passing the exception to the `log` method causes the entire stack trace to be printed, thereby allowing you to see the entire call stack of the program when the exception occurred.

35 CONCLUSION

Java is a large and complex programming language – but it is also capable of solving large and complex problems.

This book has introduced you to all the key features of Java Standard Edition (Java SE), and you are now well placed to use Java to solve interesting real world problems, and, just importantly, capable of using the very latest version of Java, and all the new features it has to offer.

In many ways, however, this book has only scratched the surface of what Java is capable of achieving. As I mentioned in the introduction, Java is now primarily used as a server-side language, and is the power behind many of the Web's most popular web sites. This power is unlocked via a set of APIs called Java Enterprise Edition (Java EE).

This book has not introduced Java EE, but it has left you in a strong position to start investigating it yourself if you choose. Before learning advanced features such as Java EE, it is essential that you have a strong grounding in the language fundamentals – and this is what this book has provided you with.

If you would like to write server-side Java applications, you actually have two choices:

Java EE

Java EE: this is a set of standard APIs defined by Java, and implemented by a variety of vendors – both commercial and open source. It includes a web framework for constructing rich websites called Java Server Faces, along with an API for creating server-side components called Enterprise Java Beans.

In order to use Java EE you need to use a Java Application Server that is compatible with these APIs. Probably the most popular open source Java application server to use in conjunction with Java EE is the JBoss application server, available from here:

http://jbossas.jboss.org/

Oracle then provides a tutorial guiding you through the process of developing Java EE applications, which is available here:

http://docs.oracle.com/javaee/6/tutorial/doc/

Spring

The Spring Framework (http://projects.spring.io/spring-framework) is a lightweight framework containing all the same key features as Java EE. Applications written with the Spring Framework are typically deployed in the open source Tomcat application server: http://tomcat.apache.org.

The Spring Framework website contains high quality documentation, and with the knowledge you have gained so far in this book you will find it reasonably straightforward to get started.

Spring also supports an API for developing rich websites called Spring MVC, along with a variety of other APIs.

Whichever direction you head with your knowledge of Java I wish you the best of luck.

Once again, as an independent publisher of computer science books, reviews are very important to us. If you could spare the time to place a public review this would be greatly appreciated.